World War II

World War II

Other Books in the Turning Points Series:

World War II

Myra H. Immell, *Book Editor*

Bonnie Szumski, *Editorial Director*
Scott Barbour, *Managing Editor*

Greenhaven Press, Inc., San Diego, California

Every effort has been made to trace the owners of copyrighted material. The articles in this volume may have been edited for content, length, and/or reading level. The titles have been changed to enhance the editorial purpose.

No part of this book may be reproduced or used in any form or by any means, electrical, mechanical, or otherwise, including, but not limited to, photocopy, recording, or any information storage and retrieval system, without prior written permission from the publisher.

Library of Congress Cataloging-in-Publication Data

World War II / Myra H. Immell, book editor.
    p.   cm. — (Turning points in world history)
    Includes bibliographical references and index.
    ISBN 0-7377-0699-6 (lib. bdg. : alk. paper)—
ISBN 0-7377-0698-8 (pbk. : alk. paper)
    1. World War, 1939–1945. I. Title: World War 2. II. Title:
World War Two. III. Immell, Myra H. IV. Turning points in world history (Greenhaven Press)

D743 .W647 2001
940.53—dc21   2001016033
                                                          CIP

Cover photo: © Digital Stock
Digital Stock: 73, 106, 174, 212
Library of Congress: 124

© 2001 by Greenhaven Press, Inc.
P.O. Box 289009, San Diego, CA 92198-9009

Printed in the U.S.A.

Contents

was not due entirely to the strategic and tactical excellence demonstrated by the Germans during the invasion and ensuing battle.

Isoroku Yamamoto. Current thought is that Yamamoto himself was responsible for the Japanese loss, largely because of a lack of proper planning and conflicting objectives.

Foreword

Certain past events stand out as pivotal, as having effects and outcomes that change the course of history. These events are often referred to as turning points. Historian Louis L. Snyder provides this useful definition:

> A turning point in history is an event, happening, or stage which thrusts the course of historical development into a different direction. By definition a turning point is a great event, but it is even more—a great event with the explosive impact of altering the trend of man's life on the planet.

History's turning points have taken many forms. Some were single, brief, and shattering events with immediate and obvious impact. The invasion of Britain by William the Conqueror in 1066, for example, swiftly transformed that land's political and social institutions and paved the way for the rise of the modern English nation. By contrast, other single events were deemed of minor significance when they occurred, only later recognized as turning points. The assassination of a little-known European nobleman, Archduke Franz Ferdinand, on June 28, 1914, in the Bosnian town of Sarajevo was such an event; only after it touched off a chain reaction of political-military crises that escalated into the global conflict known as World War I did the murder's true significance become evident.

Other crucial turning points occurred not in terms of a few hours, days, months, or even years, but instead as evolutionary developments spanning decades or even centuries. One of the most pivotal turning points in human history, for instance—the development of agriculture, which replaced nomadic hunter-gatherer societies with more permanent settlements—occurred over the course of many generations. Still other great turning points were neither events nor developments, but rather revolutionary new inventions and innovations that significantly altered social customs and ideas, military tactics, home life, the spread of knowledge, and the human condition in general. The developments of writing, gunpowder, the printing press, antibiotics, the electric light, atomic energy, television, and the computer, the last two of which have recently ushered in the world-altering information age, represent only some of these innovative turning points.

Each anthology in the Greenhaven Turning Points in World History series presents a group of essays chosen for their accessibility. The anthology's structure also enhances this accessibility. First, an introductory essay provides a general overview of the principal events and figures involved, placing the topic in its historical context. The essays that follow explore various aspects in more detail, some targeting political trends and consequences, others social, literary, cultural, and/or technological ramifications, and still others pivotal leaders and other influential figures. To aid the reader in choosing the material of immediate interest or need, each essay is introduced by a concise summary of the contributing writer's main themes and insights.

In addition, each volume contains extensive research tools, including a collection of excerpts from primary source documents pertaining to the historical events and figures under discussion. In the anthology on the French Revolution, for example, readers can examine the works of Rousseau, Voltaire, and other writers and thinkers whose championing of human rights helped fuel the French people's growing desire for liberty; the French *Declaration of the Rights of Man and Citizen*, presented to King Louis XVI by the French National Assembly on October 2, 1789; and eyewitness accounts of the attack on the royal palace and the horrors of the Reign of Terror. To guide students interested in pursuing further research on the subject, each volume features an extensive bibliography, which for easy access has been divided into separate sections by topic. Finally, a comprehensive index allows readers to scan and locate content efficiently. Each of the anthologies in the Greenhaven Turning Points in World History series provides students with a complete, detailed, and enlightening examination of a crucial historical watershed.

Introduction: A World in Conflict

In 1783, in a letter he wrote to Josiah Quincy, American statesman Benjamin Franklin wrote, "There was never a good war or a bad peace." Most people who survived World War I only to suffer through—or die in—World War II would agree with Franklin's statement about war and peace. World War I—the "Great War"—ended in 1918 with the signing of the Treaty of Versailles. It was supposed to be the "War to End All Wars." But twenty-some years later, the world was caught up in another global war. And, to the horror of the people who believed the government promises that there would never be another world war, this war was even more widespread and more destructive than the one before it. All but five countries of Europe—Ireland, Portugal, Spain, Sweden, and Switzerland—took sides. Twenty-nine countries threw their support to the Allies—Britain, France, the Soviet Union, and the United States. Seven countries backed the Axis—Germany, Italy, and Japan.

Although historians agree that World War II did not begin until September 1, 1939, the seeds were sown long before that, in part by World War I and the peace settlements that followed it. World War I had engendered antiwar sentiments in France, Britain, and other Western democracies. These sentiments ran especially high in the United States, where most people had no wish to get involved in "Europe's problems" and favored a policy of isolationism. In some other countries, disappointment, anger, frustration, and overall dissatisfaction with the outcome of World War I were the hallmarks. Germany, Italy, and Japan, for example, believed that they had been discriminated against by the peace settlements. The Germans, in particular, felt humiliated—not only by their defeat in World War I but also by the harsh punishments imposed on them by the Treaty of Versailles.

Looking Toward War: European Totalitarianism

By the 1930s, totalitarian leaders had established strongholds in Italy, Germany, and Spain. Italy had fought on the side of the Allies in World War I. The war had killed more than 500,000 Italian soldiers and had left the country in a state of economic depression, with huge war debts and high unemployment. Many Italians were unhappy with the Treaty of Versailles because it had failed to grant them the huge territories they had expected to gain from being on the winning side in the war. When, in 1922, the Italian king Victor Emmanuel named Fascist Benito Mussolini prime minister, Italy's course toward war was assured. Within a few years, Mussolini was "Il Duce"—the dictator of Italy—and Italy became a Fascist state. Mussolini could not forget Italy's long-past glory days when the nation wielded power and the rest of the known world knew and honored the Italian people. Determined to use all of the nation's resources, human as well as economic, to once again make Italy a "great power," he pushed the Italians to do whatever they had to in order to bring about the return of the nation's glory and greatness. Mussolini had no doubts about what it would take to make Italy the seat of power it once was. For Mussolini, greatness was synonymous with conquest and military glory.

In Germany, a similar scenario took place. Like Italy, Germany suffered from high unemployment and inflation, as well as political instability and violence. Political chaos had claimed the country after World War I, resulting first in a provisional government that lasted about a year and then in a democratic Weimar Republic that struggled for more than fourteen years to overcome national unrest and many other problems. The defeat they had suffered in World War I sat heavily on the Germans, as did the harsh terms and humiliations imposed on their nation by the Treaty of Versailles. The treaty demanded Germany pay such high reparations—$32 billion—that in the early 1920s the German government stated flatly that it would not—could not—pay them. Germany had started exporting heavily in an effort to try and pay its debt. But all their efforts accomplished was to upset the European balance of trade, create shortages in

Germany, and cause inflation to rise. When the French, angered by the German defaults on payment, invaded Germany's industrial Ruhr Valley and took control of the coal mines and steel mills located there, the results were devastating, ultimately raising the rate of inflation so high that it bankrupted the German government and left the German economy teetering on the brink of total ruin. The Germans' other major dissatisfactions with postwar conditions only exacerbated the situation. As a nation, Germany was no fonder of democracy than it was of war reparations. The German people were not comfortable with a democracy that had not been of their choosing but had been forced on them by military defeat. They had to find someone or something to blame for what was happening to them and for the depressed condition of their country, and many blamed democracy.

Into the chaos that was postwar Germany came many new political parties, one of which was the National Socialist Workers' Party, or Nazis. In 1932, the Nazis, until then a small and not very influential political party, became the largest party in the Reichstag, the supreme legislative body of the republic. The following year, the president of Germany asked Nazi Party leader Adolf Hitler to serve as chancellor of Germany. Despite a failed attempt for the German presidency in 1932, Hitler had the support of the German people, who he had been wooing with his promises for a number of years, telling each group of Germans what they most wanted to hear. To get their support and financial backing, he promised German workers security; told Germans suffering from the poor economy that he would get even with the Jewish bankers and Marxists, who he blamed for the German defeat in World War I; and assured German bankers and industrialists that he would get the unions under control and contain Communism.

Hitler's appointment as chancellor of Germany was, in effect, the end of the Weimar Republic and of any kind of democracy in Germany. It did not take Hitler long to become dictator of Germany and accelerate a Nazi revolution. Hitler became "Der Führer" (the leader), banned all political parties except his own, and boasted that his government, the Third

Reich (Third Empire) would last for a thousand years. He convinced the German people that they were a master race—true Aryans—superior to everyone else. Claiming that the Jews would contaminate the purity of Germany, he stripped them of their citizenship and deprived them of the majority of their human rights. He justified this by blaming them for all of Germany's ills. Then, in total defiance of the Treaty of Versailles, he initiated a program to rearm Germany and turn it once again into a strong military power. The Nazi slogan "Today, Germany; tomorrow, the world" left no doubts as to Hitler's vision for the future.

International War on the Horizon

The terms of the Treaty of Versailles, which had forbidden Germany from rearming or producing weapons, also forbade the presence of German troops in the Rhineland of western Germany, a prohibition designed to safeguard French security. In 1936, in direct opposition to the ban, Adolf Hitler sent armed German troops into the Rhineland. Hitler was taking a big chance, for he was well aware that Britain and France could stop him if they chose to take action. The inaction of Britain and France had major ramifications, not the least of which was to close the door once and for all on the Versailles treaty and the concept of collective security that was at the very heart of the League of Nations.

The changes taking place in Europe were not the only ones that would have a monumental effect on the world. Asia also was experiencing change, and it did not bode well for some groups of Asians. In 1931 Japan had moved to expand its territory by overrunning Manchuria and taking it from the Chinese. The ease with which Japan had gained military and economic control of Manchuria did not go unnoticed in Europe. Always on the lookout for ways to restore Italy to its former glory, Italian dictator Benito Mussolini saw what the Japanese had accomplished fairly easily in Manchuria and decided that Italy could be just as successful in Ethiopia. Reasoning that an Ethiopian colony would help solve Italy's ever-increasing economic problems, he looked for an excuse to overrun the African nation. A clash between Italian and

Ethiopian forces in a disputed zone on the frontier of Italian Somaliland gave him the excuse he wanted. In 1935, Mussolini sent Italian troops into Ethiopia. Ignoring protests and sanctions by the League of Nations, he persisted. By 1936, Ethiopia was formally annexed to Italy and Il Duce was its self-proclaimed emperor.

The year 1936 was pivotal: The already volatile international state of affairs was further incited by eruption of war in Spain. Actions taken by the five-year-old Republican government to limit the power of the Catholic Church and redistribute land in Spain had intensified the animosity of right-wing Spaniards and triggered a call for the return of the monarchy. The result was a civil war in Spain between Spanish Republicans—Loyalists—and right-wing Spanish nationalists led by General Francisco Franco. Interference by outside powers inflamed the situation, and what started out as a battle between Spanish nationalists and Republicans turned into a struggle for supremacy between Fascism and Communism, with Germany and Italy supporting the Republicans and the Soviets supporting the Loyalists. It was a situation that became even more distorted when sympathetic British, French, and Americans joined international brigades to fight for the Republican cause, arguing that their cause had nothing to do with Communism.

Hitler and his henchmen saw the war in Spain as an opportunity to further their own interests and those of Germany. In their view, the war offered an opportunity not only to forge a closer relationship with Italy and acquire Spanish ore and magnesium, but also to use Spain as a testing ground for new German war techniques.

When the Spanish Civil War ended in 1939 with Francisco Franco the new dictator of Spain, much of Spain was in ruins and hundreds of thousands of Spaniards were dead. Hitler, however, had achieved his goals. His newly formed all-German troops had perfected techniques and strategies that would serve Germany well the next time it went to war. To further strengthen Germany's position, he and Mussolini had joined forces, signing the Rome-Berlin Axis political and military pact, and had entered into an anti-Communist alliance with Japan. Although officially the emperor still governed Japan, the true power belonged to the military, who, with the ink still wet on the pact with Hitler and Mussolini, invaded China. The stage was now set for an all-out global war.

German Expansionism: A Step Closer to War

Austrian by birth, Hitler believed that Germany was Austria's mother country. In the early 1930s he had tried to fulfill his dream of *Anschluss*, the annexation of Austria to Germany, and had been stopped when Mussolini had mobilized Italian troops. With Mussolini now his ally, Hitler was more confident of success. In March 1938, arguing that uniting the German-speaking people of Germany and Austria would promote political stability, Hitler realized his dream of *Anschluss*. Once again, the Western democracies sat back and let Hitler have his way.

Next Hitler targeted Czechoslovakia, the only democracy in central Europe. Arguing that the 3 million Germans who lived in the Sudetenland region of northwestern Czechoslovakia were entitled to the right of self-determination, Hitler proclaimed that Germany had a right to get involved in the Sudetenland. When, to prevent Hitler from taking action, the Czech government declared martial law, the British, backed by the French, urged negotiations. Unintimidated, Hitler did not back down. Claiming that all he wanted was to unite all German people into one country, Hitler once again got what he wanted. This time, however, he had to go back on his word to British prime minister Neville Chamberlain to accomplish his objective. Chamberlain had negotiated with Hitler in good faith in what turned out to be a futile attempt to avoid a conflict that surely would lead to war. Chamberlain had made two fatal mistakes when dealing with Hitler, the first of which was believing that a policy of appeasement would truly satisfy Hitler and work to Europe's advantage. Chamberlain's second mistake was to trust Hitler when Hitler promised he would respect Czech dominion, not take any more European territory, and settle future disputes by peaceful negotiation. While a naive and misguided Chamberlain was telling the world that he had made "peace in our time" a possibility, Hitler was marching his armies into Czechoslovakia, taking control of the western region of the country and turning the eastern region into a puppet state of Germany.

Hitler's dreams of expansion had been documented years earlier in *Mein Kampf* when he wrote of creating living space—*lebensraum*—for German settlers in Eastern Europe's rich farming areas. While the Western democracies pondered what to do, Russian leader Joseph Stalin moved to protect the rich Soviet farmlands by signing a nonaggression pact with Germany. The pact was a result of Stalin's conviction that Czechoslovakia was just a stop on Hitler's path to Russia and that the Western democracies would not do anything to help him fight off Hitler when that time came. Stalin knew that the agreement would not protect Russia indefinitely but felt it was his best option at the time. Despite his distrust of Hitler, Stalin secretly made plans with the German leader to divide Poland between them, with Germany occupying western Poland and Russia governing eastern Poland.

When Hitler moved against Poland in 1939, attacking on the land and from the air, his confidence was at an all-time high. The nonaggression pact he had signed with Stalin had assured him that the Soviets would not interfere. He was equally sure that neither Britain nor France would be able to move fast enough to send troops to protect Poland in event of a German attack. Hitler's new strategy of blitzkrieg, or lightning war, premised on taking the enemy by surprise, was all he had hoped for. Between the unexpectedness of the attack and the onslaught by *Luftwaffe* bombs, Nazi Panzer armored tanks, and more than 1 million German infantry soldiers, Poland did not stand a chance. Stalin, meanwhile, moved quickly to make the Soviet presence felt first in the eastern portion of Poland and then in the Baltic Republics and Finland.

Early Axis Victories

After Poland was conquered, Germany adopted a strategy of holding fast and keeping relatively still. Throughout the winter and spring of 1939–1940, blitzkrieg was replaced temporarily by *sitzkrieg*, the period of "phony war" when nothing happened. With the Wehrmacht's successful invasion of Denmark and Norway late in April 1940, the lull came to an abrupt end.

The French, who had waited for the Germans to strike along the World War I Maginot Line, suffered a major setback when the Germans avoided the Maginot Line and, on the heels of their invasion of the Netherlands, swept into France through Belgium. German forces defeated the French in the air and on the ground, forcing Allied forces trapped in Belgium to retreat to the northern port city of Dunkirk. There, a drama was played out over a nine-day period: Hundreds of British civilian and naval boats that had crossed the English Channel evacuated hundreds of thousands of mostly British troops from Dunkirk. However, even in defeat, the British would not back down, underlining newly appointed British prime minister Winston Churchill's declaration to the House of Commons in 1940 in response to the overriding question about Britain's stake in a war against Germany: "What is our aim? I can answer in one word: Victory—victory at all costs, victory in spite of all terror; victory, however hard and long the road may be; for without victory, there is no survival."

Mussolini declared war on France and Britain within a few days after the evacuation at Dunkirk and four days before France surrendered Paris to the Germans. Meanwhile, Italian and German troops were overrunning much of North Africa. Not content with this, Mussolini sent his troops into Albania. Within a year, Italy and Germany had conquered the Balkan countries. With the fall of France, Nazi troops occupied all of the northern part of the country and the Atlantic coastline to the Spanish border. According to the terms of the armistice France and Germany signed, the French would continue governing the southern part of France. Technically, that came to pass. But, in actuality, the Vichy government headed by French marshal Henri Pétain governed as a puppet of the Germans.

With France under control, Hitler turned his attention to

Britain. He knew that he could not successfully invade Britain without first crippling the Royal Air Force. To take control of the airways, the more than a thousand German planes that took to the air were ordered to bomb and destroy Britain's most important industries and airfields. To help ensure success and crack the morale and determination of the British people, the *Luftwaffe* bombarded—blitzed—London from the air on a regular basis. The Battle of Britain was Hitler's first major defeat—all attempts to defeat the Royal Air Force failed as dismally as all efforts to demoralize the British public.

Not yet ready to give up on Britain, Hitler revised his strategy and sent additional submarines into the Atlantic to sink more British ships, hoping to cut off food supplies to the island nation and starve the British population into surrender. But once again, British determination and perseverance foiled Hitler's plans. Instead of surrendering, the British government worked out a cash-and-carry arrangement with U.S. president Franklin Roosevelt that enabled the British to pay cash for food and armaments that their own ships picked up in the United States and transported across the Atlantic back to Britain. Within a year, with the cash-and-carry arrangement replaced by a lend-lease program, the British remained undefeated. The Battle of the Atlantic continued for four more years—until 1945.

Hitler, meanwhile, opted to forget about invading or conquering Britain for the time being. The key to controlling Europe, he concluded, was to conquer the Soviet Union, which he thought would be an easy target that could be defeated quickly. He coveted the wheat of the Ukraine and oil supplies of the Caucasus, and conquering the Russian steppe would fulfill his goal of *lebensraum*. In the early summer of 1941, breaking the treaty he had signed with Stalin just two years earlier, Hitler loosed his forces on the Soviet Union.

That same year, Japan, the other major member of the Axis, launched an attack on Pearl Harbor, Hawaii, that led the United States to give up its policy of isolation and forgo its reluctance to get involved in another European war. The Japanese, determined to control the Pacific, had not been idle in the years before the attack. In 1940, announcing a plan to achieve a "new order in Greater East Asia," the Japanese government set out to establish a Greater East Asia Co-prosperity Sphere. While the Germans and Italians had been advancing across Europe, Japanese troops had taken over all of Indochina and much of China and the East Indies. Their surprise attack on the American naval base at Pearl Harbor grew out of their belief that they had to defeat the United States and prevent U.S. forces in the Philippines from threatening their control of the Pacific. As far as the Japanese were concerned, the United States posed a major threat to their plan for expansion in the East and needed to be shown just how powerful and strong the Japanese really were. The Lend-Lease Act, passed earlier that year, had disquieted the Japanese, for it provided the countries fighting the Axis with $50 billion in weapons, food, and other services. Through lend-lease, the American government could fulfill its objective of contributing to the war effort without the risk of antagonizing the American people by committing the country to active participation in a war that most Americans wanted no part of.

The crippling attack on their navy at Pearl Harbor, however, changed the prevailing American attitude about participating in the war. President Roosevelt labeled December 7, 1941, the day of the attack on Pearl Harbor, "a date which will live in infamy." Instead of reacting as the Japanese had predicted—backing off in awe at the might of the Japanese and allowing them to aggressively pursue their plans in the Pacific—the United States declared war on Japan. Four days later, Germany and Italy declared war on the United States. In a few short years, American policy had progressed from neutrality to nonbelligerency to limited participation in the war to total participation in the war. America had entered the war in Europe on the side of Britain, France, and the Soviet Union and allied with China in the war in Asia. The British, French, and American heads of state did not completely trust Stalin, but at the time an alliance with the Soviets was not only expedient but necessary as well.

Within six months after the U.S. declaration of war, the war had become truly global, with fighting in both Western and Eastern Europe, Italy and the Mediterranean, Burma and China, and the Atlantic and Pacific. Albania, Egypt, and Greece had fallen to the Italians, while Estonia, Sebastopol, and Rostov were in the hands of the Germans, who also had invaded Greece, Yugoslavia, and Crete.

The War in Europe and the Mediterranean

By the time the United States entered the war, the European Allies had been fighting the Germans for several years. They were tired and their resources were running low. The United States had the industrial strength they lacked. Whereas the Axis powers were finding it more and more difficult to produce the war materials they needed to supply their forces, American factories were churning out planes, tanks, and ships by the thousands.

At the same time the United States was jumping into war full force, the forces Hitler had sent to the Soviet Union were learning that the country they had been sent to conquer was going to conquer them. Although taken by surprise when first invaded, Stalin had recovered quickly. He ordered his people to follow a scorched-earth policy and, if they had to retreat, to destroy anything the Germans might find useful. The Germans were successful at first—capturing Kiev, laying siege to Leningrad and cutting it off from the rest of the country, penetrating as far as the outskirts of Moscow, conquering as they went. But by then the snow and bitter cold of the Russian winter was setting in. Ill equipped to deal with the severity of a Russian winter, the German armies knew their only hope was to hold their ground until spring and push forward then. Hitler's expectation of a quick defeat of the Soviets had been totally unrealistic. The Soviet Union was too large, the climate too icy and overpowering, and the Soviets too determined. It was only a matter of time until the Germans fell to defeat.

By 1943 the tide of the war had definitely turned, marking the beginning of the end for the Axis in the Soviet Union, in other parts of Europe, and in North Africa, where the Italians and German general Erwin Rommel's Afrika Korps had maintained the upper hand since 1940. From a German perspective, in 1943 everything fell apart. North Africa fell to the Allies. An Allied conquest of Sicily and southern Italy led to the downfall of Mussolini and the dissolution of the Fascist Party in Italy. Not ready to concede, the Germans rescued Mussolini and kept fighting, even though they knew they were losing. Their retreat from Rome without a fight in June 1944 confirmed that the war was taking a turn in favor of the Allies.

The fate of the Germans was sealed that same month by the Allied landings on the beaches of Normandy, France, considered by historians the largest and most carefully planned offensive of the entire war. Although the Germans knew there would be an invasion, they did not know where or when it would take place. While the Americans pushed through northern France, liberating almost all of France within about a month and a half, French Resistance forces led by French general Charles de Gaulle entered Paris, transforming it into a free city for the first time in four years.

The Soviets, meanwhile, continued to advance, liberating their country region by region and moving in to take over some countries of Eastern Europe. By the fall of 1944, almost all of east-central Europe was under Soviet control, creating uneasiness in the minds of the other Allies, who had even more reason than before to distrust Stalin. While the Soviets took control in the east, the Americans, British, French, and Canadians continued to advance in the west. The Germans were caught in the middle, unable to make any headway as the Allies pushed toward the Elbe River in Germany. Knowing full well that they had no hope of winning the war, the Germans finally admitted defeat. On May 8, 1945, V-E Day, the war in Europe officially ended. By then, Mussolini had been captured and hanged by Italian partisans, and Hitler, who had survived several assassination attempts by his own generals, had committed suicide in his underground bunker in Berlin rather than acknowledge Germany's defeat or suffer the humiliation of surrender.

The War in the Pacific and in Asia

As in Europe, the war in Asia seemed to favor the Axis at first. By late summer of 1942, the Japanese had taken control of Malaya, Singapore, and Rangoon and had occupied Burma, the Dutch East Indies, Guam, Wake Island, and the Philippines. The Japanese had dominated the Pacific almost completely and, at first, the Allies could make no headway against them on land. At sea, they fared slightly better. They did not win, but neither did they lose, the Battle of the Coral Sea in 1942, the first naval battle fought entirely in the air by aircraft based on carriers. Although the damage done in this battle ruined the Japanese plan to invade Australia, the Japanese navy did not suffer its first major defeat until the following month, when the Americans won the Battle of Midway. It was a crucial loss strategically for the Japanese, slowing their advance across the central Pacific, ending their threat to Hawaii, and, above all, costing them their naval superiority in the Pacific.

The Japanese continued to hold island strongholds in the Pacific and fought a series of ferocious battles as the Americans struggled to make their way north to Japan. The American strategy was to leapfrog, hopping from one island to the next, capturing some and bypassing others. Those that they bypassed were cut off from supplies, effectively isolating them so that they could barely survive let alone threaten anyone. Japanese culture and beliefs were alien to most Westerners, making it difficult to understand the Japanese concept of war, honor, and duty at all cost to country. As the Americans drew closer to Japan, Japanese military leaders tried to stop them by sending out kamikazes, Japanese airmen who considered it not only their duty but an honor to volunteer for suicide missions against the Americans, causing their own deaths by crashing their bombers into Allied bases and ships. Allied frustration grew as it became increasingly more evident that the Japanese would continue to refuse to admit defeat or to surrender no matter how high their losses became.

In August 1945, convinced that many American troops would continue to die unless the Japanese surrendered, the U.S. government unleashed an extremely powerful bomb—an atomic bomb—never before used in warfare. The first bomb was dropped on the Japanese city of Hiroshima. Even though it killed tens of thousands of people and virtually destroyed the city itself, the Japanese steadfastly continued to refuse to surrender. Surrender came only after a second atomic bomb was dropped on yet another Japanese city—Nagasaki. With the same devastating effects as those experienced in Hiroshima, World War II came to an end. To this day, the August 14, 1945, Japanese agreement to unconditional surrender withstanding, historians and scientists continue to debate the need to drop the bomb on Japan and the morality of the action. In his award-winning biography of Harry S. Truman, historian David McCullough asks,

> And how could a President, or the others charged with responsibility for the decision [to drop the bomb], answer to the American people if when the war was over, after the bloodbath of an invasion of Japan, it became known that a weapon sufficient to end the war had been available by midsummer and was not used?

McCullough goes on to justify Truman's decision:

> Had the bomb been ready in March and deployed by Roosevelt, had it shocked Japan into surrender then, it would have already saved nearly fifty thousand American lives lost in the Pacific in the time since, not to say a vastly larger number of Japanese lives.[1]

Nor had anyone ever doubted that Roosevelt would use it.

The United States and the War

When the United States entered the war in 1941, most Americans had no idea that the war would drag on for four more years. Surprisingly, very few foresaw how profoundly the war would change Americans and the American nation as a whole—technologically, economically, culturally, and socially. Although surprised, most Americans enjoyed the new sense of power and strength with which their country had emerged from the war.

The changes effected by the war were enormous. More than 15 million Americans volunteered or were drafted into the military. While they were preparing to fight or were actually doing battle, the Americans left on the homefront had the responsibility of providing for those in the military in addition to providing for themselves. They were faced with the need to feed, shelter, train, equip, transport, and provide medical care for American soldiers, sailors, marines, air force, and other military personnel. Out of this need came dozens of new boards, offices, and agencies to direct the effort.

American scientists went into high gear, developing new weapons such as the bazooka rocket launcher, the proximity fuse, radar, sonar, and the atomic bomb. The American economy experienced an upward spiral, pulling the nation and its citizens out of the lingering effects of the Great Depression. Industrial and agricultural productivity soared, resulting in more jobs for more people. People had more money to spend than they had in a long time, but with about one-third of the economy devoted to the production of military goods, consumer goods were in short supply. As prices rose for these goods, workers demanded higher wages, which compounded the problem. But, by 1943, the economy was settling, inflation was holding steady, and Americans were enveloped in prosperity.

The war brought about other changes as well, changes that many Americans had a hard time accepting and that led to racial unrest and conflict. As more Southerners, many of them African Americans, were lured to the industrial cities of the northern United States by the increased demand for workers, racial tensions grew, fanned in part by white Southerners who had migrated to the urban areas of the north to find work and were opposed to the idea that African Americans could hold the same jobs that they did. In California, a similar situation occurred, except that it was not southern African Americans that were on the receiving end of the prejudice but Mexican Americans who had migrated from Texas and Arizona in search of work.

The war also changed the role of women. With so many men gone, more women entered the workforce, often taking jobs traditionally filled strictly by males and considered inappropriate and unfeminine for women. Although many women who went to work to support the war effort planned to give up their jobs when the war was over and the men returned, some women had second thoughts about giving up their new lives. The war had made these women self-sufficient and independent and they saw no reason to return to the traditional role of homemaker just because the men came back home.

No one living in the United States, however, suffered greater change than the Japanese, many of whom had joined the military to fight for the United States. The Japanese attack on Pearl Harbor had increased awareness and concern about national security and defense, creating a strong sense of unease and suspicion among many Americans—the focus of their distrust being the Japanese, Germans, and Italians living in the United States who were not American citizens. In some areas of the country, such as California, all Japanese were regarded with suspicion and, in some instances, outright animosity—even those born in the United States. This distrust led to the creation of relocation centers in which more than 100,000 Japanese were interned for the duration of the war, an episode that most postwar historians consider one of the most shameful in American history. That more than half the Japanese forced to evacuate their homes and sell at a loss virtually all of what they owned were American citizens did not seem to matter to most Americans.

In the first volume of his two-volume popular history *The Glory and the Dream*, historian William Manchester summarizes the mixed emotions and the magnitude of the changes that characterized Americans and their nation during the war years:

> For tens of millions [of Americans] the war boom was in fact a bonanza, a Depression dream come true, and they felt guilty about it. Not so guilty that they declined the money, to be sure—that would have been asking too much of human nature and wouldn't have helped combat troops a bit—but contrite enough to make them join scrap drives, buy war bonds, serve in Civil Defense units, and once in a while buy a lonely soldier a drink.

> Every great war is accompanied by social revolution, and the

very dimensions of this war were to alter America greatly. Few realized that then. The *New York Daily News* really believed that GIs were fighting "to get back to the ball game and the full tank of gas" and GIs themselves sometimes thought they were in there battling for Mom and apple pie. But history does not let those who make it get off that easily. No country could have survived America's convulsive transformation of 1941–45 without altering its essence and its view of itself. The homefront was in reality a battleground of ideas, customs, economic theory, foreign policy, and relationships between the sexes and social classes. Rosie the Riveter, like Kilroy, was everywhere, and she would never be the same again.[2]

The Aftermath of War

Almost nothing was the same after World War II, except the bickering, the hidden rivalries, and the playing of politics on an international scale. British prime minister Winston Churchill summed it up after the war with a single comment: "When the war of the giants is over, the war of the pygmies will begin."

The war robbed the world of great numbers of its population, taking an even greater human toll than World War I had. More than 15 million soldiers and untold millions of civilians were killed during the six years of fighting. As part of Hitler's plan to conquer the world, the Nazis had rounded up and worked, shot, or gassed to death more than 6 million European Jews. For many, this genocide—the Holocaust— was the most shocking and inhumane aspect of the war. The Japanese had added to the death toll by indiscriminately killing men, women, and children in the countries they conquered. Millions of those who had managed to survive the war were homeless and on the verge of starvation.

Arguing that the cruelty inflicted and atrocities committed by the Nazis and the Japanese had gone far beyond that justified by war, the Allies accused top Nazi and Japanese leaders of war crimes and acts against humanity. Of the twenty-two top Nazi leaders brought before the International Military Tribunal at Nuremberg, Germany, in 1946, half were sentenced to death for their crimes. Of the twenty-eight Japanese leaders tried in Tokyo, Japan, in 1948, seven were sentenced to death. Defiant to the end, the seven condemned men shouted the Japanese battle cry *banzai* one last time as they climbed onto the scaffold on which they would be hanged.

Humans were not the only casualties of the war. Much of Europe and Asia lay in ruins, devastated by bombs and mines and tanks and battles, partially or totally destroyed. Bombed-out factories, railroads, and highways dotted the landscape. In Europe, the countries that traditionally had controlled huge empires and world trade no longer had the power they once did. They needed to be rebuilt, but their economies were as shattered as their cities and people. War had cost them many of their Asian and African colonies, the established sources of their raw materials and cheap labor, at the very time they were needed most. The leadership role enjoyed by the nations of Western Europe before 1914 was one of the casualties of the Second World War.

Defeat had cost Germany and Japan their right to survive and rebuild as independent nations. The Allies divided Germany into four zones—American, British, French, and Soviet—with each Allied nation occupying and ruling its zone. The United States occupied Japan, placing American general Douglas MacArthur in charge. Among the many changes imposed on the Japanese was the transformation from a nation controlled by the military into a democracy in which the people had the right to vote.

There was, however, hope that in spite of the war—and, perhaps, because of it—this time the peace would be lasting. The Allies had thought about this during the war and, determined to do all they could to avoid a third world war, had agreed that after the war was over they would meet to establish an organization similar to the League of Nations whose primary goal would be to prevent war. Approved by fifty-one countries in 1945, the United Nations became a reality that remains in operation today. Headquartered in New York City, with members from all parts of the globe, it now performs more than just the peacekeeping services for which it was conceived originally.

The New Superpowers

Nothing was more indicative of the shift in the balance of world power resulting from World War II than the emergence of the United States and the Soviet Union as superpowers—the world's foremost military powers and the indisputable leaders of the postwar world.

The Soviet Union, the largest country on earth, had suffered more losses than several of the other nations involved in the war combined. At the same time, however, it had an incredible abundance of natural resources and a multitude of workers to farm the land and staff the factories. The war had enabled the Soviet Union to dominate Eastern Europe and set up Communist governments that pledged the allegiance of their countries to the Soviets.

America, whose citizens had not had to suffer the devastation of bombs or the blood of the battlefront in their own nation, had been transformed by the war as much as or more than any of the battle-scarred nations of Europe or Asia. The wartime industrial efforts and productivity of the United States had made it the world's leading industrial power, with farms and factories that produced more than any other country in the world. Politically and militarily, the United States had replaced Britain and France as leader of the Western democracies.

It soon became clear that two superpowers with such differing ideologies would not—actually could not—exist amicably for any length of time. Although the two nations had been allies during the war and had worked together to defeat the common enemy, each remained committed to its own interests and concerns and harbored a nagging distrust of the other. Stalin or the leaders that followed him were not likely to forget that, for a long time, both the United States and Britain had left the Soviet Union to fend for itself, ignoring Stalin's pleas to open a second front in Europe to alleviate German pressure on the Soviet Union. As a result, over both nations, and the rest of the world, hung the threat of the atomic bomb, which in the words of one of its creators, scientist Robert Oppenheimer, "made the prospect of future war unendurable. It has led us up those last few steps to the mountain pass; and beyond there is a different country."

Because the war established the United States and the Soviet Union as superpowers, many historians claim that the cold war that grew out of their rivalry and the arms race that it engendered collectively were yet another legacy of the war. Even those historians who do not subscribe to that line of thinking acknowledge that World War II changed the world forever, impacting people and nations all over the globe and thrusting them into a compelling new era.

Notes

1. David McCullough, *Truman*. New York: Simon & Schuster, 1992, pp. 439–40.

2. William Manchester, *The Glory and the Dream: A Narrative History of America 1932–1972*, vol. 1. Boston: Little, Brown, 1973, pp. 353–54.

Chapter 1

War in the Making

In Defense of the Treaty of Versailles

Mark Mazower

The Treaty of Versailles, which formally brought World War I to an end, inflicted heavy monetary and territorial penalties on Germany and decimated its military. Over time, historians, political figures, and others have criticized the treaty settlement and have argued that it contributed to the outbreak of World War II. Mark Mazower, professor of modern history at Birbeck College, agrees that the treaty was not without defects. He also contends that the drafters of the treaty had few—if any—alternatives given the political, cultural, and national realities of the times. In Mazower's view, put forth in this selection, many of the concepts and borders formed in the Treaty of Versailles helped build the peace in 1945. The main force to emerge from World War I and the main political factor with which the creators of a new postwar settlement had to contend, Mazower writes, was the power of nationalism.

The Versailles Treaty settlement was, from the moment of its birth, unloved as few creations of international diplomacy have been before or since. [Adolf] Hitler and [Winston] Churchill were united in its condemnation; so were commentators from the American anti-Soviet diplomat and historian George Kennan to the British Marxist E.H. Carr. One is hard put to find a school textbook with anything good to say about the achievements of the Paris peacemakers. Yet curiously we still live in the world they shaped: were the foundations laid more carefully by them than we like to

Excerpted from Mark Mazower, "Two Cheers for Versailles," *History Today*, July 1999. Reprinted with permission from *History Today*.

think? The argument that the defects of Versailles led to the outbreak of another world war is commonplace; yet one might as easily argue that its virtues underpinned the peace after 1945.

Accusations Against the Treaty

Some suggest that Versailles was based on principles inconsistently applied. The charge is obviously true. The right of national self-determination was granted at Germany's expense, and the Anschluss with Austria, which Social Democrats in Vienna wanted in 1918, was prevented by the Great Powers and only achieved after the Nazis broke the League of Nations system and marched in twenty years later. But international affairs are not a matter of logic alone, and the principle of consistency must be matched against considerations of power politics or geography. National self-determination could never have been applied across the board; the basic issue is whether a better principle existed for the re-ordering of Europe.

More serious an accusation is that the peace settlement was not so much inconsistent as ineffective: it was based upon an inaccurate appraisal of the European balance of power and deprived of the means of its own defence by American withdrawal and British indifference. At Paris the Great Powers ignored the fact that the almost simultaneous collapse of Germany and Russia had produced an anomalous situation in eastern Europe. The French, who of all the Great Powers felt most immediately threatened, thought the only safeguard of their own security—if the League was not to be equipped with an army of its own—was alliance with grateful clients like the Baltic states, Poland, Czechoslovakia, Romania and Yugoslavia. But it should have been obvious that the newly independent states formed there would be unable alone to ensure stability in the region once these two Great Powers reasserted themselves. . . . After 1939, Hitler's New Order pushed the principle of German (and Russian) hegemony one brutal stage further. But this is less an argument against the Versailles settlement itself than against the refusal of the Great Powers who sponsored it to back it up with armed force before 1939.

Thirdly, it is often felt that the whole approach to Germany after the Treaty was flawed. The enemy was humiliated but not crushed, burdened by reparations yet unopposed when it rearmed and marched into the Rhineland. . . . But the economic problem after 1919 was not so much reparations as the shaky structure of international lending and, in particular, the shock of the world depression. . . .

Finally, there is the accusation common to conservatives and Communists alike that the Versailles peace settlement was overly ideological. For some, it was an extension of nineteenth-century liberal moralising, a combination of British utilitarianism and American idealism—a basically philosophical approach to the world which lacked realism or understanding of the political passions which animated people in Europe.

Alternatively, it was—behind the veil of noble sentiments—an anti-Communist crusade whose liberalism masked a fundamentally reactionary and deeply conservative goal: the containment, if not the crushing, of Bolshevism. Outflanked gradually by other more determined and forceful anti-Communist movements of the right, European liberals lost their enthusiasm for defending the Versailles order and sat back to watch fascism take over the task of saving Europe from red revolution.

The Impact of Nationalism

One question, however, confronts the critics of Versailles: what were the alternatives? It was not, after all, as if the Powers had willed this new liberal order of independent, democratic nation-states into existence. They had certainly not been fighting the Great War to this end. On the contrary, as late as 1918 most Entente diplomats still favoured the preservation of the old empires in central Europe in the interests of continental stability. Of course, after 1919 the conflicts and tensions produced by the new states of the region made many people nostalgic for what the Austrian writer Stefan Zweig, looking back to the Habsburg era [the Habsburgs ruled from the mid-1400s to 1918], called "the world of yesterday." Fragmentation since the war seemed to have harmed the region both politically and economically, especially once the world depression forced countries into an impoverished self-sufficiency.

Yet it was a rare blend of nostalgia and realpolitik which

lay behind much of the antipathy to Versailles. The makers of America's new role in Europe after 1945, for example, who had grown up looking closely at these problems, held Versailles responsible for the instability of interwar Europe. Adolf Berle, Roosevelt's assistant secretary of state between 1938 and 1944, believed that French generals had been responsible for breaking up the Austro-Hungarian Empire and wanted some kind of reconstitution of that entity to ward off the Russians. Hitler, he advised the president . . . was perhaps "the only instrument capable of re-establishing a race and economic unit which can survive and leave Europe in balance."

George Kennan . . . took a very similar view in the late 1930s. In his despatches from Prague he wrote: "It is generally agreed that the breakup of the limited degree of unity which the Habsburg Empire represented was unfortunate for all concerned. . . ."

It did not take long for someone as astute as Kennan to realise that the Nazi New Order was not going to stabilise central Europe in the way the Habsburgs had done. But the reason for this, in his mind, was not the apparently obvious one that Hitler's whole upbringing had turned him into a German nationalist critic of the Austro-Hungarian monarchy. It was, rather, what Kennan conceived as the excessively democratic character of Hitler's Germany and the limited involvement of Germany's aristocracy in the Third Reich. More aristocratic government was Kennan's answer to Europe's problems. It is hard to imagine a more far-fetched or unrealistic approach—the Habsburgs were marginalised between the wars even by Hungary's reactionary regent Admiral Horthy, and the most successful Habsburg aristocrat of that era was the bizarre and premature proponent of European union, Count Coudenhove-Kalergi. Perhaps only an American conservative intellectual like Kennan could have taken the prospect of a Habsburg restoration seriously. European conservatives, closer to the ground, had fewer illusions. "The Vienna to Versailles period has run its course," wrote the historian Lewis Namier in February 1940.

Whatever the weaknesses of the system created in 1919, a

return to previous forms is impossible. They have been broken, and broken for good.

It was not aristocrats that had kept the old empires together but dynastic loyalty, and this had vanished.

The Nazi New Order—or Communism

If dynasticism no longer offered an alternative principle to the Versailles order, then what of the rival ideologies of right and left? This was where root-and-branch critics of Versailles had to bite the bullet. Most anti-Communists between the wars had no difficulty in swallowing the idea of an authoritarian revision of the Versailles settlement. What made them hesitate was a quite different proposition; the reality of life under the Nazi New Order. . . . Above all, the New Order was based on the idea of German racial superiority, and few anti-Communists could stomach this once they saw what it meant in terms of practical politics.

If one agreed with Namier that "no system can possibly be maintained on the European Continent east of the Rhine which has not the support either of Germany or of Russia," then the only ideological alternative to Nazism was Communism, or more precisely the extension of Russian rule westwards into Europe. Just as Versailles's critics on the right had seen Germany's move east after 1933 as confirmation of their own prejudices, so critics on the left similarly interpreted the course of events after 1943 as a happy necessity. Historians like E.H. Carr saw this as realism replacing the idealism of Versailles. It was apparently not felt to be realistic to point out that all the historical evidence pointed to the unpopularity of Communism among the majority of the populations who now had to endure it. . . . Today we are unlikely to see Communism as an attractive alternative to the principles embodied in the Versailles order: yesterday's "realism" looks riddled with its own form of wishful thinking. . . .

Nationalism and the Ethnic Issue

The power of nationalism was the chief force to emerge from the First World War in Europe, and was the main political factor facing the architects of a new postwar settlement. From our perspective [today], it hardly looks as though fascism and Communism were able to handle European nationalism better than the peacemakers at Versailles. Hitler's New Order proceeded by ignoring all nationalisms except the German, and lost Europe in consequence. Communism believed that eventually nationalist antipathies would vanish, subsumed within an internationalist struggle: but time ran out for the Communists before this happened. If we want to find guidance in the past for how to tackle the problems of nationalism that remain in Europe, we cannot do better than return to the diplomats who gathered in Paris eighty years ago. . . .

Ethnic civil war emphasised in the most unmistakable way that the peacemakers in Paris were not sketching their maps on a tabula rasa [clean slate]. On the contrary, they were as much responding to circumstances as shaping them. East European critics of Great Power arrogance often forget today how far the Versailles settlement was brought into being, not by the Powers, but by local nationalist elites and their supporters. New nations were pressing their claims on paper, in the streets and by force of arms, as the war approached an end. . . .

It is to the credit of the Versailles peacemakers that they confronted the problem of ethnic violence head on. They were aware of the chief defect of the Wilsonian [referring to U.S. president Woodrow Wilson] principle of national self-determination—namely that if it was interpreted territorially and not merely as a grant of cultural autonomy, then on its own it ruled out either an equitable or a geographically coherent settlement of the problems of central and eastern Europe. No one, after all, was proposing to give the Kashubians, the Polesians, the Pomaks, or any of the other small ethnic groups of the region a state of their own. They, and several other larger peoples like the Jews, the Ukrainians and the Macedonians, would remain under the rule of others. In other words, the creation—or better, the recognition—of nation-states at Versailles was accompanied by its inescapable shadow, the problem of minorities. . . .

[In 1929] British foreign secretary Austen Chamberlain warned that, "We have not reached such a degree of solidarity in international affairs that any of us welcome even the most friendly intervention in what we consider to be our domestic affairs." This attitude discouraged the most dynamic lobbyists for Europe's minorities, the Germans and the Jews. Until 1933, they worked together in the European Congress of Nationalities to try to give the Minorities Treaties teeth. Thereafter their paths diverged. But Hitler's rise to power can be seen in the context of the failure of the League [of Nations] to protect Europe's minorities. Where the League's rather timid use of international law had failed, the Nazis used force; their "solution" involved forced population transfer, resettlement and ultimately genocide. And after 1944 many of these instruments were turned on the Germans themselves as they were driven out of Poland and the former Habsburg lands.

Yet we should not write off the peacemakers of Versailles too quickly. Despite the horrors of the 1940s, which virtually eliminated both the Jews and the Germans from much of eastern Europe, many minorities remained across the region. However, instead of building on the League's tentative efforts to construct an international regime of minority rights, the architects of the postwar order enshrined in the United Nations deliberately retreated from the problem and tried to dress up its reluctance to deal with it with meaningless persiflage about "human rights.". . .

The Reality of Versailles

The very least, then, that we can say for Versailles is that it recognised and articulated the major problems for European stability at that time. What was more, there was no palatable alternative to the nation-state then, or since. Where the peace was found wanting between the wars was in the will to uphold it. Today NATO [the North Atlantic Treaty Organization] is turning itself into the kind of force which the peacemakers of 1919 lacked. But do its political masters have a clear grasp of what kind of Europe they wish to defend? They could do worse than cast their eyes back to the work of their predecessors eighty years ago.

Totalitarianism: Prelude to War

Charles Messenger

In this selection, British historian and defense analyst Charles Messenger describes how the Treaty of Versailles and the lessons learned from World War I led Russia, France, and Britain to reorganize their militaries and amend their military theories. Messenger makes clear how the war and the terms of postwar treaties contributed to the growing political polarization and economic problems in Germany that enabled Benito Mussolini and the Fascists to take control in Italy and Adolf Hitler and the Nazis to rise to power in Germany. Both Hitler and Mussolini, along with Russian dictator Joseph Stalin, explains Messenger, took advantage of the civil war that broke out in Spain in 1936 to test their new military weapons and theories. He goes on to relate how a confident Hitler set out to expand German territory and recapture German prestige and glory.

Although the slaughter that had marked the Great War of 1914–18 had come to an end, 1919 was one of the most turbulent years that Europe had witnessed. In Russia civil war raged. . . . The Baltic states, Poland and Finland seized the opportunity to break away from the dominance that Russia had for so long exerted over them.

Austria-Hungary split apart. . . . Turkey, too, seethed as a result of the loss of the Ottoman empire. Germany suffered the anguish of civil war as the Left tried to take control. . . .

In the meantime, the victorious Allies were drawing up the peace treaties which would formally bring the Great War to an end. They also desired to create a new world in which the slaughter of 1914–18 could not be repeated. The framework was to be President Woodrow Wilson's Fourteen Points of January 1918. Some, notably the French, whose main industrial region in the north of the country had been devastated by the war, wanted to extract the maximum revenge on Germany. To a large extent their desire was met, with Germany being forced to make heavy financial reparations for the damage she had caused. Her militarism was to be crushed for all time through stringent restrictions on the size of her armed forces. Conscription was banned, with the army being limited to 100,000 men, a tenth of its 1914 strength. Germany was to be allowed no air force, no tanks, and no guns above 150 mm caliber. Her navy . . . was restricted to a few elderly cruisers and smaller vessels. The need to give Poland access to the sea caused East Prussia to be isolated from the rest of Germany. Poland also received part of mineral-rich Silesia. Finally, the Rhineland was demilitarized and occupied by Allied troops and the coal-rich Saarland given to France to administer on behalf of the League of Nations. The same happened with Germany's former African colonies.

The Treaty of Versailles, bringing a formal end to the war with Germany, was signed on 28 June 1919. The Allies celebrated this with victory parades, but in Germany the swingeing terms caused resentment among certain sectors of the population. This was directed at the Weimar government, which had been forced to sign the treaty. The myth grew like a canker that the German armed forces had been betrayed at the end of the war by the politicians and others—the so-called "stab in the back."

Other peace treaties followed. That with Austria (Treaty of St Germain) recognized the disparate races that had made up the empire and the nationalism that this had engendered. A new state of Czechoslovakia was created, while the Austrian provinces in the Balkans were combined with Montenegro and Serbia to create Yugoslavia. . . .

The last of the former belligerents to make peace was Turkey. The Treaty of Sèvres of August 1920 saw the dismemberment of the Ottoman empire, with France being granted Syria, and Britain Palestine, Transjordan and

Mesopotamia (soon to be renamed Iraq) as League of Nations' mandates. The Dardanelles were demilitarized, the Dodecanese ceded to Italy, and Greek troops allowed to occupy Turkish territory on both sides of the Bosphorus.

But the principal achievement of the peace conference was the creation of the League of Nations. . . . Contrary to French wishes, the League had no integral military element. Its purpose was merely to encourage, through disarmament agreements, mutual guarantees between nations, and international agreement not to resort to war until all other avenues had been thoroughly explored. For this the League would provide arbitration machinery. However, none of the vanquished nations was initially invited to join, and neither was Russia. Worse, as the League was setting up its headquarters at Geneva, the US Senate refused to ratify the Treaty of Versailles. . . . Thus the League of Nations had to operate without one of the leading global powers. . . .

A Change of Military Theory

Britain and France could not afford to act as the world's military policemen; 1914–18 had drained them physically and financially. They had dismantled their vast war machines as quickly as they could and were now bent on reconstruction of their exhausted economies. French defence policy was based on the need to secure her eastern borders so that Germany would not contemplate another invasion like those of 1870 and 1914. . . .

In Britain the military conservatives regarded the trench warfare of 1914–18 as an aberration and were relieved by the prospect of getting back to "real soldiering." This meant reverting to the traditional priority of defence of empire. But the need to police the mandates in the Middle East quickly placed an intolerable strain on the British Army, slowing down demobilization. It was now that the Chief of the Air Staff, Hugh Trenchard, stepped in, proposing that the newly independent Royal Air Force [RAF] take over responsibility for the Middle East at a fraction of the existing costs. The government gratefully accepted this plan, and the policy of air control was born.

Yet, in spite of seeming military stagnation, there were some who sought to draw valid lessons from 1914–18 for the future. They began with the premise that the internal combustion engine had altered the nature of war. One school of thought concerned itself with air power. Initially led by the Italian General Giulio Douhet, it argued that the aircraft, by virtue of its ability to overfly seas and armies, could strike at the very heart of the enemy—his government, industry, and, above all, the morale of the population.

The other major school of military theory concerned itself with a weapon which had been created during the war to overcome the deadlock on the Western Front. It was Colonel J.F.C. Fuller, lately chief of staff at the headquarters of the British Tank Corps in France, who led the way in arguing that the tank would revolutionize war on land, and, by increasing the pace of operations, would make static warfare a thing of the past. He was joined by a wartime soldier turned journalist, Captain Basil Liddell Hart. They likened the old style of warfare to the brute force of a cudgel directed at the enemy's mass. In contrast, armoured warfare was as the thrust of a rapier aimed at the heart of the opposing army—its command, control and communications. With these disrupted, the enemy would be unable to react in time and his defeat would be inevitable. . . .

Mussolini and Hitler Rise to Power

During the 1920s a new force began to emerge in Europe. Italy, although one of the victors of the late war, suffered in its immediate aftermath from a series of weak governments. Civil unrest, especially strikes, grew. To counter this, a right-wing movement called the *Fascisti* developed in northern Italy, with journalist Benito Mussolini quickly rising to lead it. Initially they had little popular support, but in autumn 1921 began a campaign of moving into one city after another, gaining control by taking over the public utilities. Then, in August 1922, the Socialist opposition declared a general strike. Frustrated by the central government's inability to deal with it, Mussolini and his followers took over the national transport system. Two months later the Fascists made their celebrated march on Rome and took over the reins of government, vowing to modernize the country.

The path which brought Adolf Hitler and his Nazi Party to power in Germany was, however, to be a much longer one than Mussolini's. Its start point was the German Workers Party formed in 1919. Its manifesto called for the restoration of Greater Germany, the abrogation of the peace treaties, and the denial of German citizenship to Jews. It was renamed the Nationalsozialistische Deutsche Arbeiterpartei (NSDAP) in 1921, with Hitler taking control. By early 1923 Germany was falling badly behind in reparations payments to the Allies. French troops therefore occupied the industrial Ruhr. Not only did this result in galloping inflation, but it also provided right-wing parties, like the NSDAP, with a rallying cry. Chancellor Gustav Stresemann, fearful that the country was on the verge of total collapse, declared a state of emergency and agreed to resume reparations payments. Consequently, the French withdrew from the Ruhr.

The Right saw Stresemann's action as a climbdown. In Bavaria, where feeling against him was strongest, Hitler formed an alliance dedicated to toppling the Weimar republic. . . . Hitler and his followers attempted a putsch in Munich, but it was put down by the police and the army. Hitler was imprisoned for a short time and the NSDAP banned in Bavaria. . . .

In October 1929 . . . came the Wall Street Crash. Its reverberations were felt all over the world, nowhere more so than in Germany, whose fragile economy took a severe battering. Unemployment rose sharply and with it came increased political polarization to the extreme Left and extreme Right. The elections of the following year witnessed much street violence between Communist and Nazi thugs. They also saw Hitler win over a hundred seats in the Reichstag, making his party the second largest. The government's deflationary policies caused unemployment to rise even further, thus increasing the political polarization. This enabled Hitler to challenge Field Marshal Paul von Hindenburg for the presidency in 1932. He lost, but gained over a third of the total vote. . . . That same year the Allies agreed to waive the remainder of Germany's reparations payments, but this did not prevent the NSDAP from becoming the largest party in Germany as a result of elections held that July. Hitler, however, refused to join other parties in a governing coalition and fresh elections had to be held. The Nazi vote fell slightly. . . . Von Hindenburg now appointed Hitler as chancellor. . . .

One of Hitler's first steps was to call for fresh elections, but a week before they took place there was a fire at the Reichstag. Hitler blamed the Communists, but it is almost certain that the fire had been started by the Nazis. The elections saw the Nazis win sufficient seats to gain total power and Hitler wasted little time in getting legislation passed

A Propagandist's View of the German March into Austria

Propaganda was a favorite Nazi tool. This tribute to the German march into Austria, which appeared in a 1938 issue of Die Wehrmacht, *the biweekly magazine published by the German army, is just one example of Nazi propaganda.*

Ancient German longings have been fulfilled. The dream of a great German people's Reich stretching from the Eider to the Brenner and from the Rhine to the Leitha has been realized. German soldiers always supported the drive for unity, and were always ready to bleed and die for it. . . . Adolf Hitler's German soldiers did not march into German Austria in battle. They entered German land as representatives of a general German will to unity, to establish brotherhood with the German people and soldiers there. It was a great demonstration of the community of German blood.

In this spirit the German army crossed the Austrian border at many places on the immortal morning of 12 March 1938. They were received in the same spirit by the German-Austrian population. Everywhere and without exception, there was invisible, spontaneous contact from heart to heart. . . . It was more than mere liking—it was love at first sight. Who among our soldiers in gray or blue will ever forget the joy looking his way from the eyes of all the Austrians who lined the streets of which virtually prohibited all political parties other than the NSDAP. Thus by the spring of 1933 he was in almost total control of Germany. Just over a year later, on 2 August 1934, Hitler's power became absolute on the death of von Hindenburg. By this time global peace was beginning to come under threat. . . .

German plans for rearmament had been in place for some years. General Hans von Seeckt, commander-in-chief of the Reichswehr until 1926, realized only too well that his 100,000-man army was not strong enough to defend Germany's western and eastern borders simultaneously. He therefore structured it as a cadre to provide the framework

---

the cities and villages! Who will not still hear the enthusiastic shouts that everywhere received him to the end of his days? Who does not remember the countless pastries given them by the joyous generosity of these German people! In some places, a flood of cigarette packages fell on the German vehicles.

True, they were hard, strenuous days. . . . But extraordinary military accomplishments have their rewards. Each soldier felt the proud glow of manliness, a feeling twice as strong given the admiration of their deeds one could see every hour, indeed every minute, in the eyes of the population. . . . Comrades from the former Austrian army also admired our men's achievements. Without exception they were eager to join the German army. . . .

Not only the officers and soldiers of the former Austrian army have justified expectations, but also each Austrian citizen. They all saw the German military's divisions and air squadrons not only as the representatives of the German will for unity, but also as the representatives of the new German great power. The German in Austria can raise his head more freely, proudly and self-confidently than ever before. He is German. Not only in a national political sense, but also in a governmental and military sense. He has become a citizen and soldier of the German army.

Ludwig Sertorius, "With German Soldiers in Liberated Austria," *Die Wehrmacht*, no. 6, 1938. www.calvin.edu/academic/cas/gpa/wehr01.htm.

for a massive expansion in time of war. One of its key features was the *Führerarmee* concept, which laid stress on training soldiers to fill posts at command levels higher than those they were in. This was to serve the army well during 1939–45. . . . Although Versailles prohibited Germany from having an air force, von Seeckt set up a covert air office within the war ministry.

Once the Allied Control Commission had left Germany, it became possible to begin clandestine development of modern weapons within the country. Indeed, Alfred Krupp, the German armaments tycoon, later stated that most of Germany's significant artillery weapons of 1939–45 had been developed before Hitler came to power. . . .

But while the British continued their experiments with armoured warfare, it was the Russians who made the most spectacular advances. . . .

When Stalin launched his first Five Year Plan in 1928, the primary driving force behind it was the creation of an effective munitions industry. . . .

By the mid 1930s the Red Army had a formidable armoured force. [War commissar Mikhail] Tuchachevski had also introduced paratroops and was conducting ambitious manoeuvres with combined arms. Foreign observers were impressed, although the more astute of them were aware that, as a whole, the Red Army was still an unwieldy mass—"a bludgeon, quite incapable of rapier work," as one of them wrote.

March 1935 was a momentous month for Germany. First, German troops reoccupied the Saarland, whose inhabitants had overwhelmingly voted to be restored to Germany in a League of Nations plebiscite held a few weeks earlier. Then, on the 9th, Hitler announced to the world that Germany had an air force. Suspicions that he was creating one had grown during the previous twelve months, but now it was a *fait accompli*. A week later, Hitler announced a massive expansion of the army. Versailles was well and truly dead.

Hitler saw the Luftwaffe as essentially a political weapon which he could use to further his aim of recreating a Greater Germany. To this end it had to be superior to or at least match other European air forces in numbers of aircraft.

Consequently, in 1934 a plan was drawn up calling for 4,000 aircraft by the end of the following year. Two thousand of these aircraft had already been produced by the end of 1934. As for the army, the original plan, drawn up at the end of 1933, entailed expanding it to twenty-one divisions by 1937. The additional manpower was to be found from one-year volunteers. By March 1935 Hitler was demanding a further increase, to thirty-six divisions. This could only be met by conscription. This meant drawing on those born during the so-called "white years" of 1914–18, when the birth rate fell dramatically. Furthermore, industry found it hard to increase weapons production to match the accelerated expansion. One significant example of this was that, while three Panzer divisions had been formed by October 1935, the remainder of the army had to rely largely on horse-drawn transport, and would continue to do so.

When it came to strengthening the German navy, Hitler had no wish for a repeat of the pre-1914 Dreadnought race, which would merely serve to antagonize Britain. Consequently . . . Germany agreed to restrict her surface fleet to just over a third of that of the Royal Navy, but would be allowed parity in submarines. This concession reflected a British belief that the submarine no longer posed the threat that it had during 1914–18, an attitude which they would have cause to regret.

Yet Britain and France were still uneasy and began slowly to rearm in that same year of 1935. At the time governments perceived that the main threat was the bomber. Consequently, rearmament was initially directed at increasing the size of the British and French air forces so as to provide a deterrent to the Luftwaffe.

Civil War in Spain: A Testing Ground

That 1935 marked a turning-point in European affairs during the interwar years was further reinforced in October. Mussolini had been disappointed that, unlike France and Britain, Italy had been awarded none of Germany's former African colonies. True, Italy already possessed Libya, Eritrea, and Italian Somaliland, but Mussolini wanted more

and cast his eyes on Abyssinia. . . . After peaceful overtures
had failed, Italian troops invaded the country. . . .

Taking advantage of British and French concern over
Abyssinia, Hitler sent his troops into the still-demilitarized
Rhineland in March 1936. It was a calculated gamble, since
the German army, still in the throes of expansion, was hardly
ready for war. It worked, and served to boost Hitler's confidence still further. True, as a result of the German move, the
French and British held military staff talks, but they reached
no firm conclusions on how further German expansion
might be countered.

London and Paris were further distracted in the late summer of 1936 by the Spanish Civil War. Increasing rivalry between the Left and Right in the country resulted in land
seizures, strikes and street violence. This culminated in a revolt . . . led by General Francisco Franco in July 1936. . . .

The British and French, alarmed that the conflict might
widen, declared their non-intervention and tried to persuade
other nations to do the same. Hitler, Mussolini, and Stalin,
while agreeing in principle to do so, in practice ignored the
plea. Soon each was sending ground and air contingents to
Spain. . . . For the dictatorships, Spain quickly became a
weapons-testing laboratory. In the air, German Messer-
schmitt Me109s duelled with Russian Poliakarpov I-15s and
I-16s, while on the ground German, Italian and Russian
tanks met each other in battle for the first time. . . .

The worsening situation in Europe and elsewhere caused
Britain and France to speed up their rearmament. In Britain
a bewildering series of RAF expansion plans followed one
another in rapid succession. . . . In spite of efforts to expand
the aviation industry, only 4,500 [aircraft] had been achieved
by spring 1938 and many of these were obsolescent types,
ordered under previous schemes. The French aviation industry was in a very much worse state and could only produce a fraction of the aircraft required. . . . By 1939, it was
still producing only 600 aircraft a year, while the Germans
were building 3,000.

As in 1914 the French agreed that the British should take
the lead when it came to naval operations, with the French

navy concentrating most of its effort in the Mediterranean. . . . In 1935 a plan was drawn up which called for a significant increase in aircraft-carriers, cruisers and destroyers so as to ensure that the German navy did not gain control of home waters. . . .

The French army was still firmly wedded to the Maginot Line. Yet one officer had dared to question reliance on this to the exclusion of all else in defence policy. This was Charles de Gaulle, who expounded his ideas in a book, *The Army of the Future*, published in 1933. He argued that France's falling birth rate meant that it could no longer sustain its traditional mass conscript army. Instead, the core of the army should be a 100,000-man professional armoured force. This was dismissed by most politicians, who argued that there was little point in having an offensive-based army when so much money had been spent on the Maginot Line. In any event, political suspicion of a regular army lay deep in France. . . .

Hitler Strikes Out

In Germany it was different. The *Wehrmacht* (armed forces) continued to expand. . . . Hitler was now devoting his attention to creating the Greater Germany he had dreamt of for so long. His first target was Austria. Bound to Germany by a common language, there was already a strong Nazi following within the country that for some time had been at work paving the way for a German takeover. Early in 1938 matters reached such a pitch that the Austrian chancellor, Kurt von Schuschnigg, complained to Hitler, but was rebuffed. He therefore decided to hold a plebiscite on whether the Austrian people wished to retain their independence. Fearful that it might produce the wrong result, Hitler ordered his troops across the border on 12 March, the very eve of the vote. It was a bloodless invasion, with *Anschluss* (union) being achieved in less than twenty-four hours. The only flaw was the performance of the Panzer arm, which spearheaded the invasion. Lack of organization and inexperience caused a sizeable proportion of its vehicles to break down or run out of fuel.

Hitler now turned on Czechoslovakia, especially the westernmost province of Sudetenland, which contained a significant ethnic German minority. This, as the Austrian Nazis had done, began to agitate for total autonomy at Hitler's prompting, and he made it clear that he was prepared to use force if necessary. The Czechs refused to be cowed, and mobilized. Recognizing the not insignificant Czech military strength, Hitler did not take immediate military action, even though it was clear that neither Britain nor France was prepared to go to war over Czechoslovakia. . . .

Four weeks after he had occupied Sudetenland, Hitler turned his eyes on Poland. He demanded that the Poles hand over the port of Danzig and that Germany be allowed to establish road and rail links with East Prussia across the Polish Corridor. The Poles, not unnaturally, refused. Hitler, however, was prepared to bide his time. . . . In mid March 1939 Czechoslovakia found itself dismembered between Germany and . . . Hungary. . . .

Hitler now reiterated his Polish demands, which were again turned down. Two days later, on 23 March 1939, his troops marched into the port of Memel on the Polish-Lithuanian border. The Poles immediately warned Hitler that any similar occupation of Danzig would mean war.

It was now that Britain and France finally woke up to the fact that the only way in which Hitler could be stopped was to stand up to him. Accordingly, they declared at the end of March that they would stand by Poland in the event of German aggression. . . .

Mussolini, jealous of Hitler's successes, decided to copy him and sent troops across the Adriatic to Albania, which had been under Italian influence for the past fifteen years. This continuing land-grabbing now caused US president Franklin Roosevelt to become concerned. In mid April 1939 he sought assurances from Hitler and Mussolini that they would not attack other European nations. Unfortunately, Roosevelt was on weak ground, since during the period 1935–7 Congress had passed a series of Neutrality Acts which forbade the United States from entering a war that was already raging. The two dictators were well aware of this and ignored Roosevlet's request.

The war clouds now began to loom ever larger over Europe.

Why Britain Had to Fight

Herbert Agar

On September 3, 1939, Britain, along with France, Australia, and New Zealand, declared war on Germany. For the second time in history, the world was officially at war. In this introductory chapter to his book *The Darkest Year: Britain Alone, June 1940–June 1941*, Pulitzer Prize–winning author, journalist, and editor Herbert Agar contends that German leader Adolf Hitler was proceeding on carefully planned-out actions when he went to war, contrary to the claims of some important writers and revisionist historians that Hitler went to war by accident. Agar argues that British and French leaders cannot be blamed for seeking at first to appease Hitler. They did so because of misleading and erroneous "facts" they received from respected government and civilian sources. In Agar's view, once Britain recognized that European civilization was at stake if someone did not take a stand and challenge Hitler, the British had no other choice but to promise to support Poland against the Nazis.

France had fallen on June 22, 1940, and on July 19 Hitler made the last of his "final" peace-offers to Britain. When this had been rejected by the Government and laughed at by the people, *The Times* of London reprinted this from the *New York Times:*

> Hitler has spoken and Lord Halifax has answered. There is no more to be said. Or is there? Is the tongue of Chaucer, of Shakespeare, of the King James translation of the Scriptures, of Keats, of Shelley, to be hereafter, in the British Isles, the dialect of an enslaved race? . . .

Excerpted from Herbert Agar, *The Darkest Year: Britain Alone, June 1940–June 1941* (Garden City, NY: Doubleday & Company, Inc., 1973). Copyright © 1972 Herbert Agar. Reprinted with permission from PFD on behalf of the estate of Herbert Agar.

From our own shores we cannot see the shadow over ancient gardens, over houses hoary with age, over the graves of poets and philosophers, and the tombs of the martyrs. We know only that one of the green and lovely oases of civilization in the wilderness of man's time on earth is foully threatened, and that the whole world forever more will be the poorer if it falls.

This was the mood of the West. People everywhere were watching breathlessly, unable to believe that England could resist, unable to believe that England could fall. We only knew that if she fell it would be in battle and not at a conference.

What had brought our world to this pass? Why the war and why the collapse of France? . . .

Why the war? . . . I believe that Hitler went to war by design and not by accident, and that Nazi Germany was at least as brutal as we thought in 1940. The more we learn, the more unworthy seem the Nazis to whom the German people abdicated all power during the 1930s. [Winston] Churchill wrote, with his graceful ferocity, that Hitler "called from the depths of defeat the dark and savage furies latent in the most numerous, most serviceable, ruthless, contradictory and ill-starred race in Europe." I suggest that the magic of Hitler was stranger than this. He called from the depths a group of jealous buffoons who hated each other, who crawled before their Fuehrer, and who shared the one talent of mesmerising that "ill-starred race."

A Revisionist View: War by Accident

After each war with Germany we have revisionist historians who insist that the war was not at all the way it seemed to those of us who were in it, and that we were wrong to think that we had been fighting for a worthy cause. . . . American revisionists have now entangled themselves in an effort to show that the whole thing was the fault of President [Franklin] Roosevelt. This has got them nowhere. . . .

In England, however, important writers . . . [suggest] that Hitler blundered into war almost by accident, certainly not by deep design, and that he was driven into the stance of a modern Napoleon [Bonaparte] by the stupidities of the Allies. This, I suggest, underestimates Hitler's guilt and exaggerates the faults of the unhappy "men of Munich."

The question is simple: Am I right in believing that the rough outline and the major aims of the six-years-war are to be found in [Hitler's autobiography] *Mein Kampf* and thus were long-contemplated? A.J.P. Taylor says "No." He denies that Hitler had always planned to ruin France and to make Germany lord of the Continent. In his exhilarating book, *The Origins of the Second World War*, he dismisses the threats in *Mein Kampf* as an emotional reaction to the French occupation of the Ruhr. He admits that Hitler intended to make Germans a great power in Western Europe and to gain *Lebensraum* [living space] from Russia in the East. The *Lebensraum* he agrees, must not be over-crowded; so where do the Russians go?

Hitler, says Mr Taylor, thought these good things could fall into his lap without a great war, through the folly of other people—although big threats and little wars might be needed. He had become head of the German State not by careful planning but because foolish people put him at the top intending to use him.

"Far from wanting war," writes Mr Taylor, "a general war was the last thing [Hitler] wanted. He wanted the fruits of total victory without total war; and thanks to the stupidity of others he nearly got them." So the broken victims of Nazi aggression must be blamed for their agony on the grounds of their longing for peace. Liddell Hart carries this complicated argument still further in his *History of the Second World War*. Here the Germans almost became the dupes of [British prime minister Neville] Chamberlain and Halifax [Edward Wood, British foreign secretary and Earl of Halifax].

"How, then," asks Liddell Hart, "did it come about that [Hitler] became involved in the major war that he had been so anxious to avoid?" The answer is to be found not merely, nor most, in Hitler's aggressiveness, but in the encouragement he had long received from the complaisant attitude of the Western Powers coupled with their sudden turn-about in the spring of 1939. "That reversal [i.e. the guarantee to Poland] was so abrupt and unexpected as to make war inevitable. . . . The Polish guarantee was the surest way to produce an early explosion, and a world war.'"

Liddell Hart points out that the British Government had allowed (perhaps encouraged) Hitler to believe that his search for *Lebensraum* to the East need not lead to war with the West. Also, in September 1938 the British and French Governments had turned down a Russian offer to join in the defence of Czechoslovakia, thus appearing to dismiss Eastern Europe as of small account. So Hitler felt betrayed when the decision to "support" Poland was announced. "I'll cook them a stew that they'll choke on," he shouted.

A Guarantee to Poland

Nevertheless, no matter how much we blame the Western Powers for their maundering (and the United States for selfish folly about reparations and war debts), Hitler had a consistent purpose which he had laid down in *Mein Kampf* fourteen years before he went to war and at least sixteen years before he began to go daft. The timing he left to the Fates (or their Nordic equivalent); but the plan was exact: the "betrayed Germans" in Austria, Czechoslovakia and Poland must first be rescued; then France must go, leaving England confused and ineffective; then Russia.

Obviously, Hitler hoped to do all this on the quiet, or with a few small wars; but if it meant the big war, he was content to take the chance when the hour was ripe. Liddell Hart is mistaken in thinking that the abrupt promise to Poland was a light-minded caprice. Militarily, it may have been ridiculous; but morally the guarantee (or something equally dramatic) had become necessary. The British people and their Government had seen at last that European civilisation was at stake, that Hitler and his shabby court had to be challenged. The Polish guarantee defeated nobody except the Poles; but it called a halt. It announced that the British, who are slow to wrath, admitted that their efforts to assuage the unassuageable had failed.

Ian Colvin, the *News Chronicle* correspondent in Berlin, may have influenced the choice of Poland as the place to make a stand. Late in March 1939 he told Lord Halifax that

Poland was positively the next country on Hitler's list. He added that if Britain gave clear proof that she would fight for Poland the German General Staff might call a halt to their all-aspiring Fuehrer. Like other rumours of serious resistance in Germany, this proved false; but Chamberlain made his guarantee to Poland two days after Mr Colvin's report, on March 31. He may have dreamed that the German generals would play their part and that even militarily his promise would not prove vain. Hope died slowly (first in Britain, and later in the United States) among those who thought that the Nazis could be dealt with like normal human beings.

The *Diaries* of Sir Alexander Cadogan [British permanent under secretary of state for foreign affairs] offer a more sophisticated view of the promise to Poland:

> Our guarantee could give no possible protection to Poland in any immediate attack. . . . But it set up a signpost for himself [Chamberlain]. He was committed, and in the event of a German attack on Poland he would be spared the agonising doubts and indecisions. Our military situation must have been known to them and they should have been aware of the imminence of the peril that threatened them. You may say that it was cynical. On a short view perhaps it was. But it *did* bring us into the war. . . . The poor Poles cannot be expected to appreciate the result for them.

Surely not. Cadogan seems to be suggesting that the Poles had to die in order to help Chamberlain clear his muddled mind. This sounds unfair both ways.

According to [Nazi minister of armament and ammunition] Albert Speer, Hitler always wanted to go to war over Poland and intended to provoke battle no matter how humbly the Allies might cringe. Speer quotes the Fuehrer:

> "Do you think it would have been good fortune for our troops if we had taken Poland without a fight, after obtaining Austria and Czechoslovakia without fighting? Believe me, not even the best army can stand that sort of thing. Victories without loss of blood are demoralising. Therefore it was not only fortunate there was no compromise; at the time

we would have had to regard it as harmful, and I therefore would have struck in any case."

Speer, the self-styled parent of German arms-production, is not the best witness when it comes to his own doings; but he was the nearest thing to a friend Hitler ever found. And he was in and out of Hitler's house—wherever that mobile unit might appear—more than any other man. Thus I am inclined to believe his tale which, if true, does not suggest a Hitler eager above all else to avoid a big war.

Appeasement Was the Only Option

And I find unsympathetic the theory that the proximate cause of the war was the dithering of Chamberlain, Halifax, [French premier Édourd] Daladier and Co. I see nothing base or stupid in these last, sad efforts to treat Germany as if she were sane. Granted that Chamberlain distrusted France, hated Russia and hoped for friendship with Germany; those who write off his policy as a silly result of these silly opinions forget some of the "information" which the Government had at the time and which could neither be ignored nor appraised.

[Former prime minister Stanley] Baldwin, who knew nothing about aviation, had announced that "the bomber will always get through" and Kingsley Martin of the *New Statesman*, who normally thought Baldwin a joke, believed this nonsense faithfully. Then Baldwin resigned in May 1937, just in time to avoid the fatal decisions. Neville Chamberlain, who succeeded, was shocked by the first report from the Committee of Imperial Defence. The Committee warned him that a German air attack on London lasting sixty days would kill 600,000 people and injure twice that number. This was indeed a pretty dish to set before the new Prime Minister.

Furthermore, everyone had for years been quoting figures from the Italian General [Giulio] Douhet's book of horrors. A city, said Douhet, could be destroyed by bombers in a day: then "ten, twenty, fifty cities. . . . A complete breakdown of the social structure cannot but take place in a country subjected to this kind of merciless pounding from the air. . . . The disintegrations of nations . . . will be achieved by aerial forces.". . .

During the First World War the Germans had invented "strategic bombing," or "total air warfare," or the bombing of civilians, as an indiscriminate form of terror. . . . During those first days of air warfare, the Germans dropped about 300 tons of bombs on the British Isles, causing 4,820 casualties, including 1,430 dead. Thus came the guess that in the next war "in densely populated areas such as London, there will be fifty casualties per ton of bomb dropped. Of these casualties, one-third will be killed and two-thirds wounded."

And how many tons could London expect each night? By 1937 the Air Staff estimated that within two years the Germans could average some 644 per twenty-four hours, adding that since the Germans liked to be as *schrecklich* [frightful] as possible they might start with 3,500 tons during the first twenty-four hours. Fifty times 3,500 gives 175,000 casualties, among whom a little more than 58,000 should be dead. And this on the first day, according to the best (or at any rate the only) advice.

How many light-hearted condemners of "appeasement" have tried to think themselves into 10 Downing Street at dawn, in the weakest hour of the spirit, faced with these so-called facts? What would you or I do about the 600,000 dead, or even about the 58,000 which should already have perished if the war began yesterday? Would we think it wrong to try again, in the hope that Hitler might not be implacable?

Chamberlain believed in facts, . . . and "facts" were served to him. Churchill thought facts were cranky and demanded miracles and saved the world; but if Hitler had been a little more normal Chamberlain might have saved thirty million lives plus a world-wide civil war plus the hydrogen bomb which still may prove at any hour that man is a failed experiment. Who knows? Who would like to have made Chamberlain's decisions? By the time Churchill had inherited, the war was well on its way and there were none of these problems: only victory or death.

Adding fortuitously to the indecisions and the torture of Chamberlain, General Vuillemin (Chief of Staff of the French air army) visited Germany for a week in August 1938 as [Field Marshal Hermann] Goering's guest. Vuillemin convinced himself that the Germans had nothing but friendly feelings toward France, and his hosts convinced him that the Luftwaffe and the airplane industry of Germany were unsurpassably powerful and efficient. He told François-Poncet, his Ambassador in Berlin, that the French air force would not last a fortnight against the Germans. Then he carried the news to Paris, whence it was relayed to London on the eve of Munich.

A Wealth of Misinformation

Another prophet of woe, another nuisance to Chamberlain, was Charles Lindbergh. . . . This was the American who had flown a single-engined plane from New York to Paris, and who, oddly, was regarded as an impartial authority on the world's air forces. As for his authority, . . . he was wrong on every count.

As for his impartiality, three weeks after Munich he was awarded, and accepted, the "Service Cross of the German Eagle with Star." Such was the man who undertook, in the late 1930s, to intimidate the British and the French and, incidentally, the Americans.

As a sample of what Lindbergh was saying he told [British deputy secretary of the cabinet] Tom Jones . . . that the air power of Germany was greater than that of all the European nations (including Russia, whose strength he derided) and that the Germans "could not be prevented by us or by France from laying the great capitals level with the ground.". . .

The Germans had no such power as Lindbergh suggested. Why did the British Government listen to him? The Committee of Imperial Defence, yes; it must be respected. The head of the French air force, yes. But why Lindbergh? He had taken refuge in England after his son was murdered in New Jersey and he did not even sense the imperturbable pugnacity of his mild-mannered hosts. He went on predicting Great Britain's defeat until the day America was brought into the war. His judgment on Hitler was equally odd. In the spring of 1939 he recorded in his *Wartime Journals:* "It seems to me that this man, damned almost everywhere except in his own country, called a fanatic and a madman, now holds the future of Europe in his hand. Civilisation depends upon his wisdom far more than on the action of the democracies."

Lindbergh was believed. He had youthful charm plus the maximum of physical daring. He added more than any other civilian to the French and British fear that war against Hitler meant national suicide. And he was right had the Nazis won; but he proved a misery in his underestimate of the British. Albert Speer, after 1942 the minister for production, writes:

> The obverse of Hitler's claim to world leadership was the subjugation of nations. I knew that France was to be relegated to satellite status, that Belgium and Holland and even Burgundy were to be incorporated into Hitler's Reich: I knew that the Poles and Russians were to be extinguished as nations and turned into serf peoples. Moreover, for him who wished to hear, Hitler had made no secret of his intention to exterminate the Jewish people.

This was written later, but it is not the description of a man who hoped to change the world by persuasion and by the folly of his neighbours.

Conquest: The Meaning of Nazism

We may never know how to come to terms with Hitler's tenebrous mind. [Historian] Alan Bullock, I feel, has made the wisest exploration of that secret place. He says there are two views of Hitler's foreign policy, "the fanatic and the opportunist." The first stresses mad racialism and the insistence from early days that Germany must conquer *Lebensraum* in Eastern Europe at the cost of the sub-human Slavs and the nonhuman Jews. The second view dismisses all this (and the whole of *Mein Kampf)* as fantasy-life, and stresses Hitler's opportunism. He never had a timetable, either in becoming Chancellor or in launching his aggressions. He waited for things to come his way, for the fruit to fall into his lap. And it often did.

Mr Bullock says that we should not "treat these two contrasting views as alternatives, for if that is done, then whichever alternative is adopted, a great deal of evidence has to be ignored." Hitler, Mr Bullock believes, was both fanatic and opportunist: ". . . convinced of his role as man of destiny *and* prepared to use all the actor's arts in playing it. . . . Consistency of aim with complete opportunism in method and tactics. This is, after all, a classical receipt for success in foreign affairs."

The full industrial resources of Germany were not used for rearmament even after the war began—a fact which has been used to suggest that Hitler did not intend war. The truth I think, is that he intended exactly what he got, up to 1941: a series of *blitzkriegs* carried out by troops trained and equipped for brief, stabbing, lethal attacks. Had Britain either fallen or made peace, these "short, decisive blows," as Hitler called them, could have made him master of the Western World. Alan Bullock lists the blows: "Poland, four weeks; Norway, two months; Holland five days, Belgium seventeen days; France six weeks; Yugoslavia, eleven days; Greece, three weeks." And Mr Bullock adds: "The explanation of why the German army was allowed to invade Russia without winter clothing or equipment is Hitler's belief that even Russia could be knocked out by a *blitzkrieg* in four or five months, before winter set in."

The belief might have come true had it not been for the stubborn British. . . .

Alan Bullock sums up his lecture, *Hitler and the Origins of the Second World War:* "Not only did Hitler create the threat of war and exploit it, but when it came to the point he was prepared to take the risk and go to war, and then when he had won the Polish campaign, to redouble the stakes and attack again, first in the West, then in the East."

This was the meaning of Nazism: conquest. In July 1941, in Alsace, the Administrative President for the Third Reich announced: "Providence has placed the German people at the very heart of Europe and has entrusted us with the mission of establishing order in Europe. We shall wrest from those peoples who live in our *Lebensraum* such areas as we need to accommodate and feed not only ourselves but our posterity: namely 200 million Germans. And we shall drive out of these areas all the heterogeneous peoples." These are not the words of a government that has been driven reluctantly into war by the dithering of its neighbours.

Returning to my question: is it right to condemn the Nazis as killers and to impute to Hitler an implacable thrust toward conquest? I think the answer is "yes" and that it is important to establish the "yes" (when writing about Hitler's war) before revisionist historians confuse the issue beyond hope. I also think that the pre-war rulers of Great Britain and France, in view of the "facts" presented to them, deserve some pity for their efforts to cling to peace. . . .

During the grisly last days at Bordeaux, with France prostrate, [French prime minister Paul] Reynaud turned on [his army commander Maxime] Weygand, who was insisting on an armistice. "You take Hitler for William I," said Reynaud, "an old gentleman who took Alsace-Lorraine from us and left it at that. But Hitler is Genghis Khan!" This was the whole point of the war. This is why the revisionist historians are wrong. This is why the British had to fight.

Chapter 2

Waging War in Europe

Turning | Points
IN WORLD HISTORY

The World Through Hitler's Eyes

Gerhard L. Weinberg

Scholar and award-winning author Gerhard L. Weinberg is a Kenan Professor of History at the University of North Carolina at Chapel Hill and an acknowledged expert on World War II. In Weinberg's opinion, Germany's foreign relations immediately preceding and during the war years were rooted in Adolf Hitler's distorted image of Germany and the outside world. Weinberg maintains that Hitler's worldview was very narrow and was based on the assumption that Germans were superior to everyone else. Hitler, he contends, explained other countries in terms of his own racial fantasies. For example, he reasoned that because of its mixed racial composition, the United States was weak and posed no real threat to Germany. According to Weinberg, Hitler believed that Germany would quickly dominate Britain and Russia and that U.S. actions would have little or no impact on his plans for future German supremacy.

A significant factor in the understanding of international relations is the perception of countries and issues by those in a position to make policy. The more policy formulation is restricted to one man or a small group, the more important this factor becomes. The conduct of foreign relations by a dictator can often be understood only by reference to his image of the outside world, an image that acts as a filter distorting the realities he sees. This is particularly true for Adolf Hitler whose views on most matters changed very little during his adult life, and who was little affected by experience which leads other men to adjust erroneous perceptions to facts. . . .

Excerpted from Gerhard L. Weinberg, "Hitler's Image of the United States," *American Historical Review*, July 1964. Reprinted with permission from the author.

Hitler did not leave an extensive correspondence with friends, relatives, and officials, which might provide a basis for assessing his attitudes. Nor, to judge by available evidence, did he make marginal comments on papers submitted to him for information or decision. He left two books, a few memorandums, a small number of private documents. All the rest consists of public speeches and private talk, recorded by others; even the books are really speeches reduced to writing and provided with some continuity. Since Hitler never earned a reputation for excessive veracity, the scholar faces the question of the reliability of his evidence.

There is a rule of thumb that can be used to good advantage. Before 1933 Hitler talked and wrote to gain understanding and support. Blunt, outspoken, and revealing to an extent he later regretted, this evidence of Hitler's views can generally be taken as accurate. After 1933 he was confronted with the concrete problems of a man in power and used his public utterances for tactical purposes, mixing open expressions of his views with deception to suit the occasion. From 1933 on, therefore, it is safer to depend on his secret directives and confidential talks to his friends, associates, and officials. Though at times concealing his thoughts even from those closest to him, he was, nevertheless, an inveterate talker who continued behind closed doors the practice of speaking rather openly that he had once started in the Vienna home for men. Where these sources fail us, the plans initiated in accordance with directives then secret, but now known to us, can be used to fill the remaining gaps.

Hitler's Threefold Program

During the First World War and the years immediately thereafter, Hitler appears to have given little thought to the United States. Like that of many German youngsters then and since, Hitler's youthful imagination had once been fired by Karl May's novels about American Indians, but Hitler's world in the first years of his political activity hardly extended beyond the Atlantic. As one student of the earliest National Socialist concepts of foreign policy has concluded: "The astounding narrowness of his horizon is also evidenced by the fact that Hitler hardly noticed a world power like the United States of America." Interested like so many Germans in explaining that Germany had really won the war, rather than trying to understand its defeat, he paid no particular attention to American matters beyond constantly repeating the condemnations of President [Woodrow] Wilson that were then fashionable in Germany. . . .

Mixing a crude simplification of social Darwinism with authoritarian views, a general inversion of historical reality, and some fantasies about the Germans and other peoples, Hitler expounded a world view based on the assumption that Germans were somehow superior to all others. They would maintain their superiority first by eliminating the allegedly alien Jewish element in their midst, and second by assuring themselves of adequate space on which to live and proliferate as farmers. This meant the conquest of space in Eastern Europe. The people in that space would be killed or expelled: the soil, not the people, was to be Germanized. Since this program would require war with Russia, the fact that the Communists had taken over in that country was a stroke of good fortune in Hitler's eyes because they had removed the only element in Russian society, the allegedly Germanic state-forming upper class, that might have made for effective opposition. Before this war could be launched, however, it would be necessary to make war on the eternal enemy France, a venture in which Italy and possibly Great Britain were expected to participate. There was thus a threefold program: first, an internal division of Germany into those Hitler considered the real Germans and those who could not qualify; second, a war against France; and third, after that war had freed Germany from the threat to its rear, a war against Russia. This program, expounded at length in [Hitler's autobiography] *Mein Kampf*, was also the main theme of Hitler's public speeches in the 1920's. With politics as his full-time occupation, he preached this same set of ideas in every town where he could find listeners—listeners, it may be added, who paid to hear this nonsense expounded.

A few years later, in the summer of 1928 . . . Hitler dictated a second book. . . . The years since the writing of *Mein Kampf* had been good, economically. German production, employment, and income were rising substantially, and Hitler, whose political chances were hardly helped by this fact, gave the subject some careful thought. In the first place, the availability of a large land area now appeared to him to have industrial as well as agricultural advantages for the people living there. This was illustrated by the second factor: the conspicuous presence of large numbers of American automobiles in Germany. Always intrigued by things connected with roads and motor vehicles, Hitler was greatly impressed by the fact that in spite of its high wages and great distance, the American automobile industry was so obviously successful in the European market. This was owing, he thought, to America's great space, resources, and domestic market.

Once the United States had caught his attention, the whole apparatus of Hitler's racial determinism had to be applied to explaining that country. Somehow it had to be integrated into his view of the universe. His analysis was as follows: The United States was the product of emigration from Europe. Who had emigrated? Always the most restless, those with the greatest initiative, and therefore the best in each country. Who were the best in each country? Why, of course, the Nordic element. The United States was, therefore, the great meeting place of the Nordics, who were protecting their racial purity by excluding Asiatics and by other immigration legislation. . . . Far from being the melting pot Americans imagined it to be, the United States was in fact a homogeneous country, a gathering in of the finest Nordic racial stock from each European country. This not only explained why Americans had made such good use of their living space; it also led to the conclusion that they were exceedingly dangerous people. With a racial headstart over everyone else—especially the European countries drained of their best blood by the same process that had made America strong—and with a vast living space on which to proliferate, the Americans were the real threat to German predominance in the world. Hitler's deduction from this analysis was simple: only a Eurasian empire under German domination could successfully cope with this menace. A third war was now added to the original two. After the first two wars had enabled it to construct a continental empire from the Atlantic to the Urals, Germany would take on the United States. One of the major tasks to be performed by the National Socialist movement, therefore, must be the preparation of Germany for this conflict.

A New Perspective

In the years between 1928 and 1933 Hitler was engaged in the bitter struggle for power in Germany, a struggle that he won, but that hardly allowed him much time for reflection on areas in any case peripheral to his major concerns. . . . In the years 1933–1934 and during the subsequent decade his evaluation of the United States was entirely negative, by contrast with the analysis just presented. . . . Once again the evidence indicates that the economic situation affected Hitler's thinking. The world depression was on everyone's mind, and it was a prominent subject of international negotiations. . . . It is clear . . . that Hitler was tremendously impressed by the fact and impact of economic depression in the United States. This came to be one of his favorite topics and a major theme of National Socialist propaganda. . . .

This new perspective required a new analysis in terms of Hitler's racial fantasies. He now concluded that the United States was a racial mixture after all—a mixture from all over, including Negroes and Jews, and what were undoubtedly the inferior exiles from every country except Germany. This mongrel society, in which the scum naturally floated to the top, could not possibly construct a sound economy, create an indigenous culture, or operate a successful political system. No wonder they were thrown into a panic by Orson Welles's reports on the arrival of invaders from Mars. The only hope in America's past had been smashed when the wrong side won the Civil War. . . . If this was what had happened to America's past, the only hope for its future lay in the German element that might someday take over. To quote Hitler once more: "The German component of the American people will be the source of its political and mental resurrection."

This analysis in turn led to different conclusions. The

United States was hopelessly weak and could not interfere in any way with the realization of Hitler's plans. Deprived by its racial decomposition of the ability to produce an effective military force, it would eventually fall naturally within a German empire that would also include Mexico (in which Hitler was interested because of the oil resources), and such portions of South America as caught his fancy. In this process, the German-Americans as well as those of German descent in Latin America could play an important role if they would only awake to their true destiny.

Thus Hitler went forward in the 1930's unconcerned about and generally uninterested in the United States. . . . In the spring of 1938, when reminded of American influence in the Far East, Hitler contemptuously asserted that the United States was incapable of waging war and would not dare go beyond empty gestures in international affairs.

These views were undoubtedly reinforced by the continuing underestimation of American military potential by Germany's military leaders in general, and by the German military attaché in Washington in particular. . . .

America Distorted and Underestimated

Public opinion in the United States, and particularly the American press, which showed open disapproval of Germany's racial policies, merely confirmed Hitler's evaluation of American degeneracy. In his eyes, the Americans were not only too stupid to get in out of the rain; they even objected to anyone who did. Furthermore, by racial arithmetic Hitler concluded in November 1937 that the United States was held together by fewer than twenty million Anglo-Saxons, and in November 1938 that there were fewer than sixty million persons of valuable racial stock in the United States. Thus even in regard to population Germany was far ahead, especially after the annexation of Austria and the Sudetenland. It is not surprising that with such an outlook Hitler was receptive to reports containing the wildest distortions of American reality. . . .

The negative assessment of America's power potential was further reinforced by the neutrality legislation. These laws, designed to remove what some people thought had been the causes of America's entry into World War I, only encouraged Hitler to start World War II by assuring him that none of his prospective European enemies would be able to secure supplies from across the Atlantic even by purchase. As Hitler was to put it in an exposé for his military leaders: "Because of its neutrality laws, America is not dangerous to us." Contemplating war at a gathering in March 1939, he envisaged a conquest of the United States following the defeat of Britain and France. His cavalier dismissal of [President Franklin] Roosevelt's peace appeal of April 1939 thus merely reflected his actual assessment of the power potential of the United States. His attempt to ridicule the United States in the public glare of a *Reichstag* session was an echo of his private thoughts.

The outbreak and early course of the war again confirmed Hitler's low assessment of American strength and potential. . . . Confident that isolationist sentiment would keep the United States neutral for some time, Hitler determined to strike in the West quickly. By direct subsidy and special propaganda themes, Germany attempted to strengthen the isolationist elements in America. The pro-Allied sympathies and hopes of a large segment of the American public, on the other hand, had neither brought down any of his dive bombers nor stopped one of his tanks. Surveying the world in triumph after the fall of France in June 1940, Hitler and his associates were confident that they could cope with the United States easily enough. Looking beyond the surrender of Great Britain that appeared imminent to them, they planned to construct thereafter a large navy of battleships that would enable them to move effectively against the United States in the only sphere of power that might present a problem. Simultaneously, the defeat of

Hitler in Paris

France seemed also to open the way to German naval bases on and off the coast of Northwest Africa for appropriate use by the prospective battle fleet.

Playing the Odds

All these prospects were replaced by other plans in the late summer and fall of 1940, as Britain refused to give in. Trying to understand the reasons for such foolhardy unwillingness to acknowledge defeat, Hitler concluded that the British must expect others to fight for them in the future as replacements for the French. Assuming that the Russians and Americans provided this distant hope for England, he decided to take this opportunity to attack Russia. After the German victory in the West, this looked like a simple undertaking that could be accomplished in a few weeks. It would not only destroy Britain's hope of aid from that quarter, but it would immobilize the United States as well. As Hitler put it: "Britain's hope lies in Russia and the United States. If Russia drops out of the picture, America, too, is lost for Britain, because elimination of Russia would tremendously increase Japan's power in the Far East. Russia is the Far Eastern sword of Britain and the United States, pointed at Japan." In other words, once Japan was relieved of the Russian threat at its back door, it would move ruthlessly forward in Asia, thereby keeping the United States occupied in the Pacific.

If the first part of Hitler's speculation proved illusory, in that the war against Russia turned out to be neither as short nor as simple as he had expected, his anticipations about Far Eastern events proved at least partially correct. The collapse or weakening of those European powers with colonial possessions in the Far East encouraged Japan to move southward in the summer and fall of 1940, while the German attack on the Soviet Union in the following year emboldened Japan even more.

It is true that in urging Japan to move forward in Asia, Germany preferred that the Japanese concentrate on Great Britain, while leaving the United States alone for the time being. The Tripartite Pact of September 1940 was in part designed to frighten the United States from intervention in the conflict, but the hasty conclusion of the treaty without regard to the details of the text indicates that the propaganda and publicity role of the pact was more important in German eyes. . . .

It is true that during 1941 Hitler had hoped to postpone war with America. . . . Throughout the winter of 1940–1941 Admiral Erich Raeder had urged drastic steps, at the risk of war, against American shipping; Hitler had regularly put him off, preferring to concentrate on the preparations against Russia. . . .

Hitler's view was that the United States was really a feeble country with a loud mouth. The Americans were probably doing as much by aiding Britain as they would ever be able to do; thus there was no longer any point in waiting for the United States to intervene at its convenience. There was, furthermore, the danger that Japan might make a deal with the United States if not supported by its allies. In any case, as the German Foreign Minister explained to one of his associates: "A great power does not allow itself to be declared war on; it declares war itself."

All the evidence indicates that the outbreak of war between Germany and the United States left Hitler's view of America unchanged. One month after Pearl Harbor he said: "I'll never believe that an American can fight like a hero." He expressed his "feelings of hatred and deep repugnance" for Americanism and added: "I don't see much future for the Americans. In my view it's a decayed country." That America's entrance into the war might seriously affect its outcome does not seem to have occurred to him.

France Defeated

Alistair Horne

In the spring of 1940 France fell to its German invaders. In this selection, former foreign correspondent, historian, and prize-winning author Alistair Horne maintains that France was on "the road to disaster" since 1936, when no one stopped Adolf Hitler from occupying the Rhineland. France, Horne writes, was not yet over the pain of World War I and was on the brink of civil war when its demoralized armies went unenthusiastically to war with Germany once again. Horne contends that when the French refused to help Poland in 1939, they isolated themselves, leaving them with no choice but to remain on the defensive and wait for Germany to attack. In Horne's view, what the French lacked most of all in 1940 was time—the Germans moved so fast that the French could not put the proper plans or resources into action.

For Hitler, as for many of his soldiers, the war was over. France, the arch-enemy, was prostrate at last; Britain no longer counted, she would fall like a plum from a tree in due course. Russia did not exist; America did not exist. Ever since that day of humiliation at Versailles, it was France alone that had obsessed German thoughts. Karl-Heinz Mende summed them up well when, writing home about the Armistice, he said: "The great battle in France is now ended. It lasted twenty-six years.". . .

The Flaws of Victory

Soon Hitler's astounding achievements in France would turn to dust as the diamond brilliance of *Sichelschnitt* [the German surprise assault against Holland, Luxembourg, Belgium, and

Excerpted from Alistair Horne, *To Lose a Battle: France 1940*. Copyright © Alistair Horne 1969, 1990. Reprinted with permission from PFD on behalf of the author, and by Macmillan.

France] was shattered by the fatal flaw latent within it. In his appreciation drawn up for the Kaiser, which prepared the ground for the German attack on Verdun in 1916, Falkenhayn, the German Chief of Staff, had recognized Britain to be Germany's principal enemy. By "bleeding white" the French Army at Verdun, he had argued, Britain's "best sword would be knocked out of her hand." The U-boat blockade would do the rest, in due course. Now Hitler had succeeded where Falkenhayn and all the Kaiser's generals had failed. Britain's "best sword" lay shattered on the ground. But Hitler and the planners of genius who had created *Sichelschnitt* had in reality thought no further ahead than Falkenhayn; no contingency plan had been prepared whereby a tottering Britain might be invaded immediately after success had been achieved in France. By mid July, when the first O.K.H. [army] plan was drafted, it was already too late. The Germans had missed the bus. . . . The two great errors of the otherwise perfect *Sichelschnitt*—this original fault of high strategy, and the tactical fault of the 24 May "Halt Order" which allowed the B.E.F. [British Expeditionary Force] to escape from Dunkirk—in conjunction added up to one thing. Britain would remain at war, inviolate. And as long as Britain was there, it was inevitable that sooner or later the immense power of the United States would be brought in too. But like so many of his generation of Germans, their vision blinkered by the memories of 1914–18 and of the shame of Versailles, Hitler could see only France and "the last decisive battle" which would have to be fought there.

In fact, as one now sees it in the perspective of time, Hitler's astonishing triumph over France was to be the direct source of his greatest disaster. After France, the mighty warrior nation which had defeated Germany in 1918, had been overthrown with such ease, what nation on earth could stand up to the Wehrmacht? So Hitler in 1941 was convinced that, while reducing his war production and demobilizing part of his forces, and without furnishing his cohorts with any winter equipment, he could knock out Russia in one lightning campaign. But although in many ways their doctrine of war may initially have been as faulty as that of the French, the

Russians would be able to make a retreat equivalent to a French withdrawal from Sedan across the Pyrenees and down to Saragossa, before launching any major counter-offensive. . . . Even more lethal to the Germans than their self-assuredness derived from the easy success in France was the supreme reliance Hitler now placed in his own infallibility. He saw himself as having been proved right in his audacity over the cautiousness of his professional advisers during the planning of *Sichelschnitt*; and, in retrospect, he saw how wrong had been the strategic assessment in battle of even those . . . whose judgement he trusted most. In his unquenchable animosity towards the O.K.H., he could not admit that it was in fact not he but [army chief of staff general Franz] Halder who during the campaign had been right. So Hitler became less and less inclined to accept the advice of his military experts, and more and more to rely on his own intuition, until finally it led him to the point of no return at Stalingrad.

France's Road to Disaster

For four grim years, France disappears from the forefront of the battle. "The choice is always between Verdun and Dachau," wrote a severe French critic of 1940, Jean Dutourd. Unable to face the prospects of another Verdun in 1940, it was indeed Dachau that became France's fate. In their hundreds of thousands, Frenchmen were shipped off to the concentration camps or to slave labour inside the Reich. With superb psychological cunning, the Nazis divided the conquered country geographically in two, thereby imposing yet another enduring source of division upon those that already plagued France. In the act of liberation, her old and new Allies would inflict at least as much damage upon France's cities and countryside as had the Luftwaffe, and the prostrate nation could hardly be subjected to greater humiliation. But there were many Frenchmen who did not agree that the final battle to save national "honour" . . . had yet been fought. Using every device and subterfuge they slipped off to join [Charles] de Gaulle's Free French in England, or the "Normandie-Niemen Squadron" in Russia. . . .

Who, and what, were responsible for France's catastrophe in 1940? Could the game have been played differently? At what point did disaster become irremediable? The questions are still asked and re-asked, and the answers become no simpler with time. But post-mortems are irresistible. The Riom Trials, held under the auspices of the Vichy Government in 1942, attempted to saddle the blame for the lost war upon earlier French Governments. The questions asked were loaded; no official record was made of the proceedings; the "trials" were finally adjourned and then dropped. Equally inconclusive and incomplete were the 2,500 pages of the "Serre Report," based on the findings of the French official Commission of Inquiry which sat from 1947 to 1951. It did its best to exculpate the politicians of the period, but it could not even agree as to whether it was the breakthrough on Corap's or Huntziger's [French Generals] front which precipitated the military catastrophe on the Meuse. However . . . more than any individual or set of individuals was to blame. Two doctrines and two philosophies and the past events of a generation were involved. Since the "day of glory" of 14 July 1919, almost every throw of the dice had resulted in advantage to Germany and loss to France. Upon Hitler's reoccupation of the Rhineland, unchallenged, in 1936, the road to disaster was clearly signposted. Three years later France went reluctantly to war, while she was herself still close to a state of civil war, with morale . . . "sapped by the feeling of the last twenty years that there would be no war because France could not stand another bleeding like that of 1914," and . . . with a French Army of 1918 facing a Wehrmacht of 1939.

Before the decisive battle itself opened, there were two other chronological milestones on France's road to disaster. In August 1939, the signature of the Ribbentrop-Molotov Non-Aggression Pact effectively removed any prospect of Germany's military potential being split by a war on two fronts; a month later, this was compounded by France's unwillingness to come to the aid of her solitary Polish ally, by launching an offensive in the west. Thus, from October 1939 onwards, France had no option but to remain on the defensive and wait to be attacked. When the attack came the following May, the preponderance of strength—with all factors taken into account—was immeasurably greater on the German side than at any time during the First World War. Therefore, there is a fatalistic view which regards the Battle of France as having been lost even before it was begun. Might France still have been defeated even if the Germans had not marched to the masterly blueprint of *Sichelschnitt*, if they had simply utilized a crude replay of the Schlieffen Plan of 1914? Possibly.

On the other hand, in war Fate contains many surprises. For all its impressiveness, the Wehrmacht of 1940 was a more fragile instrument, less consistently solid throughout, than the Kaiser's Army of 1914; nor did it have the same weight of resources behind it. On almost every occasion when Allied troops in 1940 came up against the ordinary infantry divisions which comprised the great mass of the Wehrmacht, they held their own. Acutely limited in their fuel supplies, the Panzers could not have fought a protracted campaign without a major reorganization. Then there is the prime consideration of the steadfastness of the German High Command, about which much has already been said. It is always held that the Younger Moltke [General Helmuth von Moltke] lost the First War on the Marne because his nerve failed. Yet there were times during both the Norwegian and the French campaigns when the German High Command of 1940 revealed itself to be potentially little less impressionable than Moltke. What, then, if the steel tip provided by the few Panzer and motorized divisions could have been blunted, that vulnerable wooden spear-shaft slashed into by determined Allied armour-led flank attacks, the nerves of the German High Command shaken by one sharp reverse? Might the German onslaught have been brought to a temporary halt, perhaps long enough for the Allies to reorganize their forces into a more coherent defence? The impact [Field Marshall Karl von] Rundstedt's Ardennes Offensive of 1944 made upon the Allies indeed suggests how even such a last-gasp effort (and against a far greater relative superiority than the Germans possessed in May 1940) can at least win time.

It was *time* that was the vital element which—more than

weapons, even perhaps more than morale—France most lacked in 1940. After the battle had been engaged, the afternoon of 15 May, the sixth day of fighting, marks the moment of almost certain military defeat. This was the decisive day that saw the failure of the first French counter-attacks, to which had been dedicated the main weight of her armoured reserves, and the day on which it was clear that the Germans could not be prevented from breaking out of their Meuse bridgeheads. For the French armour to have concentrated for a blow effective enough to have halted the Panzers on the 15th, the necessary dispositions would have had to be decreed by the 12th. But with the essential French reserves dispersed as they were in the line-up for the Dyle-Breda Plan's advance into Belgium, this would have proved virtually impossible. The French ripostes were almost bound to be too late. The speed with which Panzer warfare developed in 1940 certainly proved the validity of the dictum of Moltke the Elder [Field Marshall Helmuth von Moltke]: "*One* fault only in the initial deployment of an Army cannot be made good during the whole course of the campaign." On top of this must be added the tremendous significance of the Luftwaffe's supremacy in the air, which (although later in the war the Germans were able to conduct an imposing defence in the teeth of far greater Allied tactical air superiority) constituted a decisive factor at this stage of the Second World War. Apart from the lethal effect of the close-support Stukas, the Luftwaffe's far-ranging medium bombers were what finally denied the French High Command the time it needed to commit its reserves to battle, at the right moment and the right place.

The odds against France opposing *Sichelschnitt* in 1940, with any successful defence and even allowing for the element of the unexpected, remain enormously high. When all is said and done, the strategic brilliance of the German plan and tactical skill with which it was executed will always make it one of the classic campaigns of history. Certainly, few between great powers have ever been determined so swiftly, or so decisively. For a recent comparison, one needs to search back, beyond the defeat of France in the Franco-Prussian War of 1870, to Napoleon's triumph of Austerlitz in 1805.

The Battle of Britain

Richard Hough and Denis Richards

The Battle of Britain lasted about sixteen weeks, from July to October 1940. Commonly asked questions about the battle are, "Why did the Germans lose?" and "Why did the British win?" Internationally recognized author Richard Hough and air historian and author Denis Richards credit the British victory and German loss to multiple factors, not the least of which were inefficiencies and lack of communication and leadership within the German Luftwaffe, fatal flaws in the German equipment, the scientific system of defense built up over the years by the British, and the strength and persistence of British resistance. Hough and Richards insist that, contrary to what many people have said, written, or believe, the Battle of Britain was fought not just by Royal Air Force (RAF) fighter pilots but by most of the British population, who held on in the face of overwhelming pressure.

Fifty years on, the pattern of the Battle of Britain appears very much as it did at the time: appears, that is, to the interested British. The Germans, less well pleased with the outcome, for long affected to regard the campaign as of minor importance and swept it under their historical carpet. . . .

Equally clear at the time, and since, is that the Germans had been trying to destroy the RAF, and particularly Fighter Command, as the necessary preliminary to invasion. What was not so clear, until post-war access to German records, was the relationship between the air attacks and the timetable of invasion. . . .

Why the Germans Lost

Though there was ample evidence from every kind of source of the German preparations to invade, and later of the dispersal of invasion shipping from the Channel ports, even the Enigma decrypts did not directly point to Hitler's decision, taken on 12 October, to postpone "Sealion" until the following spring. On that day the Fuehrer had also decreed that preparations should be actively continued, in order to keep Britain under pressure. It was these continued preparations that the Enigma intercepts mostly reported, not the strategy behind them—a matter discussed in closed rooms or by landline, not over the ether. But because the threat to Britain seemed to continue, yet nothing happened, the British public began to wonder whether there had ever been any serious intention to invade at all. So began the first, mildest and shortest-lived of the controversies associated with the Battle of Britain. Did the RAF really save Britain from invasion—or was Hitler only bluffing all the time? Post-war investigation amply confirmed that Hitler was far from bluffing, but that he knew he had to beat the RAF first. He tried to do precisely that, and failed.

The reasons for that failure were, of course, manifold. The switch to London was certainly one. The superiority of [Sir Hugh] Dowding as a commander-in-chief to the increasingly self-indulgent and remote-from-reality [Luftwaffe commander Hermann] Goering was another. So too was the extraordinary weakness of German intelligence—a surprising feature in view of its excellence before and during the Battle of France. While Fighter Command knew precisely what faced it, the Luftwaffe was ill-informed not only about the complexity and methods of the British defensive system, but also about Fighter Command's locations and strength. At the lower levels, too, there was a singular lack of information. Fighter pilots in a *Staffel* [a squadron of 12 to 16 aircraft] never saw an intelligence officer; these, to be found in every British squadron, existed only at *Geschwader* [a group of 100 to 160 aircraft] level for the Germans. The result was that throughout the swiftly moving battle vital experience and information about the British spread among the German crews only casually and informally, sometimes through adjutants or commanding officers, but usually by word of mouth from pilot to pilot.

There were reasons for the German defeat more fundamental than any of these. The British fighters were part of a scientific system of air defence evolved over many years, operating in exactly the role for which they were designed. The German bombers and fighters, in contrast, were attempting an unfamiliar task by a series of improvisations. The Luftwaffe had not been equipped or trained for a campaign of attrition against long-distance, fixed targets, as Luftwaffe doctrine had not for many years envisaged such a campaign. . . . In Poland, Norway and France it had played its part with ruthless efficiency, eliminating the opposing air forces as a preliminary to unleashing its full might against enemy troops, communications and strong points. But those opposing air forces had all been weak. In the Battle of Britain it had to face powerful and determined opposition—and there was no German Army at hand to follow up such successes as it achieved.

For the Battle of Britain, there were also fatal flaws in the German equipment. Against German expectations, the bombers proved too vulnerable to operate by themselves and had to be escorted. But the long-range Me 110 could not live with the Hurricane or Spitfire skillfully handled, and the excellent Me 109 had only short endurance. Over London, having wasted fuel while escorting slower bombers there, it had only some ten minutes' combat time remaining. If it flew beyond the capital more than a few miles, it simply could not fight. To fighter commanders like Adolf Galland, this was the decisive factor in the German failure.

There were also other factors which told against the Luftwaffe. There was the dreaded Channel, waiting to swallow up damaged aircraft on the return flight; and there was the certainty of the prison camp for any German pilot who baled out over England. By contrast, British pilots who "took to the silk" were usually quickly reunited with their squadron. Such factors, together with their rising losses and the prolonged British resistance, had their inevitable effect on even such consistently brave and determined men as the Luftwaffe aircrews. Flushed with their success over France, they began with an abundance of confidence, which they progressively lost. The RAF pilots, with for most of them the spur of fighting in direct defence of their homeland, maintained with few exceptions a magnificently high morale throughout.

But for its task in hand, perhaps the Luftwaffe's greatest weakness was one not commonly appreciated. Though it had a big general numerical advantage over Fighter Command, its advantages in the vital single-engined fighters was by no means overwhelming. Against skillful and determined opponents operating as part of a scientific system of air defence, the Luftwaffe proved to be simply not strong enough. Quite apart from the collapse of the invasion project, its losses alone were sufficient to force the diversion into the safety, at that time, of night bombing. . . .

One Battle, Many Contributors

From the controversies surrounding the Battle it is a relief to turn to the myths, which have flourished freely. . . . If a group of the more persistent of these myths were to be embodied in a pantechnicon sentence it might conceivably run something like this: "The Battle of Britain, despite Fighter Command's being down to its last few aircraft, was won by unfailingly cheerful young officers flying Spitfires magically produced by Lord Beaverbrook and directed by 'Stuffy' Dowding, who first had to beat the Air Ministry, Winston Churchill and the French before he could beat the Germans."

Most of these myths have received some attention. . . . Of one which has not, about the unfailingly cheerful young officers, it is perhaps sufficient to point out that very often the officers were non-commissioned ones, in the rank of sergeant; and that though these young men, mostly in their early twenties, were indeed incredibly cheerful, they were not invariably so. Particularly not when, as was always happening to someone, they were dog-tired from flying and long hours at readiness, or tense with nervous strain from repeated danger, or badly wounded, or burnt. . . .

It would be too much to describe as a myth the popular impression that the Battle was won by Dowding and a thousand or so dashing young fighter pilots. There is a world of truth in that, but it is an incomplete truth. For the more one studies the Battle, the more one becomes aware of all the complex forces and factors which had to cohere perfectly to get those young men into the air in the right place and at the right time and with the right weapons to deal with the enemy.

Moreover, there were vast organisations right outside the RAF which helped to shape and win the Battle. Quite apart from bombarding the invasion ports, maintaining watch round the British coasts with 200 or more craft on daily patrol, and keeping the sea lanes open, the Royal Navy by its sheer existence constituted the prime obstacle to Germany's hopes. Since the German Navy could not expect to master the Royal Navy, the Luftwaffe had to do so instead, and for

German Bombs Fall on London

In late September 1940 the Germans lifted the main weight of their attack from the RAF, and from then until May 1941 applied it to bombing (or "blitzing") British citizens by night in a futile attempt to intimidate the civilian population. American correspondent, Edward R. Murrow writes:

This is London, 3:45 in the morning. Tonight's attack against the central London area has not been as severe as last night; less noise, fewer bombs, and not so many fires. The night is almost quiet—almost peaceful. The raid is still in progress and it is, of course, possible that we may see a repetition of last night when the weight of the attack developed in the two hours before dawn. . . . A couple of air-raid wardens standing out in the open were discussing whether the stuff coming down was a flock of incendiaries or high explosives. . . .

Later we went out to see a fire. A block of cheap little working-class houses had been set alight by fire bombs. As we walked toward the blaze, gusts of hot air and sparks charged down the street. We began to meet women. One clutched a blanket, another carried a small baby in her arms, and another carried an aluminum cooking pot in her left hand. They were that it had first to master the RAF. It was this single fact alone which determined the enemy's strategy for the Battle.

Whether the Navy, in actual fact, would have intervened in the Channel in the full strength feared by the Germans, is an interesting question. At a meeting to discuss the anti-invasion plans at the end of July Admiral of the Fleet Sir Charles Forbes, Commander-in-Chief of the Home Fleet, stated firmly that in no circumstances would his heavy ships operate south of the Wash. Churchill, expected to explode by the others present, merely met this "with an indulgent smile." The Royal Navy, he asserted, invariably undertook the impossible when the situation demanded: "If two or three nurses were wrecked on a desert island, the Navy would rush to their rescue, through typhoons and uncharted seas: and he

---

all looking back over their shoulders at that red glow that had driven them out into the streets. They were frightened. . . .

At dawn we saw Londoners come oozing up out of the ground, tired, red-eyed, and sleepy. The fires were dying down. We saw them turn into their own street and look to see if their house was still standing. I shall always wonder what last night did to that twenty-one-year-old boy who had flown so many bombs over Germany but had never heard one come down before last night. Today I walked down a long street. The gutters were full of glass; the big red busses couldn't pull into the curb. There was the harsh, grating sound of glass being shoveled into trucks. In one window—or what used to be a window—was a sign. It read: SHATTERED—BUT NOT SHUTTERED. Near by was another shop displaying a crudely lettered sign reading: KNOCKED BUT NOT LOCKED. They were both doing business in the open air. Halfway down the block there was a desk on the sidewalk; a man sat behind it with a pile of notes at his elbow. He was paying off the staff of the store—the store that stood there yesterday.

Edward R. Murrow, *This Is London*. 1941. Reprint, New York: Schocken Books, 1969.

had not a shadow of doubt that if the Germans invaded the south coast of Britain we would see every available battleship storming through the Straits of Dover." And while Churchill was in charge, no doubt they would have done. . . .

The Army, too, contributed much to the victory, not only by its preparations to meet the invader, in which it would have had stout support from the Home Guard, but by its expertise in the highly dangerous work of dealing with the hundreds of unexploded bombs . . . and by providing most of the vital ground defences. The anti-aircraft gunners, especially those at Dover and the airfields, played an important part from the beginning, the searchlight crews an increasingly useful one as the German night offensive developed. Without these ground defences, far more low-level attacks would have been made, and far more damage done to aircraft factories and Fighter Command installations. Anti-aircraft fire also disturbed the concentration of bombers at higher level on the vital run up to the target. And though the guns hurled a vast quantity of steel and explosive into the sky for every aircraft they shot down, the mere sight and sound of them was a valuable boost to civilian morale.

It should also be recalled that the civil defence services were already highly active during the Battle well before they performed so long and magnificently during the "blitz." The air-raid wardens, full-time and part-time, of both sexes; the heavy rescue services, recruited mainly from the building trades; the firemen, professional and auxiliary; the ambulance teams; the police, whose work was so vastly extended when raids occurred; the Women's Voluntary Service, who in their green suits and purple blouses (bought at their own expense) seemed to be everywhere, and to undertake anything . . . —all these organisations and many more made their essential contribution. And so, of course, did the workers in the aircraft and other factories and in the fields. . . .

Some of these groups were more closely associated with the RAF than others. The Post Office War Group, for instance, did magnificent work in restoring shattered landlines and keeping each part of the whole complex defence system in touch with the next. And the 30,000 or so members of the Observer Corps, women as well as men, and mostly part-time, were as essential to the Battle as the RAF's own radar stations.

There were many more such bodies. The Civilian Repair Organisation, involving scores of garages and workshops, performed an invaluable service in rebuilding damaged aircraft, as many as 150–200 a week. . . .

Most closely associated of all with the RAF, since they worked alongside, were the members of the Women's Auxiliary Air Force [WAAF]. At the time of the Battle they were still admitted to only half-a-dozen trades, but whether "admin.," or cooks, or clerks or "drivers (petrol)" or telephonists or balloon fabric repairers, they played an essential part. . . .

Perhaps those most often affected by the cries that came over the air were the girls of the Y (Interception) Service, who monitored R/T [radio telephony] over the Channel and southern England. They heard the shouts and screams of the German pilots as well as the British. . . .

These bare references illustrate the immense contribution to the Battle made by literally millions outside the RAF. And within the RAF itself, the Battle was by no means only the work, as is so often thought, of Fighter Command. Coastal Command, by its reconnaissance, anti-invasion patrols and bombing, played a vital part: Coastal aircraft photographed the assembly and dispersal of the invasion craft. . . . No less involved was Bomber Command, with its attacks on Berlin, German communications and airfields, and the invasion ports.

In its passive role, Balloon Command also played a most useful part. The balloons could not rise high, but they made it difficult for the enemy to come down below 5,000 feet, where he could bomb more accurately, and they were a death-trap to dive-bombers. . . .

But when tribute is duly paid to the many contributors to the victory who are sometimes overlooked or forgotten, the mind rightly and inevitably comes back to those superb fighter pilots and their commander-in-chief. Perhaps more than any other victory in history, this one was achieved by a scientific system of defence built up over many years. . . .

As the daylight Battle faded, and the bombs descended in full force by night, a new phase of Britain's resistance began.

In the words of [author-poet-editor] Angus Calder, "it was the battle of an unarmed civilian population against incendiaries and high explosive: the battle of firemen, wardens, policemen, nurses and rescue workers against the enemy they could not hurt. The front-line troops were doctors, parsons, telephonists. . . . Where the bombs fell, heroes would spring up by accident. . . ."

Many of the heroes, as is so often the case, were heroes by force of example. This was a fact which the Prime Minister, himself a hero with a sense of humour even in the most difficult circumstances, tried to impress on Nelson, the black cat at No. 10 Downing Street. When Nelson showed fright at the sound of the guns, Churchill chided him for being unworthy of the name he bore, and added: "Try to remember, Nelson, what those boys in the RAF are doing."

A week later, on 15 October, Churchill warned the War Cabinet that it would be two or three months before there could be any substantially better results against the night bombers. He added: "The people of Britain must stick it out."

With no little inspiration from those who had saved them in the great air battles earlier, they did, to the enduring benefit of their country, and the world.

U-Boats: The Scourge of the Atlantic

Samuel Eliot Morison

A Harvard University Trumbell professor of American history and a rear admiral in the U.S. Naval Reserve, Samuel Eliot Morison won international recognition for his fifteen-volume *History of United States Naval Operations in World War II.* In 1963 Morison published a one-volume history—*The Two-Ocean War*—based on his monumental work, and it is from this short history that the following selection is taken. In it, Morison argues that the Americans should have anticipated German U-boat attacks on American and Allied ships and better prepared for antisubmarine warfare. A few hundred submarines, he explains, cost the Americans and the British a two-year major naval effort, enormous sums of money, and tens of thousands of lives. Morison relates how the need to combat the U-boats resulted in improvements in some military weapons and devices, such as depth charges and sonar, and the invention or development of others, such as radar.

A convoy is beautiful, whether seen from a deck or from the sky. The inner core of stolid ships in several columns is never equally spaced, for each has her individuality; one is always straggling or ranging ahead until the commodore becomes vexed and signals angrily, "Number So-and-so, take station and keep station!" Around the merchant ships is thrown the screen like a loose-jointed necklace, the beads lunging to port or starboard and then snapping back as though pulled by a mighty submarine elastic; each destroyer nervous and questing, all eyes topside looking for the enemy, sound gear below listening for him, radar antennae like cats' whiskers feeling for him. On dark nights only a few shapes of ships a little darker than the black water can be discerned; one consults the radar screen to ascertain that the flock is all there. To one coming topside for the dawn watch, it is a recurring wonder to see the same ships day after day, each in her appointed station, each with her characteristic top-hamper, bow-wave, lift and dip; the inevitable straggler, the inveterate smoker, the vessel with an old shellback master who "knew more about shipping forty years ago than any goddam gold-braid in a tin can," and whose sullen fury at being convoyed translates itself into belated turns, unanswered signals and insolent comebacks. When air cover is furnished there are darting, swooping planes about the convoy; upon approaching port, the stately silver bubble of a blimp comes out, swaying in the breeze and blinking a cheery welcome.

There is nothing beautiful, however, about a night attack on a convoy, unless you see it from a submarine's periscope. A torpedo hit is signaled by a flash and a great orange flare, followed by a muffled roar. Guns crack at imaginary targets, star shell breaks out, a rescue ship hurries to the scene of the sinking, and sailors in other ships experience a helpless fury and dread. If the convoy has a weak escort it can only execute an emergency turn and trust that the rest of the wolf-pack will be thrown off or driven down; if the escort is sufficient a "killer group" peels off, searching relentlessly with radar and sonar, while everyone stands by hoping to feel underfoot the push of distant depth charges that tells of a fight with a submerged enemy. . . .

U-Boats: Terrors of the Atlantic

A prompt attack by U-boats on American coastal shipping should have been anticipated, since they had done just that during World War I. No U-boats happened to be in position to raid American coasts when Germany declared war on the United States in December 1941, but [German] Admiral [Karl] Doenitz chose five of his best "aces" (and followed them by six more) to devastate the American East Coast shipping lanes. . . .

Operation *Paukenschlag* ("Roll of the Drums"), as the Germans called it, opened on 12 January 1942, when a British steamer was torpedoed and sunk about 300 miles east of Cape Cod by U-123. Two days later, enemy submarines moved into the shipping bottleneck off Cape Hatteras. Three tankers in succession were sunk on 14 and 15 January. Next day the U-boats sank a Canadian "Lady boat" and two freighters, then three tankers in succession and three more before the end of the month. Thirteen vessels in all, measuring 95,000 gross tons (and 70 per cent of this tanker tonnage), were lost in a little over two weeks.

No more perfect setup for rapid and ruthless destruction could have been offered the Nazi sea lords. The massacre enjoyed by the U-boats along our Atlantic Coast in 1942 was as much a national disaster as if saboteurs had destroyed half a dozen of our biggest war plants. The damage in the Eastern Sea Frontier was wrought by no more than 12 U-boats operating at any one time, and every month the Germans were building 20 or more new 740- and 500-tonners. Each U-boat carried fourteen torpedoes, including some of the new electrically propelled type that showed no air bubbles in the wake, so could not be sighted or dodged. In addition they carried guns of sufficient caliber to sink most merchant vessels by shellfire alone. The 500-tonners carried enough fuel for a cruise of at least 42 days. Allowing two weeks for the outward passage and the same for homeward to a French port, they could spend two weeks in the Atlantic coastal lanes. Their usual tactics, in the early months of 1942, were to approach a trade route at periscope depth, lie in wait on the surface at night, and launch torpedoes from seaward against a vessel whose silhouette might be seen against shore lights.

One of the most reprehensible failures on our part was the neglect of local communities to dim their waterfront lights, or of military authorities to require them to do so, until three months after the submarine offensive started. When this obvious defense measure was first proposed, squawks went all the way from Atlantic City to southern Florida that the "tourist season would be ruined." Miami and its luxurious suburbs threw up six miles of neon-light glow, against which was silhouetted southbound shipping that hugged the shore to avoid the Gulf Stream. Ships were sunk and seamen drowned in order that the citizenry might enjoy pleasure as usual. Finally, on 18 April 1942, the Eastern Sea Frontier ordered waterfront lights and sky signs doused, and the Eastern Defense Command of the Army ordered a stringent dimout on 18 May.

If one or two torpedoes did not fatally hole the attacked ship, the submarine finished her off by shellfire. In the spring, when the nights became shorter and the ineffectiveness of our antisubmarine warfare had been demonstrated, the U-boats became bolder and attacked in broad daylight, even surfaced. Although they invariably attacked without warning, they commonly gave the crew a chance to get away before opening gunfire, and refrained from machine-gunning survivors in lifeboats, as had been done freely in the early part of the war. Survivors were often questioned as to the identity of the ship and the nature of her cargo, were sometimes offered water, provisions or cigarettes and dismissed with a standardized joke about sending the bill to [President Franklin] Roosevelt or [British prime minister Winston] Churchill. The healthy and sunburned German submariners appeared to be having a glorious field day. They later referred to this period as "the happy time."

A Need for Convoys

This assault temporarily stunned the defense forces of the United States and Canada. Such protection as the Navy furnished to shipping was pitifully inadequate. Destroyers could not be spared from the transatlantic route. . . . Consequently there were no escorts to organize coastal convoys; and [American] Admiral [Ernest] King judged, rightly, that a convoy without escort was worse than no convoy at all. The question has often been asked why the Navy was so unprovided with these indispensable small craft for antisubmarine warfare. The reason was its desperate concentration on building destroyers and larger ships to fight an impending two-ocean war. Small craft were neglected in the belief that they could be improvised and rapidly reproduced in quantities at small shipbuilding yards. It was the same with anti-submarine aircraft. . . .

The total number of Allied, American and neutral merchant vessels sunk in the North Atlantic in January 1942, between our coast and the Western Approaches to the British Isles, was 58; only three of these were in transatlantic convoys. . . .

A poor substitute for coastal convoys, nicknamed the "bucket brigade," was set up on 1 April 1942. . . . By August a completely interlocking convoy system had been organized: two main lines (New York–Guantanamo and New York–Key West) with local branch lines from all important points on the East Coast, Gulf, Caribbean, Brazil and West Africa feeding in.

As soon as Admiral Doenitz learned that coastal convoys were being organized along the Eastern Sea Frontier, he diverted U-boats southward, into the Gulf Sea Frontier. Organized 6 February 1942, with headquarters at Key West, this naval frontier covered the Straits of Florida, most of the Bahamas, the entire Gulf of Mexico, the Yucatan Channel and most of Cuba. . . .

The Navy was not idle while these things went on. Every submarine spotted was hunted; but the hunters, few in number, had not yet acquired the necessary technique to kill. . . .

Admiral Doenitz was naturally delighted with the performance of his boys. On 15 June he reported to Hitler the gratifying number of sinkings compared with the small number of submarines employed, and predicted "vast possibilities through the rapid increase in number of U-boats and the use of supply submarines." He dwelt on the poor quality of American defenses, the heavy destruction of tankers and the failure of new construction to replace shipping losses. In a press interview that summer Doenitz declared: "Our submarines are operating close inshore along the coast of the United States of America, so that bathers and sometimes entire coastal cities are witnesses to that drama of war, whose visual climaxes are constituted by the red glorioles of blazing tankers."

No frantic boast, this; burning tankers were not infrequently sighted from fashionable Florida resorts, and on 15 June two large American freighters were torpedoed by a

U-boat within full view of thousands of pleasure-seekers at Virginia Beach.

Antisubmarine Warfare: Ahead-Throwns and Sonar

The amount of study, energy and expense necessary to combat a few hundred U-boats is appalling. The major naval effort of the Allied navies in the Atlantic was so employed for two years. In money terms alone, counting the sunken ships and cargoes, time lost at sea, and expense of operating naval vessels and planes to protect the seaways, the efforts of the American republics and the British Empire amounted to some hundreds of billions of dollars; whilst the lives lost by submarine action reached tens of thousands. Beaten Nazis may take comfort in reflecting that no army, fleet or other unit in World War II, with the exception of their own people who murdered defenseless civilians, wrought such destruction and misery as the U-boats.

There was no administrative center of the Navy's efforts against the U-boats until March 1942, when Admiral King designated Captain Wilder D. Baker to set up an antisubmarine section of his staff in Washington. This section was responsible for matériel, supply, development and training.

An important step toward unified control of merchant shipping was taken on 15 May 1942, when the Convoy and Routing Section of C.N.O., headed by Rear Admiral M.K. Metcalf, became a section of Cominch headquarters. About 1 July "C. and R." assumed full responsibility for the routing and reporting of all merchant shipping in the United States strategic area, and for troop convoys. Cinclant, Admiral Ingersoll, provided the escorts and many of the transports; C. and R. organized the convoy, and, in conjunction with the British Admiralty, laid down its route. . . .

Besides improved depth charges, which were tossed off a vessel's stern, two ahead-thrown weapons were adopted by the United States Navy in 1942: "hedgehog" and "mousetrap." Hedgehog . . . consisted of a steel cradle from which projected six rows of spigots firing 24 projectiles. As the ship fired these ahead before breaking her sound contact with a submarine, it gave her a better chance of inflicting damage. Depth charges went off at the determined depth, whether they hit anything or not, but hedgehog shells exploded only on contact. . . . Anti-submarine ships also mounted the usual types of naval ordnance suitable for their burthen. Machine guns proved to be useful in clearing a surfaced submarine's deck, but there is no record of any U-boat being sunk with a gun smaller than 3-inch.

Both the British and ourselves, between the two wars, invented supersonic echo-ranging sound which they called "asdic" and we named "sonar." Housed in a streamlined retractable dome which projected beneath the ship's bottom but was operative only at moderate speeds owing to water noises, sonar could be employed in two ways: listening for the U-boat's propeller noises, and echo-ranging with a sharp "ping" which the U-boat's hull returned, the time giving the range and the direction indicating the bearing. The echo reached the operator with varying degrees of pitch, depending on the nature and movements of the target. This variation in the pitch, known as the "doppler effect," told a trained operator with a sensitive ear whether the target was a ship or a whale, whether it was stationary or moving, and its direction and speed.

In order to thwart sonar, German submarines were equipped with *Pillenwerfer*. This device shot out from a special tube a multitude of small, stationary gas bubbles, which returned an echo similar to that of a submarine. Trained sound operators, however, could detect a submarine's echo from that returned by *Pillenwerfer*. There were many other pitfalls for inexperienced operators. Schools of blackfish, whales, wrecks, coral reefs, and even a layer of water of different temperature echoed in a way which only an expert could distinguish from echoes on a steel hull. Snapping shrimps on the ocean bottom made a curious crackling noise that disturbed sound-listeners. The Navy's monthly *Anti-Submarine Warfare Bulletin* had to print special articles about the habits of cetaceans and crustaceans in order to diminish false alarms. . . .

Scientists of Asworg

In every aspect of this planetary struggle, men of science worked in laboratories, inventing, developing and testing new weapons, devices and military equipment for the armed forces. One group of civilian scientists worked side by side with naval officers, even on board ships and in planes. This was the Anti-Submarine Warfare Operations Research Group (Asworg), an offshoot of the National Defense Research Committee. James B. Conant, then President of Harvard University, and other scientists, visited England during the Battle for Britain and returned convinced that one of the main factors which saved England from destruction under the long sustained assaults of the Luftwaffe was a group of "operational" scientists, working closely with Royal Air Force (R.A.F.) fighter command to coördinate coast warning radar with fighter plane defense. . . .

Asworg was organized 1 April 1942 with Professor Philip M. Morse, sound physicist of M.I.T., as director. Asworg was centered at Washington. . . . It sounds odd today, when all armed services are scientifically indoctrinated; but in 1942 "practical seamen" had a deep suspicion of "long-haired scientists" that had to be overcome. Dr. Morse, however, "sold" Asworg by laying down the principle that no scientist was to claim credit for anything, since he took no responsibility for the ultimate decision; that his duty was simply to help the fighting Navy improve its antisubmarine technique.

The Asworg mathematicians and analysts worked out a whole complex of search problems, including patterns of "box search" by ships, on Greek key patterns, for regaining underwater contact with a submarine; they worked up data on effective search speed, altitude, and airborne time for patrol planes; they proved that three destroyers searching abreast were more than three times as effective as a single destroyer, that an "air umbrella" over a convoy gave far less protection than a wide-ranging air search on front and flanks; they drafted blueprints for the Atlantic Narrows air patrol that caught several German blockade runners, and for the Straits of Gibraltar patrol; they worked up countermeasures which stymied the German acoustic torpedo as soon as it appeared.

The High Value of Radar

Radar was invented by Sir Robert Watson-Watt, but some of its developments and refinements were produced in the

United States from sheer necessity. By the summer of 1942 almost every combatant ship in the Atlantic Fleet had been equipped with some form of radar, and an improved model, the SG—in which the scope gives a picture of what lay ahead—had passed the test of experiment and was ready to be installed in October. For aircraft, the value of radar was even greater than for ships, because it enabled planes to pick up a surfaced submarine far beyond visible distance, to deliver a surprise attack, and to home in other planes and ships. The first sets installed in planes were on meter-wave. The Germans invented a search receiver for it which ended its usefulness as a detecting device, and inventing a microwave plane radar to take its place became urgent. That was done, and a variety of 10-cm sets did the trick; the Germans never could figure out a way to detect or jam these. Microwave radar made possible the large number of kills by aircraft in the spring and early summer of 1943. Hitler referred to it peevishly, in his New Year's 1944 address, as "one invention of our enemy" which had thwarted his submarine fleet.

A convoy is no stronger than its ears and eyes. Radar furnished our convoys with cat's eyes, sonar with ears, while the high-frequency direction-finders (HF/DF, pronounced "Huff-Duff"), by picking up and plotting radio transmissions of U-boats at sea, acted as highly sensitive, elongated cat's whiskers. The Royal Navy was the first to adopt this method of locating submarines. Estimated positions of U-boats, plotted at Washington and London, were sent out to sea on "Fox" schedule, which was a secret radio bulletin transmitted several times a day on a fixed schedule. While HF/DF fixes were seldom accurate within 50 or 100 miles, they enabled an escort commander to order an evasive change of course which, by Admiral Doenitz's admission, frequently frustrated his wolf-packs. . . .

U-Boats Remain a Menace

The Army Air Force, which controlled almost the entire supply of United States military land-based planes in 1941, did not expect to include antisubmarine warfare among its duties. Army pilots were not trained to fly over water or protect shipping or bomb small moving targets like submarines. And the Navy did not have the planes to fill the rôle so successfully assumed by the British Coastal Command. This was due not to lack of foresight, but to a principle decided on in 1920, that the Army should control land-based and the Navy sea-based aviation. Consequently the Army received the entire American production of military land planes; while the Navy received the entire production of seaplanes and carrier types, and the numbers were inadequate for both kinds. When British experience showed the value of large land-based bombers in antisubmarine warfare, the Army modified this agreement. . . .

By June of 1942 the United States Navy and the Army Air Force were coming to grips with the U-boat problem, but were far from attaining mastery. The shortage of escorts was still critical; no DE [destroyer escort] had yet joined the Fleet. No killer groups of escort carriers had yet been organized. On the other side, Admiral Doenitz had not exhausted his repertoire, and tough days were to come for the convoys. . . .

Looking backward, the increasing number of escorts, uniform doctrine, the training and analysis systems set up, and plain hard experience seem to be the most important contributions toward controlling the U-boat menace during the first half of that woeful year 1942. Convoys were increasingly successful in protecting trade routes, but escorts were not killing enough U-boats. Only 21 of these, together with seven Italian submarines, were sunk by both Allied navies during the first six months of 1942; and only five of these kills were by United States forces. During the same period Germany built 123 new U-boats, and in June 1942 there were 60 of them, on an average, patrolling the Atlantic.

This period of antisubmarine warfare closed with a stern warning, delivered by [American] General [George] Marshall to Admiral King on 19 June 1942:

> The losses by submarines off our Atlantic seaboard and in the Caribbean now threaten our entire war effort. The following statistics bearing on the subject have been brought to my attention.

Of the 74 ships allocated to the Army for July by the War Shipping Administration, 17 have already been sunk. Twenty-two per cent of the Bauxite fleet has already been destroyed. Twenty per cent of the Puerto Rican fleet has been lost. Tanker sinkings have been 3.5 per cent per month of tonnage in use.

We are all aware of the limited number of escort craft available, but has every conceivable improvised means been brought to bear on this situation? I am fearful that another month or two of this will so cripple our means of transport that we will be unable to bring sufficient men and planes to bear against the enemy in critical theatres, to exercise a determining influence on the war.

Chapter 3

The War Expands

The Holocaust: A Crisis of Human Behavior and Values

George M. Kren and Leon Rappoport

The Holocaust of World War II, which took the lives of millions of Jews, Gypsies, and other minorities the Nazis regarded as undesirable, remains a subject of heated debate to this day. According to academician and psychohistorian George M. Kren and psychologist Leon Rappoport, the Holocaust was the major historical crisis of the twentieth century. They disagree with the popular theories that anti-Semitism, biblical judgment, and mystical revelation were primary causes of the Holocaust. Kren and Rappoport argue that the Holocaust is unique, that no previous mass destruction was accomplished in the same way or had similar emotions associated with it. The Holocaust brought into being a quality of violence significantly different from that which characterized any earlier episode of mass destruction. It was, according to the authors, a "massively selective program conducted more like a large-scale industrial enterprise than anything else."

Between 1941 and 1945, the Nazi government of Germany systematically killed millions of men, women, and children because they were Jews, Gypsies, or Slavs defined by racist ideology as threatening to Germanic ideals. This event has come to be called "the Holocaust." Ever since it happened, the culture-makers of Western civilization—writers, artists, scholars, scientists, and thoughtful people generally—have wondered why it happened, how it happened, and what it means for human society.

These questions have led to documentation and soul-

Excerpted from George M. Kren and Leon Rappoport, *The Holocaust and the Crisis of Human Behavior*, revised edition (New York: Holmes & Meier, 1994). Copyright © 1994 Holmes & Meier Publishers, Inc. Reprinted with permission from the publisher.

searching recorded in a seemingly endless literature. . . .
Among all the material already available, however, there is
no better expression of the hardly expressible challenge to
meaning posed by the Holocaust than that written by
Dwight Macdonald in 1945, when the ashes were still hot.

> Something has happened to Europe. . . . What is it? Who or
> what is responsible? What does it mean about our civiliza-
> tion, our whole system of values?

> The Nazis have not *disregarded* human life. They have, on
> the contrary, paid close attention to it. . . . There was no ul-
> terior motive behind . . . [the Holocaust], no possible advan-
> tage to its creators beyond the gratification of neurotic racial
> hatreds. What had previously been done only by individual
> psychopathic killers has now been done by the rulers and ser-
> vants of a great modern state. This *is* something new.

The Uniqueness of the Holocaust Historically

. . . It is generally acknowledged that the Holocaust was
unique in quantitative terms, a matter of more innocent victims being deliberately killed per unit of time than ever before. But this having been said, the events are then very frequently shunted into the familiar stream of history wherein
wars, massacres, and persecutions are notoriously salient and
apparently unchanging, except insofar as applied science
provides new possibilities for mass destruction.

When viewed in this fashion, and accompanied with the
proper citation of other historical horrors (the religious cru-
sades, the slaughter of the Albigensian heretics, the Turkish
decimation of the Armenians, and even the British invention
of concentration camps during the Boer War), it becomes all
too convenient to see the Holocaust as "unique"—but normal, after all. The long European tradition of anti-Semitism
adds further plausibility to the idea that killing off whole
populations is an ugly but familiar fact of historical life. And
if anyone takes issue with this orderly view of things, they
will usually be patted on the head and sent off to do their
historical sums, i.e., count the casualties.

Such intellectually comfortable perspectives on the Holocaust must be rejected on historical grounds. Psychologically, however, . . . it is essential to recognize very early on that like all emotional defense mechanisms, the tendency to normalize extraordinary events reduces anxiety only by falsifying reality. . . .

Distrust . . . may begin with correction of the popular myth that traditional German anti-Semitism was a major cause of the Holocaust. The myth goes as follows: Nazis began by elevating anti-Semitism to an article of political and cultural faith. Action was first limited to simple abuse. Later, with enactment of the Nuremberg laws, the Jews lost most of their legal rights, and they were encouraged to emigrate on the condition of leaving all of their possessions to the state. Later still, they were put in concentration camps. Finally, mass killings were started in special extermination camps.

This makes the death camps appear to be merely the last, atrocious rung on the ladder of anti-Semitism. The Nazi euphemism "final solution" also contributes to the appearance of a logical causal chain. What could be simpler? Given the Nazi premise that Jews were an inferior race corrupting humanity, it follows that with increasing Nazi power there would be an increasingly harsh program of repression.

The only problem with this reassuringly neat analysis is that it is wrong. Prior to the advent of Hitler, and even for some time after his appearance, German anti-Semitism was not much different from what prevailed throughout Europe. . . . Anti-Semitism is a European tradition. It was never confined to Germany, nor was it more intense in Germany than elsewhere. Yet complete destruction of the Jews was never made a state policy, let alone attempted on a broad scale, anywhere except in Germany. Consequently, although historical anti-Semitism was clearly relevant to the Holocaust, it cannot be accepted as a primary cause.

Personal Experience of the Holocaust

The uniqueness of the Holocaust also stands out when the focus of inquiry is shifted from historical trends to the level of personal experience. All of the surviving victims who have been able to describe their experiences have their own idiosyncratic perspectives to convey, but the major theme they agree on is the uncanny atmosphere of the death camps. To call it a nightmare quality is inadequate; by all accounts it was another world in which everything previously considered human and meaningful was turned upside down. . . .

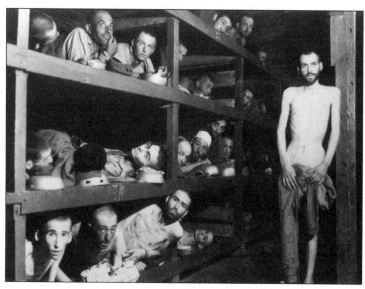

The atmosphere of concentration camps was beyond nightmarish. The horrific conditions defied the imagination.

It may well be true that the qualitative nature of the death camps and many other aspects of the Nazi genocide program must remain a mystery for those without firsthand experience. But this does not mean that intense qualities of experience generally reported by survivors should be ignored. On the contrary, it is only by attempting to work through various patterns of individual experience that certain crucial issues of meaning may be identified.

Some writers disagree, however. Faced with the extraordinary revealed horrors, their response has been to place the Holocaust in a religious or metaphysical context, treating it either as a massive testing of faith analogous to the sufferings of Job, or a biblical judgment associated with restoration of the Jewish homeland.

Looking very broadly over previous reactions to the uniqueness of the Holocaust, therefore, it seems clear that two extreme alternatives have predominated, and both have served to block the way toward careful interpretative analysis. Thus, if the genocide is seen in the cold light of normal history, chiefly remarkable for the large number of innocent victims, then there is no special challenge to critical inquiry, and historians may conduct business as usual, gathering facts and examining how they may be articulated as explanations for specific actions. If, on the other hand, the Nazi genocide program is seen in the passionate light of mystical revelation, then it will appear to be manifestly beyond critical study.

Taken together, both of these viewpoints go a long way toward explaining why the essential human questions arising from the Holocaust have largely gone unanswered: Neither view leads to constructs of meaningfully human dimensions. At one extreme, human actions are overshadowed by impersonal historical forces (e.g., anti-Semitism); at the other, they are overshadowed by metaphysical principles (e.g., God's will). We reject both. . . .

A New Level of Mass Destruction

In many relevant historical examples, it is apparent that the victims usually have been either a real or a potential danger to their oppressors. . . . This point deserves special emphasis because it defines the outer limit of the qualitative scale on which all mass violence prior to the Holocaust may be comprehended. Passion, calculated terrorism, and the liquidation of people who threaten to make trouble or who are just in the way of something believed to be more important than they are—these three levels of destruction are all understandable in the light of historical precedents and the accumulated knowledge of political rationality.

None of this can be applied in an explanatory fashion to the Holocaust. Comparison shows that the Holocaust must be conceptualized as a fourth and genuinely new level of mass destruction because the quality of violence it brought into being was manifestly different than anything that had occurred before. Unlike the American Indians or other native populations in colonialized areas of the world, for example, the Jews posed no physical challenge to Nazi authority. Unlike the Christian Armenians seeking independence from the Ottoman empire, they claimed no territory. And unlike the various groups of heretics slaughtered through the ages, the Jews as such posed no threat to prevailing religious or cultural orthodoxies. Indeed, there is even some evidence to the contrary, because SS and Wehrmacht records indicate that in various conquered territories, the manual and skilled slave labor of Jews made an appreciable contribution to the German war effort.

It is also false to conceive of the Jews as standing in the way of any particular economic, political, or military activity. Insofar as they were judged to be occupying an excessive number of professional or entrepreneurial positions in Germany and the conquered territories, they could be, and they were, easily forced out of these positions. Insofar as they were a troublesome physical presence, they could be, and they were, transported out of the way and exploited for material gain in the process. It is, moreover, quite clear that Jews and other groups such as the Gypsies were not killed in order to terrorize others, because the killing program was kept as secret as possible.

Finally, the Holocaust stands apart from all previous mass killings because the victims could do nothing to save their lives by capitulation, collaboration, or conversion. Historically, people killed as heretics usually had some opportunity to save themselves by renouncing their beliefs. . . . But Jews caught in the Holocaust were ticketed for certain death. It was an explicit policy, furthermore, that those selected to perform work assignments in the death camps instead of being killed immediately were eventually supposed to be killed. No one was to be left alive to tell the tale.

Turning from the policies which defined the victims in a historically new fashion to the means employed for their destruction, it is obvious that the highly organized methods required to funnel millions of people into gas chambers constitute yet another unique aspect of the Holocaust. The gas chamber–crematoria technology and the procedures associated with it add up to unprecedented mass murder organized according to industrial production criteria of efficiency. Nothing is more revealing of this fact than the SS recycling program for the eyeglasses, clothing, gold teeth, and hair "produced" by the victims.

What were the emotions of those assigned to operational planning and execution of the Holocaust? So far as the SS headquarters and staff people were concerned, various sources of evidence all indicate that they were relatively indifferent. Practically all of the lower echelon clerks and officers had inklings if not direct knowledge of what was going on under the euphemisms of "anti-partisan warfare," "relocation," and "final solution," but their own anxiety about these notions, added to the official regulations forbidding discussion and rumors suggesting that people who knew too much or did not keep quietly in their place might wind up on the Russian front, combined in such a way that most of these people tried not to know about the meaning of their work. . . .

Taking all the material together, however, the results of qualitative comparisons reveal the uniqueness of the Holocaust in human terms quite apart from the numbers involved and the metaphysical significance it may hold. The reasons leading to it, the methods by which it was accomplished, and the emotions associated with it were all manifestly different from anything that had ever happened before. If the qualitative difference between the Holocaust and prior acts of mass destruction can be named at all, the only appropriate term for it is *dehumanization*. Although modern mass violence must frequently appear dehumanized compared with what occurred earlier simply because of the instrumentalities made available by modern science, this consideration does not invalidate our description of the Holocaust, for the character of the mass death inflicted by bombings or missile attacks, nuclear or otherwise, is far different from the Nazi death program. In order to make even an approximate analogy, one would have to postulate bombs or missiles designed so that they would seek out and destroy only Jews. In short, the uniqueness of the Holocaust is underscored by the fact that it was a massively selective program conducted more like a large-scale industrial enterprise than anything else. . . .

A Major Historical Crisis

Ever since it occurred, the Holocaust has been a terrible, frightening enigma, an open wound in the body of Western culture, because it has stubbornly resisted definition and explanation according to commonly accepted standards of meaning. One proof of this is that Dwight Macdonald's questions . . . are as challenging today as when he first raised them in 1945. Another is that as succeeding generations of sensitive young people come of age in our society and "discover" the Holocaust, their reactions are always the same. Their questions—How are such things possible?—are always predictable, and the answers they find available are always inadequate, conveying little besides the warning that the human condition can be more terrible than they ever imagined.

In the face of these realities, which have persisted despite strenuous scholarly and intellectual efforts to the contrary, it must finally be concluded that the Holocaust will never be assimilated—given substantial meaning—in terms of the familiar, normative thought structures provided by Western history and culture. . . .

The naive, how-are-such-things-possible questions most people ask about the Holocaust are ultimately correct, for according to the fundamental tenets of Western civilization, such things are not possible. This is crucially important. Practically no one can believe Auschwitz—let alone the full scope of the Nazi genocide program—unless in one form or another they see it with their own eyes. But many who did see it with their own eyes while it was happening have testified time and time again that they could not believe what they were seeing; their eyes could accept the images as real but their minds could not. . . .

Our thesis is that the Holocaust has been the major historical crisis of the twentieth century—a crisis of human behavior and values. If this has not yet been widely acknowledged, it is because the consequences of such a crisis—unlike economic, political, and ecological crises—tend to be impalpable, especially when they are masked by a language that seems unable to express them and a public rhetoric that seems unwilling to try.

Did Roosevelt Want Japan to Attack Pearl Harbor?

Morton A. Kaplan

On December 7, 1941, the Japanese launched a surprise attack on the American naval base at Pearl Harbor in the Hawaiian Islands. The role President Franklin D. Roosevelt played in the infamous attack remains an issue of controversy to this day. Morton A. Kaplan, Distinguished Service Professor of Political Science Emeritus at the University of Chicago and editor and publisher of *The World & I*, argues that Roosevelt wanted Japan to attack Pearl Harbor. Kaplan maintains that while Roosevelt was convinced that the United States had to enter the war in order to protect American democracy, he knew that the American people wanted no part of the war and would oppose getting actively involved in it. According to Kaplan, Roosevelt's plan was to maneuver the Japanese government into overtly attacking the United States, supposedly without any provocation, giving him the excuse he needed to secure a declaration of war.

For fifty years I had dismissed the argument by World War II revisionists that Roosevelt placed the fleet at Pearl Harbor to be sunk by the Japanese. Each subsequent book on that subject, even by serious scholars, failed to shake my conviction that the claim was without merit. Yet that thesis has now been shown by Robert Stinnett in his recent book *Day of Deceit: The Truth About FDR and Pearl Harbor* to be the most likely explanation of that event. If Roosevelt was the mastermind of this plot, as I now believe, and if it can be justified, as I will argue, then serious issues of democratic account-

Excerpted from Morton A. Kaplan, "Why Roosevelt Wanted Japan to Attack Pearl Harbor," *The World & I*, October 2000. This article is printed with permission from *The World & I*, a publication of The Washington Times Corporation, copyright © 2000.

ability will turn out to be murkier than most constitutional lawyers would acknowledge.

It would be generally agreed that the president has no constitutional authority to surreptitiously lead the nation to war, even if there is not, as there was in this case, a clearly expressed statutory and public commitment to staying out of foreign wars. There are exceptions to every set of rules, however, and the conditions of the period created exceptional obligations on the part of a president who understood how much was at stake.

I never did believe FDR in 1940 when he said that he wanted to keep the United States out of the war. I understood that this prevarication was a necessity in a United States that had passed neutrality acts in 1935, '37, and '39 and that in 1940 had approved a military draft by only a single vote in the lower house. FDR did persuade the public to support lend-lease and the bases-for-destroyers deal. But a great majority of the public, supported by three consecutive statutes, wanted no part of a foreign war. If there had been even a hint that Roosevelt wanted to enter the war . . . then Wendell Willkie would have been elected in 1940. Yet Roosevelt knew that protecting American democracy required American entrance into a war against Nazi Germany and its allies. . . .

Roosevelt's Plan to Anger Japan

Stinnett presents massive evidence that Roosevelt intended to goad the Japanese into an overt attack. The basis of the plan was an eight-point memorandum by Lt. Cmdr. Arthur McCollum. This memorandum, each element of which was implemented, was admittedly designed to produce a Japanese attack. Although it went from McCollum to FDR's military advisers, the routing slips show Roosevelt was on a list to receive it. If this otherwise outrageous scheme of a subordinate to precipitate a war had been objectionable, or even inconsistent with understood objectives, McCollum would have been rebuked and perhaps removed. Roosevelt would not have been kept in the dark about a matter of utmost importance to him, and the records show that he personally took charge of "D," sending warships into waters adjacent to Japanese activity. "I don't mind losing one or two cruisers, but do not take a chance on losing five or six," Roosevelt stated. Clearly he was trying to anger Japan. The Japanese in fact formally protested the cruisers, which were just off the island of Shikoku, next to Japanese fleet units.

The object of the plan—and of the November "peace proposal," which was a disguised ultimatum that would be read as such by the Japanese but not by the American public—was to leave the Japanese a Hobson's choice: either to surrender all their objectives, including the coprosperity sphere, in the Pacific or to attack the United States. No Japanese government could have survived such a debacle, and it would have deprived them of what they saw as their rightful role in a Pacific area in which European imperialists had carved up China. Indeed, the Meiji revolutionaries, who copied European institutions and international practices to protect Japan from the fate of China, saw their role, at least in part, as protecting Asia from European domination. . . .

To secure a declaration of war, it was vital to Roosevelt that a Japanese attack on the United States appear unprovoked. The Pearl Harbor command was under orders to do nothing to provoke an attack. Admiral Richardson was removed when he refused to station a vulnerable capital fleet there . . . because, as he correctly said, it would have endangered naval personnel. Roosevelt then appointed Adm. Husband Kimmel to the command post, and Kimmel agreed to station important elements of the fleet there, even though American contingency plans indicated Pearl Harbor was a possible point of Japanese attack. Kimmel's plans for a training exercise in the area north of Hawaii—the route to an attack upon Pearl Harbor—were vetoed by Washington. The seas along this attack route . . . were cleared of both civilian and naval vessels, thus assuring that the Japanese fleet could not be detected by American or Allied vessels.

We possess no records of the calculations that led to these decisions, but we can speculatively reconstruct them. Placing the battleships at Pearl Harbor would present a tempting target to the Japanese because if they could cripple the fleet they could secure the supplies of Asia without fear of American naval interference. The risk to our forces likely seemed acceptable. The more modern vessels, including our carriers, had been removed from the area. Moreover, it was believed that torpedoes would not be effective in shallow waters. The massive naval construction program that Roo-

A Date Which Will Live in Infamy

On December 8, 1941, the day after the Japanese attack on Pearl Harbor, President Franklin Delano Roosevelt asked Congress to declare the United States at war with Japan. That same day, he addressed the American people over the radio, telling them what he had told Congress.

Yesterday, Dec. 7, 1941—a date which will live in infamy—the United States of America was suddenly and deliberately attacked by naval and air forces of the Empire of Japan.

The United States was at peace with that nation and, at the solicitation of Japan, was still in conversation with the government and its emperor looking toward the maintenance of peace in the Pacific.

Indeed, one hour after Japanese air squadrons had commenced bombing in Oahu, the Japanese ambassador to the United States and his colleagues delivered to the Secretary of State a formal reply to a recent American message. While this reply stated that it seemed useless to continue the existing diplomatic negotiations, it contained no threat or hint of war or armed attack.

It will be recorded that the distance of Hawaii from Japan makes it obvious that the attack was deliberately planned many days or even weeks ago. During the intervening time, the Japanese government has deliberately sought to deceive the United States by false statements and expressions of hope for continued peace.

The attack yesterday on the Hawaiian islands has caused severe damage to American naval and military forces. Very many American lives have been lost. In addition, American ships have been reported torpedoed on the high seas between San Francisco and Honolulu.

Yesterday, the Japanese government also launched an attack

sevelt had got through Congress would eventually produce a fleet that could attack Japan after Germany was defeated.

The argument that we thought the Japanese attack would be to the south is a half-truth. We had evidence of a sepa-

---

`.

...ght, Japanese forces attacked Hong Kong.

Last night, Japanese forces attacked Guam.

Last night, Japanese forces attacked the Philippine Islands.

Last night, the Japanese attacked Wake Island.

This morning, the Japanese attacked Midway Island.

Japan has, therefore, undertaken a surprise offensive extending throughout the Pacific area. The facts of yesterday speak for themselves. The people of the United States have already formed their opinions and well understand the implications to the very life and safety of our nation.

As commander in chief of the Army and Navy, I have directed that all measures be taken for our defense.

Always will we remember the character of the onslaught against us.

No matter how long it may take us to overcome this premeditated invasion, the American people in their righteous might will win through to absolute victory.

I believe I interpret the will of the Congress and of the people when I assert that we will not only defend ourselves to the uttermost, but will make very certain that this form of treachery shall never endanger us again.

Hostilities exist. There is no blinking at the fact that our people, our territory and our interests are in grave danger.

With confidence in our armed forces—with the unbending determination of our people—we will gain the inevitable triumph—so help us God.

I ask that the Congress declare that since the unprovoked and dastardly attack by Japan on Sunday, Dec. 7, a state of war has existed between the United States and the Japanese empire.

Franklin Delano Roosevelt, "Pearl Harbor Speech," December 8, 1941. http://www.pbs.org.

rate attack force that was directed at Pearl Harbor. We had broken all the Japanese codes, both military and political. Contrary to claims that the Japanese maintained radio silence—and even contrary to Yamamoto's orders to maintain radio silence—it was not possible to move such a large array without communications. . . .

Although most copies of this radio traffic were destroyed or hidden . . . there were still enough remnants of the intercepts to support Stinnett's claims, which were then verified by the radio operators who had received the Japanese signals. Although this traffic was sent to the Philippines, again verified by Stinnett, most of it was not sent to Kimmel and Short. The Japanese spy who monitored the Pearl Harbor installations was covered by American intelligence. His transmissions to Japan of the locations of our capital ships at Pearl Harbor were not provided to Short and Kimmel. Nor was Yamamoto's uncoded broadcast to his two fleets, "Climb Mount Niitaka," the highest mountain in Japan. This was a clear signal to both attack fleets . . . that their attack orders were now being implemented.

Setting the Stage for an Attack

Short and Kimmel were told that war was expected soon, not that it was imminent, and they were instructed to take due measures. However, the orders to them put the emphasis on preventing sabotage, even though the authorities knew a Japanese fleet was on its way. They also were instructed to do nothing that would alarm the local population. Since Pearl Harbor was open to civilians from the highways, this meant they could not go on a visible alert. In short, their orders were likely a concocted cover story, designed to show that Washington had alerted them, although in fact ensuring that they would do nothing effective. The only thing left was to make sure that the onus for war fell completely on the Japanese. Kimmel and Short were the "fall" guys.

Some of the Stinnett book's reviewers, who are now convinced that the intercepts of the Japanese fleet's transmissions did occur, have said that, despite the normal routings of the intelligence information, Roosevelt may not have re-

ceived the reports of the tracking of the attack force. Given
the length of time the tracking continued and the fact that
the issue was at the top of FDR's agenda, this is extremely
unlikely. Given Roosevelt's plans and all the preceding ma-
nipulation, which made little if any sense in the absence of
provoking a Japanese attack, it is irrelevant. . . . No intelligence officer could have missed the fact that one attack fleet
was en route to Southeast Asia and that the other fleet was
large, contained several carriers, and was moving on the natural route for an attack on Pearl Harbor. This was not a matter of choosing from a welter of conflicting reports but a
matter of consistent tracking of actual military moves.

Roosevelt and his military advisers knew on December 6
that the incoming message to the Japanese Embassy, which
was instantly translated by American code breakers and sent
to them, was a declaration of war. They knew that both fleets
were part of a coordinated attack that would be in striking
distance of Pearl Harbor by the following morning and the
Philippines shortly thereafter. Yet Gen. George Marshall did
nothing Saturday night and took his regular Sunday horseback ride. Thus, he was sure not to be present in time to give
a warning to Short and Kimmel that would have enabled
them to take measures that might have deterred or blunted
the attack even if the Japanese had been able to deliver the
ultimatum in the early morning.

The reviewers I have read, although disturbed by Stinnett's evidence, attempt to cast doubt on his thesis by showing that individual pieces of evidence can be given a different
interpretation. Yes, we cannot prove, for instance, that Washington deliberately withheld from Hawaii the evidence that
the Japanese had secured the naval grids at Pearl Harbor. But
there are often no smoking guns such as the Nixon tapes. If
we cannot prove a case beyond any doubt, this does not mean
that we should reject a highly likely explanation. . . .

MacArthur as a Diversionary Tactic

Let me now deal with a few of the additional questions the
Stinnett book raises. Why was fuller information sent to
Gen. Douglas MacArthur in the Philippines, whom Mar-

shall neither liked nor trusted, and not to Short and Kimmel in Hawaii? Could Washington have viewed the Pearl Harbor attack fleet as the kind of diversion created by Gen. George Patton with his phantom army in 1944?

Patton's phantom army made it difficult for Hitler to concentrate his forces at the point of attack. The situation in the Pacific was quite different. The American military, as the Japanese knew, was in no position to reinforce MacArthur. Therefore, deception with regard to the attack on the Philippines was of minor importance and could not have justified the massive size of the Pearl Harbor attack fleet. If the Japanese intended to attack only the Philippines and Southeast Asia, many of the ships in the Pearl Harbor fleet would have been better disposed with the main attack. No reasonable intelligence officer would have suspected that this second fleet was designed to disguise the object of attack.

It was safe to keep MacArthur better informed because nothing he did or did not do would stop the Japanese from attacking an essential and indefensible target. How do I know the Philippines were indefensible? In 1941 I headed a student organization that supported American entry into the war. I had been reading widely on our military capabilities in the Pacific, including Gen. Johnson Hagood's book *We Can Defend America* (Doubleday, 1937), which detailed the then current indefensibility of our island outposts. . . .

In Support of Stinnett's Thesis

The attack on Pearl Harbor, . . . although important to the Japanese war effort, depended on a host of favorable circumstances for success. If the Japanese thought the attack had been detected by the Americans, even as late as Saturday night or Sunday morning, they might have called it off, the better to protect their forces for the crucial effort to the south. It was questionable whether an attack on the Philippines alone would have produced a declaration of war in a nation with such antiwar sentiment. Although the Philippines were a dependency, they were not part of the United States proper. MacArthur was an officer in the Philippine army, not the American, at the time of the attack. At the least, the attempt to get a declaration of war would be contentious and divisive, thus increasing the already present risk that the main enemy, Nazi Germany, would escape a declaration. Thus, an attack on Pearl Harbor would have been an important component of Roosevelt's plan because it would inflame public sentiment sufficiently to unite the country and to produce not merely a declaration of war but one supported by the entire Congress.

Stinnett did not prove his case beyond any doubt, but a whole laundry list of factors—including the controversial stationing of the fleet at Pearl Harbor, the refusal to let Kimmel carry out an exercise on the attack route, the Vacant Seas order, the failure to let Short and Kimmel know about Japanese intelligence on the grids at Pearl Harbor, the orders to Short and Kimmel to concentrate their efforts on sabotage, the failure to attempt to alert them on December 6, when the White House was in possession of the translated declaration of war, and Marshall's absence from his office on the morning of December 7—surely builds a powerful case that cannot be contravened by the mere possibility of some other explanation for individual pieces of evidence. . . .

Let me make one more effort to undermine Stinnett's thesis. Is it possible that Washington thought the second fleet was directed to Midway and not to the Hawaiian islands? This seems unlikely but possible. However, even if Washington thought this were the more likely alternative, they could not have ruled out Pearl Harbor. Even if they thought Midway were the only possible objective, and this is close to inconceivable, why did they not alert the fleet to take defensive measures? This makes no sense.

History is always subject to revision on the basis of new evidence, but Stinnett's thesis must be regarded as sustained on the basis of the available evidence. Although it is always possible to put a different "spin" on each individual piece of evidence, it defies reason to reject a thesis in which the parts fit so well.

In Defense of Roosevelt

Who were Roosevelt's fellow conspirators? Not Secretary of War Henry Stimson and Secretary of State Cordell Hull. The evidence suggests that Roosevelt used them. They were too straightforward, and his conversations with them strongly indicated that, in his usual manner, he was concocting a cover story. Very likely, Generals Marshall and Bedell Smith and Adm. Ernest King were among the overt conspirators. I always wondered why Marshall was horseback riding on the morning of December 7 when he knew that a likely declaration of war was being transmitted. Now we know that he knew as early as the previous evening that Japan had transmitted a declaration of war. Making himself unavailable probably was his way of ensuring that Pearl Harbor would not be alerted in time.

Roosevelt was a great president. My first vote, a military absentee ballot, was for Roosevelt. I would cast the same vote again. He understood that the fate of the world rested on stopping the Axis powers. Indeed, apart from any military threat, American democracy might not have survived isolation in a fascist world. The president's duty to "preserve, protect, and defend the Constitution" includes preserving, protecting, and defending the institutions and values the Constitution is designed to support. These can be in conflict with a strict interpretation of its clauses. However, this last argument can be so dangerous to preserving, protecting, and defending the Constitution that it should be invoked only in the most stringent circumstances. . . .

Undoubtedly Roosevelt saw himself as doing what his office demanded: protecting American institutions and values. If this technically breached the democratic process, that was an acceptable price for saving it in a war that liberalized and enriched it. . . .

Roosevelt was a master manipulator and a great actor. He positively enjoyed lying to people and using them. The potential casualties at Pearl Harbor would not have been a significant consideration to him. . . .

Do I approve of the strategy? I think I would have alerted the fleet in order to reduce casualties and hoped that the public would still support war. But then I am a professor and editor. Roosevelt was the master politician upon whom, in Harry Truman's phrase, the buck rested. A result so important may justify the means.

Midway: Yamamoto's Most Complete Failure

James C. Ryan

In June 1942 American and Japanese forces clashed in the Pacific in the naval and air battle at Midway Island. Defeat at Midway cost the Japanese their advantage in the Pacific. In this selection, historical writer James C. Ryan argues that the Japanese loss at Midway was the result of the tactical and strategic errors made by Admiral Isoroku Yamamoto. Ryan contends that Yamamoto split his forces, positioned the seven battleships of his main force in a way that wasted precious fuel, compounded communications problems during the battle by sailing with the fleet, and confused his forces with conflicting objectives. Ryan concludes that Yamamoto, the architect of the surprise attack on Pearl Harbor and a national hero, failed completely in his planning for the conduct of the Battle of Midway and was instrumental in Japan losing the war to the Allies.

One of the enduring myths of World War II is that Admiral Isoroku Yamamoto, author of the attack on Pearl Harbor, was one of the great naval strategists of all time. In truth, Yamamoto was responsible for some of the most grievous errors, both tactical and strategic, committed by the Japanese leadership. . . . The greatest of his failures came six months after the sneak attack and 1,300 miles to the west [of Pearl Harbor], at Midway.

Why Japan Went to War

In the summer of 1941, Japan resolved to go to war in the Pacific in spite of a seemingly unending war in China and se-

Excerpted from James C. Ryan, "Was Japanese Admiral Isoroku Yamamoto a Strategic Genius or the Architect of His Nations' Ruin?," *World War II*, May 1999. Reprinted with permission from The Gale Group.

rious raw material shortages, exacerbated by the American oil and steel embargo that began in July of that year. The latter event, however, was a major factor in Japan's decision to go to war with the United States.

Japan's aggressive stance in the 1930s and '40s was fueled by a host of other factors. The population of the rocky and mountainous country was growing so rapidly that it was outstripping food production, and its rapid industrial expansion required massive raw material imports. Perhaps most important, Japan had a national inferiority complex. The slights, both real and imagined, they had suffered at the hands of the Western powers had begun with the forced opening of feudal Japan by U.S. Commodore Matthew Perry's naval squadron in 1854. Later, they felt they were shortchanged in the peace treaty brokered by U.S. President Theodore Roosevelt to end the Russo–Japanese War in 1905 and in the division of spoils by the Treaty of Versailles after World War I. Finally, they felt affronted by the 5-to-5-to-3 ratio of capital ships allowed the United States, Britain and Japan by the Washington Naval Conference of 1921. That seemed an equitable ratio to the United States and Britain, which were obliged to maintain two- and three-ocean navies with global commitments while Japanese interests were confined to the Pacific. Nevertheless, the Japanese felt slighted.

With no end yet in sight for the war with China, the Japanese Imperial General Staff cast about for the next target. . . . As part of their strategy of conquest, they decided war with the United States was inevitable. Yamamoto, who had lived and studied in the United States, argued against taking on a country of such vast industrial and military potential. Once the decision was made, however, he dutifully committed himself to finding the best way to clinch a quick victory before the United States could bring its full resources into play. Logically, the first strike would be against U.S. bases in the Philippine Islands, but Yamamoto, named commander in chief of the Combined Fleet in August 1939, proposed a far more daring plan.

Yamamoto conceived an attack by carrier-borne aircraft on the U.S. naval base at Pearl Harbor. . . . In proposing his plan, Yamamoto added an ominous warning: "In the first six to twelve months of a war with the United States and Great Britain, I will run wild and win victory after victory. But then, if the war continues after that, I have no expectation of success."

The Imperial General Staff was so opposed to Yamamoto's risky venture that they at first refused to sanction it. But Yamamoto said that he might resign if the plan was not approved. His prestige was so great that his superiors relented.

The Pearl Harbor raid succeeded beyond its author's wildest dreams. . . . The Japanese had cut the head from the Hydra, but two heads, submarine and carrier warfare, grew in its place.

Conflicting Objectives at Midway

Nowhere did Yamamoto fail more completely than in his planning for and conduct of the Battle of Midway. The plan was opposed by the Imperial General Staff, but Yamamoto again quelled his opposition by saying he might resign if they refused to sanction the operation.

Midway was flawed from its inception. Although the armada Yamamoto sent should have been capable of subduing the small garrison of the atoll and any opposing U.S. naval forces, Japan lacked the shipping capacity to support such a far-flung outpost, even without the interference of marauding U.S. submarines. Some historians have theorized that if the Japanese had secured Midway as a base for long-range bombers, they could have made Pearl Harbor an untenable holding, requiring a U.S. strategic withdrawal to the West Coast. In fact, Sand and Eastern islands, the only islets in the atoll capable of supporting airfields, have a total of about five square miles of swampy ground, and the atoll has no freshwater supply. In any case, Boeing B-17 Flying Fortress bombers based at Pearl Harbor would have made Midway an untenable liability to the Japanese.

After determining to proceed in spite of those potential difficulties, Yamamoto prepared a battle plan calculated to neutralize nearly all the advantages he enjoyed. First, he split his forces, sending a significant share of his striking power north to launch a diversionary attack in the Aleutians. Second, he kept his Main Force, including seven battleships, well astern of the First Carrier Striking Force. In that position, they were wasting fuel, a commodity that was the number one limitation for the Japanese from day one of the war. Had Yamamoto grouped the Main Force with the Carrier Force, the vastly increased anti-aircraft defenses might well have made a critical difference. Furthermore, Yamamoto decided to sail with the fleet, even though being at sea would impose radio silence upon him. That compounded the communications problems during the battle.

It is ironic that history has viewed Yamamoto as a visionary champion of carrier warfare. His operational plan for Midway called for the carrier forces to neutralize the air defenses on Midway, along with any U.S. carriers that should appear on the scene, after which his mighty battleships would charge in and destroy any remaining U.S. ships. He had apparently not planned how his slower battleships were to chase down the swift carrier task forces.

Even Yamamoto's pared-down Carrier Striking Force had conflicting objectives. Its supposed mission was to attack and subdue Midway to clear the way for an invasion, but he also hoped that this attack, combined with the Aleutian strike, would compel the U.S. Navy to respond by sending separate forces to both locations, providing an opportunity to destroy the last of the American fleet. Instead, the U.S. Navy, which had learned of his plan beforehand, concentrated its carrier force to confront him at Midway, negating the diversionary attack on the Aleutians.

Admiral Isoroku Yamamoto

Disaster in the Making

Yamamoto's contradictory objectives magnified the potential for disaster. Japanese doctrine called for different battle formations for different actions. For land attacks, all carriers steamed in a tight box formation to allow visual communication between ships and preserve radio silence. For fleet engagements, the carriers were to disperse, so any attacking enemy aircraft that located one carrier might not find the others. When the American attack came, three of the four Japanese carriers—*Akagi*, *Kaga*, and *Soryu*—were still steaming in close formation. The fourth, *Hiryu*, was some distance away, which gave her a reprieve.

Unlike Yamamoto, Admiral Chester Nimitz, commander in chief of the U.S. Pacific forces, did everything right. First, he kept his carrier forces loosely coordinated so that they could provide mutual support while staying separated so that discovery of part of the force would not endanger the rest. Second, knowing that victory or defeat would rest solely on his carriers, Nimitz not only refused to send his battleships into harm's way, he even sent all seaworthy battlewagons back to the West Coast. . . . Third, he stayed at Pearl Harbor, where he would have access to shore-based intelligence and could communicate freely with his commanders at sea. Finally, he gave the commanders of Task Forces 16 and 17, Rear Adms. Raymond Spruance and Frank Jack Fletcher, a clear objective: They were to cover Midway and prevent its capture by the Japanese. As a secondary objective, they were to inflict damage on the Japanese fleet wherever the opportunity presented itself, but not if such actions would place their primary objective at risk. Those clear orders allowed his commanders tremendous flexibility. American cryptographers may have enabled Nimitz to divine Yamamoto's intentions, but it was the U.S. commander's strategic genius that enabled him to make the most of that advantage.

From the time it commenced with an air strike on the atoll on June 4, 1942, the Battle of Midway was largely out of Yamamoto's hands. His commander of the Carrier Striking Force, Nagumo, was hesitant as to whether he should launch another strike on the island garrison, and he had his second-strike aircraft switch from torpedoes to bombs and back to torpedoes during a series of abortive American torpedo attacks. As a result of those repeated weapon changes, the carrier decks were packed with fueled aircraft and littered with improperly stored bombs and torpedoes when the American Douglas SBD-3 Dauntless dive bombers struck. Their bombs triggered chain reactions among the parked aircraft, bombs and fuel, dooming *Akagi*, *Kaga*, and *Soryu*. . . .

In spite of the disasters suffered by the end of the first day, Yamamoto still had a chance to snatch victory from the jaws of defeat. He first ordered his heavy cruiser force forward to bombard Midway, hoping for a night surface engagement—the kind of contest in which the Japanese excelled. Spruance, however, avoided such a fight by steering a leisurely course eastward.

Realizing that his cruisers would be unable to reach Midway or bring the American task force to battle before daylight, Yamamoto ordered them to turn west again. That change of course brought the ships into contact with the patrolling U.S. submarine *Tambor*, and while they were evading its torpedoes, heavy cruisers *Mogami* and *Mikuma* collided in the dark. . . .

Even then, Yamamoto had three light carriers close at hand and two others deployed to the north, less than three days' journey away. Altogether, those ships carried more than 130 serviceable combat aircraft. Yamamoto also had the most powerful surface fleet in the world. Facing the Japanese were two carriers that had lost a significant share of their air complements. But Yamamoto had had enough. Bloodied by an enemy he had grossly underestimated, he turned for home.

A History of Strategic Failures

From that day forward, the Americans would dictate the course of the war. On August 7, 1942, they seized the initiative Yamamoto had lost when they invaded Guadalcanal. Time and again during the bloody six-month struggle for that island, Yamamoto's naval forces would turn nominal tactical victories into strategic defeats by failing to press the issue. This was hardly in keeping with the tradition of *Tennozan*—the staking of all on a single, winner-take-all battle.

Guadalcanal became the pivotal battle of the war in the Pacific because Yamamoto was unwilling to treat it as such.

Midway was not Isoroku Yamamoto's last failure, but it was his most complete. He was killed when U.S. Army Lockheed P-38 Lightning fighters intercepted his Mitsubishi G4M Betty bomber during an inspection tour on April 18, 1943, and shot it down. Instead of being called to account for his failures at Midway, Guadalcanal, and elsewhere, he became a national martyr.

Disaster in North Africa

William L. Shirer

In the summer of 1942, the Axis powers were winning the war. Then came two major defeats for the Germans— Stalingrad in Russia and El Alamein in North Africa. Foreign correspondent, news commentator, and historian William L. Shirer reported much of the rise of the Nazis from Berlin and, as a war correspondent, covered the Nazi fall to defeat. In this selection from Shirer's critically acclaimed history of Nazi Germany, *The Rise and Fall of the Third Reich*, he describes German general Erwin Rommel's earlier successes in North Africa and the circumstances that contributed to his defeat at El Alamein. Shirer explains how Hitler's decision not to complete the conquest of Malta resulted in a shortage of crucial supplies for Rommel. According to Shirer, Hitler did not understand the situation in North Africa and undermined Rommel's efforts there. When Rommel was forced to withdraw in defeat from El Alamein, Shirer writes, it was the beginning of the end for Hitler.

At first, that summer of 1942, the fortunes of the Axis prospered. . . . A sensational victory was scored in North Africa. On May 27,1942, General [Erwin] Rommel had resumed his offensive in the desert. Striking swiftly with his famed Afrika Korps (two armored divisions and a motorized infantry division) and eight Italian divisions, of which one was armored, he soon had the British desert army reeling back toward the Egyptian frontier. On June 21 he captured Tobruk, the key to the British defenses, which in 1941 had held out for nine months until relieved, and two days later he entered Egypt. By the end of June he was at El Alamein, sixty-five miles from Alexandria and the delta of the Nile. It seemed to many a startled Allied statesman, poring over a map, that nothing could now prevent Rommel from delivering a fatal blow to the British by conquering Egypt and then, if he were reinforced, sweeping on northeast to capture the great oil fields of the Middle East and then to the Caucasus to meet the German armies in Russia. . . .

The Axis Win and Lose Malta

It was one of the darkest moments of the war for the Allies and correspondingly one of the brightest for the Axis. But Hitler . . . had never understood global warfare. He did not know how to exploit Rommel's surprising African success. He awarded the daring leader of the Afrika Korps a field marshal's baton but he did not send him supplies or reinforcements. Under the nagging of Admiral [Erich] Raeder and the urging of Rommel, the Fuehrer had only reluctantly agreed to send the Afrika Korps and a small German air force to Libya in the first place. But he had done this only to prevent an Italian collapse in North Africa, not because he foresaw the importance of conquering Egypt.

The key to that conquest actually was the small island of Malta, lying in the Mediterranean between Sicily and the Axis bases in Libya. It was from this British bastion that bombers, submarines and surface craft wrought havoc on German and Italian vessels carrying supplies and men to North Africa. In August 1941 some 35 per cent of Rommel's supplies and reinforcements were sunk; in October, 63 per cent. . . .

It was decided to neutralize Malta and destroy, if possible, the British fleet in the eastern Mediterranean. Success was immediate. By the end of 1941 the British had lost three battleships, an aircraft carrier, two cruisers and several destroyers and submarines, and what was left of their fleet was driven to Egyptian bases. Malta had been battered by German bombers day and night for weeks. As a result Axis supplies got through—in January not a ton of shipping was lost—and Rommel was able to build up his forces for the big push into Egypt. . . .

The drive from Libya was to begin at the end of May and

Malta was to be assaulted in mid-July. But on June 15, while Rommel was in the midst of his initial successes, Hitler postponed the attack on Malta. . . . Malta could be kept quiet in the meantime, he advised, by continued bombing.

But it was not kept quiet and for this failure either to neutralize it or to capture it the Germans would shortly pay a high price. A large British convoy got through to the besieged island on June 16, and though several warships and freighters were lost this put Malta back in business. Spitfires were flown to the island from the U.S. aircraft carrier *Wasp* and soon drove the attacking Luftwaffe bombers from the skies. Rommel felt the effect. Three quarters of his supply ships thereafter were sunk.

He had reached El Alamein with just thirteen operational tanks. "Our strength," he wrote in his diary on July 3, "has faded away." And at a moment when the Pyramids were almost in sight, and beyond—the great prize of Egypt and Suez! This was another opportunity lost, and one of the last which Hitler would be afforded by Providence and the fortunes of war.

Axis Victories Grow

By the end of the summer of 1942 Adolf Hitler seemed to be once more on top of the world. German U-boats were sinking 700,000 tons of British-American shipping a month in the Atlantic—more than could be replaced in the booming shipyards of the United States, Canada and Scotland. Though the Fuehrer had denuded his forces in the West of most of their troops and tanks and planes in order to finish with Russia, there was no sign that summer that the British and Americans were strong enough to make even a small landing from across the Channel. They had not even risked trying to occupy French-held Northwest Africa, though the weakened French, of divided loyalties, had nothing much with which to stop them even if they attempted to, and the Germans nothing at all except a few submarines and a handful of planes based in Italy and Tripoli. . . .

On the map the sum of Hitler's conquests by September 1942 looked staggering. The Mediterranean had become practically an Axis lake, with Germany and Italy holding most of the northern shore from Spain to Turkey and the southern shore from Tunisia to within sixty miles of the Nile. In fact, German troops now stood guard from the Norwegian North Cape on the Arctic Ocean to Egypt, from the Atlantic at Brest to the southern reaches of the Volga River on the border of Central Asia. . . .

The German Defeat at El Alamein

The Desert Fox, as he was called on both sides of the front, had resumed his offensive at El Alamein on August 31 with the intention of rolling up the British Eighth Army and driving on to Alexandria and the Nile. There was a violent battle in the scorching heat on the 40-mile desert front between the sea and the Qattara Depression, but Rommel could not quite make it and on September 3 he broke off the fighting and went over to the defensive. At long last the British army in Egypt had received strong reinforcements in men, guns, tanks and planes (many of the last two from America). It had also received on August 15 two new commanders: an eccentric but gifted general named Sir Bernard Law Montgomery, who took over the Eighth Army, and General Sir Harold Alexander, who was to prove to be a skillful strategist and a brilliant administrator and who now assumed the post of Commander in Chief in the Middle East.

Shortly after his setback Rommel had gone on sick leave on the Semmering in the mountains below Vienna to receive a cure for an infected nose and a swollen liver, and it was there that on the afternoon of October 24 he received a telephone call from Hitler. "Rommel, the news from Africa sounds bad. The situation seems somewhat obscure. Nobody appears to know what has happened to [Acting Commander] General Stumme. Do you feel capable of returning to Africa and taking over there again?" Though a sick man, Rommel agreed to return immediately.

By the time he got back to headquarters West of El Alamein on the following evening, the battle, which Montgomery had launched at 9:40 P.M. on October 23, was already lost. The Eighth Army had too many guns, tanks and

Fireworks at El Alamein

For some British soldiers, the battle at El Alamein was their first real battlefield experience. Sid Martindale, a soldier with the First Battalion Argyll Sutherland Highlanders, describes his experience at El Alamein below.

After doing our various guard duties in Alex [Alexandria, Egypt] we were sent into action with the rest of the 8th army at El Alamein. The North African war at the time I arrived in Egypt was not going in our favor. Rommel, the desert fox, had driven General Wavells 8th army all the way across North Africa to a line not far from Alex, where the Afrikakorps had halted their advance because their supply lines were over-stretched. People in Alex started to panic, thinking the Afrikakorps would be at the city walls very soon. But the British line held and we were able to build up our reserves.

This was the situation when we arrived at the front line. During the first week at the front line two of us from each platoon were sent forward to do stag duty in the forward observation post [OP] in no-mans-land, to observe the enemy movements and would have to stay there for 24 hours. We never really saw Jerry [the Germans] while up at the OP but he could see us because the enemy would send over few shells that would explode pretty near to us but we were just out of range of their guns, but still it was very frightening.

While not at the forward observation post the battalion were stationed just behind the lines. Everyday the Luftwaffe would bomb us using Ju 87 Stuka dive bombers. This is when we suffered our first casualties. The Germans introduced a new idea to the terror of war, they added sirens to the Stuka's fixed wheels calling them "Jericho's Trumpets." The wine from the sirens as the Stuka's dived was a very terrifying sound and when you heard this you wanted to find the biggest hole possible, get in it and stay there. The Luftwaffe managed to destroy a lot of our rear transport, killing a few of our blokes at the same time. The Stuka quickly gained my respect as something that would lighten my chances of getting back home alive. I was learning what war was all about very quickly. . . .

The Battle of El Alamein began on the night of 23rd October 1942 with 882 field and medium guns opening fire at once, pounding the German and Italian artillery positions. The whole sky was lit up by this artillery barrage. It was like daylight and the noise was deafening. This Artillery fire signaled the start of the biggest British attack of the desert war. We watched this spectacular sight from our positions in the carriers. It was the biggest fire work display I've ever seen in my life and I'd have hated to be on the receiving end of all that hot lead that was flying though the air. The barrage went on until 4 in the morning and then the troops advanced. . . .

We saw hardly anything of the battle raging in front of us. It all seemed to be a very confusing time, with no lights to guide us we had to rely on directions from the officers who seemed to be holding their maps upside down. The more we advanced the more we realized that the Italians did not have much fight on them after putting up a strong resistance to our overwhelming advance and they started surrendering to our lead troops in droves. There was not much action to see but we came across lots of burnt out Italian tanks that had been destroyed by our tanks. I had never seen a battlefield before and the sight of so many dead was sickening.

We captured hundreds of Italian soldiers in the next few days without them putting up too much resistance as they knew that the battle was lost for them. They had been abandoned by their German Allies and the British armour was superior than their tanks and we had more of them. I felt sorry for the Italian soldiers because it seemed that they had been left to fend for themselves by their German Allies. We got talking to some of the prisoners we captured and started bartering with them using cigarettes and bully beef. One Italian gave me a wooden carving of Mussolini in exchange for a pack of Victory Vs cigarettes which were bloody awful. . . . After four days the Battalion was withdrawn from the battle and the next day Monty [British general Bernard Montgomery] had won his battle, Jerry was on the run and I had survived my first encounter with the enemy.

Sid Martindale, "Sid's War: The Story of an Argyll at War."

planes, and though the Italian-German lines still held and Rommel made desperate efforts to shift his battered divisions to stem the various attacks and even to counterattack he realized that his situation was hopeless. He had no reserves: of men, or tanks or oil. The R.A.F. [British Royal Air Force], for once, had complete command of the skies and was pounding his troops and armor and remaining supply dumps mercilessly.

On November 2, Montgomery's infantry and armor broke through on the southern sector of the front and began to overrun the Italian divisions there. That evening Rommel radioed Hitler's headquarters in East Prussia two thousand miles away that he could no longer hold out and that he intended to withdraw, while there was still the opportunity, to the Fûka position forty miles to the west.

He had already commenced to do so when a long message came over the air the next day from the Supreme warlord:

To Field Marshal Rommel:

I and the German people are watching the heroic defensive battle waged in Egypt with faithful trust in your powers of leadership and in the bravery of the German-Italian troops under your command. In the situation in which you now find yourself, there can be no other consideration save that of holding fast, of not retreating one step, of throwing every gun and every man into the battle. . . . You can show your troops no other way than that which leads to victory or to death.

Adolf Hitler

This idiotic order meant, if obeyed, that the Italo-German armies were condemned to swift annihilation and for the first time in Africa, . . . Rommel did not know what to do. After a brief struggle with his conscience he decided, over the protests of General Ritter von Thoma, the actual commander of the German Afrika Korps, who said he was withdrawing in any case, to obey his Supreme Commander. "I finally compelled myself to take this decision," Rommel wrote later in his diary, "because I myself have always demanded unconditional obedience from my soldiers and I therefore wished to accept this principle for myself." Later, as a subsequent diary entry declares, he learned better.

Reluctantly Rommel gave the order to halt the withdrawal and at the same time sent off a courier by plane to Hitler to try to explain to him that unless he were permitted to fall back immediately all would be lost. But events were already making that trip unnecessary. On the evening of November 4, at the risk of being court-martialed for disobedience, Rommel decided to save what was left of his forces and retreat to Fûka. Only the remnants of the armored and motorized units could be extricated. The foot soldiers, mostly Italian, were left behind to surrender, as indeed the bulk of them already had done. On November 5 came a curt message from the Fuehrer: "I agree to the withdrawal of your army into the Fûka position." But that position already had been overrun by Montgomery's tanks. Within fifteen days Rommel had fallen back seven hundred miles to beyond Benghazi with the remnants of his African army—some 25,000 Italians, 10,000 Germans and sixty tanks—and there was no opportunity to stop even there.

This was the beginning of the end for Adolf Hitler, the most decisive battle of the war yet won by his enemies. . . .

When the first reports had come in of Rommel's disaster, the Fuehrer's headquarters had received word that an Allied armada had been sighted assembling at Gibraltar. . . . Hitler was inclined to think it was merely another heavily guarded convoy for Malta. . . .

The Allies Land in North Africa

On November 5, OKW [the high command of the armed forces] was informed that one British naval force had sailed out of Gibraltar headed east. But it was not until the morning of November 7, twelve hours before American and British troops began landing in North Africa, that Hitler gave the latest intelligence from Gibraltar some thought. The forenoon reports received at his headquarters in East Prussia were that British naval forces in Gibraltar and a vast fleet of transports and warships from the Atlantic had joined up and were steaming east into the Mediterranean. There was a long discussion among the staff officers and the Fuehrer. What did it all mean? What was the objective of such a large naval force? Hitler was now inclined to believe, he said, that the Western Allies might be attempting a major landing with some four or five divisions at Tripoli or Benghazi in order to catch Rommel in the rear. . . . Something had to be done. Hitler asked that the Luftwaffe in the Mediterranean be immediately reinforced but was told this was impossible "for the moment.". . . All that Hitler did that morning was to notify [the] Commander in Chief in the West to be ready to carry out "Anton." This was the code word for the occupation of the rest of France.

Whereupon the Supreme Commander, heedless of this ominous news or of the plight of Rommel, who would be trapped if the Anglo-Americans landed behind him, . . . entrained after lunch on November 7 for Munich, where on the next evening he was scheduled to deliver his annual speech to his old party cronies gathered to celebrate the anniversary of the Beer Hall Putsch! . . .

Anglo-American troops under General [Dwight D.] Eisenhower hit the beaches of Morocco and Algeria at 1:30 A.M. on November 8, 1942. . . .

For about twenty-four hours Hitler toyed with the idea of trying to make an alliance with France in order to bring her into the war against Britain and America and, at the moment, to strengthen the resolve of the [Vichy French] government to oppose the Allied landings in North Africa. . . .

Hitler won the race against Eisenhower to seize Tunisia, but it was a doubtful victory. At his insistence nearly a quarter of a million German and Italian troops were poured in to hold this bridgehead. If the Fuehrer had sent one fifth as many troops and tanks to Rommel a few months before, the Desert Fox most probably would have been beyond the Nile by now, the Anglo-American landing in Northwest Africa could not have taken place and the Mediterranean would have been irretrievably lost to the Allies, thus securing the soft undercover of the Axis belly. As it was, every soldier and tank and gun rushed by Hitler to Tunisia that winter as well as the remnants of the Afrika Korps would be lost by the end of the spring.

The Fall of Mussolini

Henri Michel

In 1943 the Allies invaded Italy. French academician
Henri Michel, former president of the International Historical Committee for the Second World War, explains
why the landing in Sicily was so important to Allied efforts
and how the Italians and the Germans reacted. In Michel's
view, by this point everyone knew what a disaster the war
had been for Italy and for Italian Fascism. He writes that
although Adolf Hitler and Benito Mussolini still were
close personal friends, much friction and animosity existed between the Italians and the Germans. According to
Michel, the Italians wanted to get out of the war and, in
their view, the only way to accomplish this was to get rid
of Mussolini and break the alliance with Germany. Michel
recounts how Italian king Victor Emmanuel III collabo-
rated with disgruntled members of the Fascist Council to
bring down Mussolini and how, even though Mussolini's
fall was a great moral and political victory for the Allies,
armistice with the Allies led to increased discord in Italy.

In May 1943 in Washington, at the suggestion of the British
and in spite of American reluctance, the Allies decided to
follow up their success in Africa by putting Italy out of action. However, because of shortage of shipping and lack of
experience, in order also not to jeopardise the major landing
across the Channel, which still had priority, an operation of
minor importance was planned. . . .

The Sicilian Campaign

They therefore settled for a landing in Sicily. . . .
    Operation "Husky," the code name given to the landing

Excerpted from Henri Michel, *The Second World War*, translated by Douglas
Parmee. Copyright © 1968 Presses Universitaires de France, translation copyright
© 1975 André Deutsch.

in Sicily, needed very intricate gearing, for it involved the Army, Navy and Air force, and both British and American troops—the French did not take part. . . .

The landing took place during the night of July 9–10, 1943, and although it could not achieve any surprise effect, it was nevertheless virtually a complete success. . . . The only difficulties arose from "false beaches" which they had failed to detect or banks of pebbles not properly reconnoitred, on which some craft were smashed; some paratroopers were dropped too soon and fell into the sea.

But there was virtually no reaction from the enemy. And yet the Italians had ten divisions in Sicily; it is true that their strength had been reduced and that half of them . . . consisted of older men. . . .

In his usual presumptuous and boastful way, [Italian dictator Benito] Mussolini had declared that "no enemy will leave the island alive"; in actual fact the Italian troops had stampeded; only the Germans clung on to Etna long enough to enable their troops to be evacuated from the island, a move which for once Hitler himself had decided upon. . . .

On August 5 the British entered Catania; on the 16th the Americans entered Messina. Although they achieved their objective, their success was not complete because the Germans managed to bring back almost all their troops and equipment to the Italian mainland, that is to say 50,000 men and 10,000 vehicles; the 200,000 prisoners were Italians.

Being unable to prevent this evacuation was the only comparative failure of the Allies in this Sicilian campaign. . . .

In short, the Allied force proved irresistible only against the Italians; with the Germans it was a different matter. Hitler made no secret of his apprehensions to Mussolini. . . . It was absolutely necessary that Italy should hold on, he said, now that the Soviet offensive had been launched. The Duce [Mussolini] promised everything the Führer wished; but he was no longer in a position to prevent the collapse of Fascist Italy. And his days were numbered.

By July 1943 there was no longer any shadow of doubt that the war was a disaster for Italy. Not only had she not achieved any of the objectives for which she had entered it but she had lost her empire. . . .

From the economic point of view, industrial output had dropped by 35 per cent since 1939 and agricultural output by 20 per cent; imports had decreased. . . . The national debt had risen. . . . Thanks to strict control, prices had theoretically only doubled but a black market in every commodity was flourishing in all regions; and the population was suffering from a growing scarcity of foodstuffs. . . .

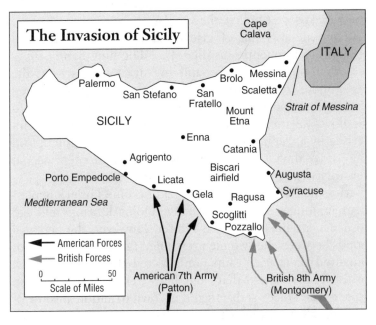

This disaster was shown in the Duce's physical condition. His stomach ulcer made him anxious and nervous and necessitated a debilitating diet and long periods of rest which were not really compatible with a position of absolute power. He had less will-power and even his reflexes seemed to have slowed down; his relatives were astonished to see a strange inertia, an almost complete apathy come over the old warrior; he seemed to be more and more indifferent, as if resigned to what was happening to him and to what lay in store for him. He retained the demagogue's confidence in words; he continued to believe that a speech was action; he took refuge in commonplaces and superficial judgments; he excused his failures by lashing out against the Italian people who had to be "driven into battle by kicks up the behind."

The régime which Mussolini had created had fallen into a similar decline. . . . Only the militia and some young Fascists still believed in the régime and its leader; the most intelligent officials turned from ironic criticism to scepticism and moral defection; they were wondering how to desert the sinking ship in time with their weapons and kit. "Fascism was dead long before 1943," wrote Guido Leto, the chief of the Fascist secret police, the OVRA.

Everyone was full of grievances against Germany and these were frequently justified. . . . The humiliating thing was that both in Greece and in Africa it was only the last-minute intervention of the Germans which had saved the Italian troops, and this the Italians found difficult to swallow. Relations between the two armies were characterised by a display of arrogance, brutality and contempt on the part of the German officers which the Italians' pride and sensitivity found impossible to tolerate. . . .

Mussolini chafed because he had become Hitler's henchman, no longer had any active say in joint decisions and had to dance attendance on the Führer. However, the personal bonds between the two men remained firm; disaster had not impaired their friendship nor affected their trust in each other. They realised that their fates were sealed. Hitler, in spite of the Duce's setbacks and his own irritation at some of Mussolini's decisions which had been particularly inappropriate, continued to admire his ally; he wrote to him that "by carrying on his heroic struggle he had become a symbol for the whole world." But their staffs were coming to hate each other more and more. . . .

How could Italy continue the fight? She was desperately short of resources. Mussolini had decided to raise a million men; national service was made compulsory for men between the ages of fourteen and seventy and for women between fourteen and sixty; but these measures were carried out rather unenthusiastically and they would have been effective only if the Italians had been willing to fight; but they were weary and becoming more and more indifferent to the

"Fascist war," from which they dissociated themselves. . . .

The only obvious solution was *sganciamento*, a breakaway from Germany. Could Mussolini persuade Hitler to agree to Italy's becoming nonbelligerent again? How would he even dare to ask him, when the war was *his* war and the alliance with Germany *his* alliance? To withdraw from the one or to break the other would be tantamount to a denial of himself. All that he could do was to try to persuade Hitler to put an end to the fighting in the USSR. . . .

Bringing Down Mussolini

It was up to the Italians and the Italians alone to find a solution to the two interrelated problems of the existence of Fascism and of Italy's participation in the war; and as a necessary prerequisite, Mussolini had to be ousted. . . .

Three groups were going to endeavour to bring down Mussolini. They made no attempt to co-ordinate their action; they each had only a few scraps of information about the plans and programme of the others; as a result, though the operation succeeded it was going to cause chaos all over Italy, split the country up between various authorities and lead to civil war.

The first and weakest group was the one formed by former politicians from pre-Fascist days. . . .

King Victor Emmanuel had the constitutional power to dismiss Mussolini—after all, the Duce was only the president of the Council summoned by him—and he was the titular commander of the armed forces which, if they followed him, would be capable of controlling any possible violent reaction by the last hard core of Fascists. But Victor Emmanuel had seriously compromised himself with the régime and he had never at any time protested against its excesses. . . .

[Another] group was formed by anxious Fascists who had been ousted. . . . These Fascists were, of course, relying on benefiting from the national union which would follow their leader's downfall; they would thus save their skins and perhaps their portfolios. . . .

Distinct plots were thus developing simultaneously, each only partly aware of the other; true, one alone was enough to bring down the Duce, who was both gullible and overcome by inertia. But what about afterwards? They had at one and the same time to avoid civil war, prevent or forestall the wrath of the Germans and win the confidence of the Allies. Was this not attempting the impossible? Hypocrisy and secrecy could not be the complete answer, even though Victor Emmanuel seemed to be establishing a kind of record for duplicity; on July 22, having already decided to have Mussolini arrested, he told him that he would be "the last person to desert him.". . .

Mussolini Falls from Power

At 5:15 P.M. on July 24 the members of the [Fascist] Grand Council met attired in Fascist ceremonial dress—the dress of the political movement whose demise they were plotting—black tunic, grey-green breeches and boots. Mussolini's statement was a long, rambling lukewarm speech in his defence; those present were struck and perhaps encouraged by the Duce's weariness, his ashen face and his obvious resignation. Mussolini's conclusion, however, was quite clear: the grave failures had been due to the fact that the Army had not always obeyed him.

[Council chairman Dino] Grandi replied with an indictment of the way in which the régime, which, he said, was completely out of touch with the country, was slowly collapsing and disintegrating. He held Mussolini responsible; he accused him of failing to give any real direction to his policy through having taken on too many minor tasks. He then read his motion, which suggested "a return to the Constitution" in order "to unite all Italians morally and materially in this hour of crisis for the nation's future," that is to say that the King should again take over actual command of the armed forces and "complete initiative in any decisions." Mussolini would devote himself solely to being leader of the Party; he would make it once again into a "block of granite" which would one day be able "to overcome their difficulties."

The régime's senior officials were therefore not bent on self-destruction; they were trying to extricate themselves from dire straits by changing their navigator. It was not for them but for the King to decide whether or not Mussolini continued to be Prime Minister; they probably reckoned that the King could not break completely with a régime to which he owed so much. Moreover, they all solemnly protested their friendship for the Duce whose burden they said they merely wished to lighten. Mussolini could have proposed an amendment to the motion and even refused to let it be put to the vote. He did no such thing; the result of the vote, which was taken verbally, was nineteen in favour and eight against with one abstention. Mussolini did not seem to have any illusions about its meaning. He stated: "You have plunged the régime into a state of crisis," and he refused the traditional "Salute to the Duce" when he closed the meeting after ten hours of dramatic discussion. . . .

Victor Emmanuel knew what had happened at the meeting of the Grand Council. . . . He knew that from now on Mussolini was alone, abandoned by everyone and weary of everything, and that he could now strike at him without risk. To make himself look taller, this dwarf of a man put on military uniform for the occasion. Mussolini trusted the King implicitly and came without any special protection; he had completely failed to grasp what was happening that day; he was not only paralysed but blind. The interview lasted twenty minutes. The King informed the Duce that he was dismissing him. . . . Then, under the pretext of ensuring his safety he had him arrested in the Quirinal gardens by a captain of the *carabinieri* [elite police regiment]; the Duce meekly got into the car which left the Quirinal by a back exit while his escort was waiting calmly at the main gate, convinced that the King had invited his Prime Minister to stay to dinner. For his "safety," Mussolini was to be imprisoned first in one of the Lipari Islands and then in a chalet in the Gran Sasso in the Apennines. . . .

Italy Surrenders

Mussolini's fall was a great moral and political victory for the Allies; it had considerable symbolic significance—had not the Duce, the founder of European Fascism, declared that the twentieth century would be Fascist? . . .

[Hitler] regarded the fate of his friend Mussolini as a personal insult. Without more ado the German troops replaced the Italians guarding the railways and bridges—a sign of how quickly they would intervene if the occasion arose; one Panzer division crossed the Brenner. Hitler had contemplated abandoning the south of Italy but the Allies' inactivity made him decide to hold on there. . . .

[Italian Prime Minister Pietro] Badoglio, however, had succeeded in gaining time. On August 5 secret negotiations with the Allies had begun in Sicily. On August 18 in Quebec, Churchill and Roosevelt had drawn up the Allies' policy and strategic plans with regard to the new Italian government; Eisenhower was to seize Corsica and Sardinia and secure air bases close to Rome and if possible beyond; but at the same time, paradoxically, units and boats were taken away from his command, the former for the great attack across the Channel and the latter for the Pacific. In these circumstances Eisenhower thought it impossible to achieve the objectives which he had been set.

On the diplomatic level, there was a difference of views between Americans and British. The Americans would have liked to leave Eisenhower a free hand to impose a military armistice on the Italians as he thought fit, in order to retain the possibility of securing their help and to ensure the most favourable conditions for landing on the peninsula. But the British, who agreed with the Soviets on this point, attached scarcely any importance to Italy's contribution to the Allied war effort; they wanted to inform Italy straightaway of the harsh punishment she deserved—the desire to secure control of the sea in the Mediterranean was not far from British minds.

They compromised. Eisenhower was to deliver a brief and strictly military text to the Italians. A second document consisting of forty-four articles and containing the political and economic terms would be communicated to the Italian negotiators in Malta on September 29; in the meantime the landing would have taken place and the Italians put to the test. . . .

The armistice was a *Diktat* [a harsh settlement imposed on the defeated nation] in which the Italians had no say and which was presented to them on August 31 in the form of an ultimatum; it was take it or leave it. . . .

On September 3 the armistice was signed in Cassibile; the terms remained secret; they would not be disclosed until the day of the [Allied] landing. The Italians thought they had several days in which to find their feet and make preparations; they hoped particularly to separate the Italian troops from the German troops who were around Rome and to take control of the airfields on which the expected Allied division would be dropped. . . . During the night the landing took place [on September 8], but a long way from Rome, south of Naples, in Salerno.

It was obvious that the Allies had merely wished to avoid being fired on by the Italians, but they were in for a nasty shock, for they found the Germans forewarned and firmly ensconced. . . . On September 16 SS commando went to free Mussolini in the Gran Sasso: the *carabinieri* who were guarding the Duce let the planes land and the SS advance towards them without firing a shot. With German support Mussolini was to try to reunite the last followers of Fascism on the side of the Germans in a movement which he called "Fascist, Republican and Revolutionary." Italy was going to be ravaged by civil war. . . .

Almost everywhere the Italian troops, demoralised and abandoned, allowed themselves to be disarmed and captured; in Toulon several thousand soldiers were made prisoner by a handful of German sailors. But on the Greek island of Cephalonia, the Italian units, when consulted by their leader, General Gandin, decided to break with the Axis; fighting broke out between the former allies, with the Germans gaining the advantage after seven days. . . . All the Italian officers . . . were massacred after they had surrendered; nearly 3,000 soldiers were packed on to pontoons in an area that was mined and died in the resulting explosions. . . .

Italy was too heavily committed in Hitler's war to withdraw from it without loss. For her, the armistice brought anything but peace; for eighteen months, throughout its length and breadth, the peninsula was to be the theatre of desperate fighting between the Allies and the Germans, but also between the Italians.

War in the Pacific: Why Japan Lost

Martin Caidin

For almost two of the four years the United States and Japan fought one another, the Japanese made major inroads in the Pacific. In 1943, however, the balance shifted. According to celebrated author Martin Caidin, in spite of their many military successes, the Japanese were doomed to defeat from their 1941 attack on Pearl Harbor. Caidin maintains that Japan did not win the war for a number of reasons. The Japanese, he writes, lacked the scientific know-how and resources to keep up with the United States and, with the exception of the Zero fighter plane, could not produce even comparable weapons and war matériel. He contends also that, in addition to misunderstanding and underestimating the United States, Japanese strategists and technicians had an unrealistic and outdated view of war and their role in it. The principal reason for defeat, Caidin reasons, was the Japanese failure to understand the meaning of total war.

On the first day of World War II, the United States lost two thirds of its aircraft in the Pacific theater. The Japanese onslaught against Pearl Harbor effectively eliminated Hawaii as a source of immediate reinforcements for the Philippines. And on those beleaguered islands, enemy attacks rapidly whittled down our remaining air strength until it could no more than annoy a victory-flushed foe.

Japan controlled as much of the vast China mainland as she desired at the time. She captured Guam and Wake. She dispossessed us in the Netherlands East Indies. Singapore fell in

Excerpted from Masatake Okumiya and Jiro Horikoshi, with Martin Caidin, *Zero!* Copyright © 1956 Martin Caidin.

humiliating defeat, and brilliantly executed Japanese tactics almost entirely eliminated the British as combatants. Within a few months fearful anxiety gripped Australia; its cities were brought under air attack. Japanese planes swarmed almost uncontested against northern New Guinea, New Ireland, the Admiralties, New Britain, and the Solomons. Enemy occupation of Kavieng, Rabaul, and Bougainville not only threatened the precarious supply lines from the United States, but became potential springboards for the invasion of Australia itself.

From Victory to Defeat

No one can deny that during those long and dreary months after Pearl Harbor the Japanese humiliated us in the Pacific. We were astonished—fatally so—at the unexpected quality of Japanese equipment. Because we committed the unforgivable error of underestimating a potential enemy, our antiquated planes fell like flies before Japan's agile Zero fighter.

At no time during these dark months were we able to more than momentarily check the Japanese sweep. The bright sparks of the defenders' heroism in a sea of defeat were not enough. There could be no doubt that the Japanese had effected a brilliant coup as they opened the war.

It is astonishing to realize, then, that even during this course of events Japan failed to enjoy a real opportunity for ultimate victory. Despite their military successes, within one year of the opening day of war the Japanese no longer held the offensive. The overwhelming numerical superiority which they enjoyed, largely by destruction of our own forces with relative impunity, began to disappear. By the spring of 1943 the balance clearly had shifted. Not only were we regaining the advantage of quantity; we also enjoyed a qualitative superiority in weapons. The Japanese were on the defensive.

The majority of the Japanese military hierarchy could not agree to this concept. They viewed the setbacks in the Pacific as no more than temporary losses. They basked in their successes of the first six months and reveled in a spirit of invincibility. Enhanced by centuries of victorious tradition, cultured by myths and fairy tales, and bolstered by years of one-track education, Japanese confidence of victory was even greater than our own.

The Zero Was Not Enough

There are many reasons why the Japanese failed in their bid to dominate half the world. One reason, it has been said, is that while Japan fought for economic gain, we fought a strategic war of vengeance, a war which promised a terrifying vendetta for the people of Japan.

We can be much more specific than this. The Japanese failed, primarily, because they never understood the meaning of total war. Modern war is the greatest co-operative effort known to man; the Japanese never were able to fuse even their limited resources into this effort. They limped along with a mere fraction of our engineering skill. Throughout the war they were constantly astonished at the feats of our construction crews which hacked airfields out of solid coral and seemingly impenetrable jungle, at the rapidity with which we hurled vast quantities of supplies ashore at invasion beachheads. Air logistics in the form of a continued flow of airborne supplies was unknown to them.

The Japanese lacked the scientific "know how" necessary to meet us on qualitative terms. This was by no means the case early in the war when the Zero fighter airplane effectively swept aside all opposition. In the Zero the Japanese enjoyed the ideal advantage of both qualitative and quantitative superiority. The Japanese fighter was faster than any opposing plane. It outmaneuvered anything in the air. It outclimbed and could fight at greater heights than any plane in all Asia and the Pacific. It had twice the combat range of our standard fighter, the P-40, and it featured the heavy punch of cannon. Zero pilots had cut their combat teeth in China and so enjoyed a great advantage over our own men. Many of the Allied pilots who contested in their own inferior planes the nimble product of Jiro Horikoshi literally flew suicide missions.

This superiority, however, vanished quickly with our introduction of new fighter planes in combat. As the Zeros fell in flames, Japan's skilled pilots went with them. Japan failed to provide her air forces with replacements sufficiently trained in air tactics to meet successfully our now-veteran airmen who made the most of the high performance of their new Lightnings, Corsairs, and Hellcats.

At war's end half of all the Japanese fighter planes were essentially the same Zero with which the Japanese fought in China five years before.

An Outdated Conception of War

In the critical field involving the development of new weapons Japan was practically at a standstill while we were racing ahead. Her few guided missiles were never used in combat. She had in preparation *one* jet airplane, and that flew but once. Japanese radar was crude. They had nothing which even approximated a B-17 or a B-24—let alone a B-29. And Japan constantly was perplexed and bewildered by a profusion of Allied weapons—air-to-ground rockets, napalm, computing sights, radar-directed guns, proximity fuses, guided missiles, aerial mines, bazookas, flame throwers, and brilliantly executed mass bombing. It was the Japanese inability to counter these weapons, let alone produce them, which had them on the ropes during the last two years of war.

The Japanese failed because their high command made the mistake of believing its own propaganda, to the effect that there was internal dissension in the United States, that we were decadent, that it would require years for us to swing from luxury production to a great war industrial effort. This in itself was a fatal error for, despite the drain of the fight against Germany, even by sheer weight of arms alone we eventually would have overwhelmed an enemy whose production was never ten per cent of our own at its peak.

Japanese strategists and tacticians fought their war entirely out of the rule books. These were never revised until ugly experience taught the Japanese that the books were obsolete, that we were fighting a war all our own—on *our* terms. The enemy became dumbfounded; they were incapable of effective countermeasures.

The Japanese high command was inordinately fond of the

words "impregnable, unsinkable, and invulnerable." That such conditions are myths was unknown to them.

Their conception of war was built around the word *attack*. They could not foresee a situation in which they did not have the advantage. Once on the defensive, they threw away their strength in heroic *banzai* charges where massed firepower slaughtered their ranks. Sometimes when the trend was against them they lost their capacity for straight thinking and blundered, often, with disastrous results.

Japanese Vulnerability

The Japanese failed because their men and officers were inferior, not in courage, *but in the intelligent use of courage.* Japanese education, Japanese ancestor worship, and the Japanese caste system were reflected time after time in uninspired leadership and transfixed initiative. In a predicted situation which could be handled in an orthodox manner, the Japanese were always competent and often resourceful. Under the shadow of frustration, however, the obsession of personal honor extinguished ingenuity.

The execution of Japanese plans was totally unequal to the grandiose demands of their strategy. Never was this so true as in the Japanese failure to understand the true meaning of air power. Because they themselves lacked a formula for strategic air power, they overlooked the possibility that it would be used against them and so were unprepared to counter it. Japanese bombers never were capable of sustaining a heavy offensive. To the Japanese, the B-17s and B-24s were formidable opponents; the B-29 was a threat beyond their capacity to counter.

The collapse of Japan brilliantly vindicated the whole strategic concept of the offensive phase of the Pacific War. While ground and sea forces played an indispensable role which can in no sense be underestimated, that strategy, in its broadest terms, was to advance air power to the point where the full fury of crushing air attack could be loosed on Japan itself, with the possibility that such attack would bring about the defeat of Japan without invasion.

There was no invasion.

Japan was vulnerable. Her far-flung supply lines were comparable to delicate arteries nurtured by a bad heart. The value of her captured land masses and the armed forces which defended them was in direct proportion to the ability of her shipping to keep them supplied, to keep the forces mobile, and to bring back to Japan the materials to keep her factories running. Destroy the shipping, and Japan for all practical purposes would be four islands without an empire . . . four islands on which were cities made-to-order for destruction by fire.

Destroy the shipping and burn the cities. We did.

Doomed to Defeat

To the submarines goes the chief credit for reducing the Japanese merchant fleet to a point where it was destroyed or useless. Air power also played a great part in this role by sinking ships at sea (the A.A.F. destroyed more than one million tons in 1944) and sealing off Japanese ports with aerial mines.

We burned the cities. The B-29s reaped an incredible harvest of destruction in Japan. Her ability to continue the war collapsed amid the ashes of her scarred and fire-trampled urban centers. The two atomic bombs contributed less than three per cent of the destruction visited upon the industrial centers of Japan. But they gave the Japanese, so preoccupied with saving face, an excuse and a means of ending a futile war with honor intact.

The full story of the vast Pacific War, however, never has been told. It is one thing to study that war from your own viewpoint, but quite another to examine it from that of the enemy.

Chapter 4

The Fall of the Axis

Turning | Points
IN WORLD HISTORY

D-Day from a German Perspective

Hans Speidel

On June 6, 1944—D-Day—the Allies landed on the beaches of Normandy, France, a major step in the invasion of Europe and the greatest amphibious operation ever staged. Hans Speidel, a lieutenant general in the German army and Field Marshal Erwin Rommel's chief of staff, was in command of the army when the Allies invaded. In this selection, he explains why the Allied invasion was so successful. According to Speidel, prior to and during the invasion the Allies had advantages the Germans did not, including effective sources of information and superiority on land, at sea, and in the air. At the same time, Speidel argues, much of the blame for the German defeat at Normandy belongs not to the Allies or to the German soldiers but to the German supreme command's "amateurishness" and Adolf Hitler's indecision, mistakes, and refusal to face facts.

The Western Allies regarded the invasion of Normandy as an operation that would decide the whole war. Their preparations for it went back as far as mid-1942. The technical preparations were extraordinary both with respect to inventiveness and execution. The Allies actually worked out with mathematical exactitude how much could be left to chance. The inventors and engineers of two hemispheres succeeded in accomplishing feats that had previously been thought impossible. Artificial harbors made landing operations and supply independent of the capture of French ports. Nothing more advantageous than the pipeline "Pluto," which carried fuel under the Channel waters, could have been thought of. The expendable wealth of the outside world could be utilized for these achievements. Artificial landing strips on improvised airfields in the bridgeheads made possible the closest co-operation between the air forces and the army and naval units.

Allies Hold the Advantage

The Allies had all the advantages in close- and long-range reconnaissance during the years of preparation for the invasion. For the Germans the wireless services were almost the only effective source of information, whereas the Allies used their air supremacy to good advantage. They combined bombing behind the German front with their reconnaissance missions, both of which they thought essential for the success of the invasion.

The British and Americans had at their disposal an established and well-trained world-wide intelligence service. In the invasion areas they also used the forces of the resistance in the occupied countries, which supplied them with the necessary details about German fighting strength and kept them constantly up to date.

Before the war Hitler had forbidden any preparations for building up an intelligence service in Great Britain. When, at the last moment, it was attempted to establish such a system, it was too late.

The Americans and British had an overwhelming superiority on land and sea and in the air. Their air forces were technically highly developed and well trained and commanded; these air forces were the decisive factor for the Allied victories in the invasion and subsequent operations. The air-ground co-operation was rehearsed to the last detail, and it must be acknowledged that it stood every test in practice. To this it must be added that the Allied ground forces were equipped with excellent weapons, were exceptionally well supplied, and were highly mobile. The British and American divisions started the invasion with their strength undiminished by warfare, and were carefully trained on the basis of the lessons learned during five years of war. The German Army, in contrast, had behind it the campaigns in Poland, Norway, France, Africa, Italy, the Balkans, and Russia; it had

The Invasion of Normandy

bled itself white and was exhausted. It was undernourished; its supplies were inadequate. The winter of Stalingrad had inflicted some half a million irreplaceable casualties and had broken the back of the German Army.

The power of the Luftwaffe had been consumed by the Battle of Britain, and its subsequent development did not keep step with modern requirements.

Three Forces, One Strategic Goal

The words of [Prussian army officer Carl von] Clausewitz on the moral greatness of a cause in war can be applied to the Allies. "The material forces seem only to be the wooden scabbard," he wrote; "the moral forces are the noble metal, the sharp and gleaming sword." The moral strength of the Allied cause was greater than that of the German. The transgressions of Hitler had created a moral vacuum. The purely military leadership of the Allies lagged behind their amazing technical preparations and achievements. They succeeded best in matters of organization and leadership, particularly in the co-ordination and command of the three services. There is hardly a case in history that shows less of the inevitable friction and tension between allies in a coalition than appeared in the military leadership in the invasion of Normandy.

The Allied leadership on the continent was tactically and strategically methodical. It complied with [French] Marshal [Ferdinand] Foch's insistence upon *"sûreté de la manoeuvre,"* and it sought to eliminate every risk, keep casualties down to a minimum, and put into practice the attack *à coup sûr* [with sure stroke].

The Allied armies therefore resembled a rigid line that pushed their enemy backward, like a steamroller that was slowly but surely to crush him.

The Allied command repeated its mistakes of the North African landings of 1942 in failing to exploit fully its great strategic opportunities; otherwise the war would have ended in 1944. As examples of missed opportunities one might mention the failure to roll back the Seine front after the battle of the Falaise pocket, and the failure to break through the Westwall and strike across the Rhine into the interior of Germany in September 1944. [American] General [George] Patton, under General [Omar] Bradley's command, was the only Allied general who dared exceed the limits of safety with his army in the endeavor to carry out large-scale operations; but he could not impart his impetus to the over-all Allied command, and he earned little thanks for his generalship.

These observations do not alter the importance of the invasion to the slightest degree; it broke up the German front in the west and rolled it back. It took so much pressure off the Soviet Union that it made possible the successes of the Red Army in 1944 and 1945. The technical support of the United States played a part in those victories too—the Russian heavy T-34 tank was powered by American engines. The United States was producing two thousand tanks per month merely for her own use even before the invasion began.

The invasion of Normandy will forever remain an event

of the first order in the history of war. It was the first big operation to succeed fully in bringing together and leading the forces of all three services to attain one strategic goal.

Overtaxed Resources

The German High Command did not take the necessary steps to adapt its structure to the need for combined operations on land and sea and in the air.

The "war lord" Adolf Hitler thought in terms of the Continent and was enmeshed in memories of the static fronts of the first World War. A war of all three services against the whole world, with the heavy demands for equipment for land and air warfare, simply overtaxed the industrial and technical resources of Germany. This Hitler did not want to admit. Divisions dependent on horses for transport, of the type used in the first World War, had to fight a mechanized enemy; sixty out-of-date divisions were not enough to "defend" the entire length of 2,500 miles of foreign coasts and frontiers. An "air force" consisting, at the beginning of the invasion, of ninety fighters and seventy bombers was supposed to maintain supremacy of the air, to reconnoiter, and to afford close support for the ground forces. The High Command was forced to issue an order early in 1944 that "every airplane in the sky is to be considered hostile."

Unscrupulousness was balanced by amateurishness in the German Supreme Command.

The Führer and the High Command of the Armed Forces directed operations from Berchtesgaden in the first weeks of the invasion, and then from East Prussia. There were grave disadvantages in these distances, particularly as air communication was impossible. . . . No German leader came to the Normandy front; on the Allied side, [British premier] Winston Churchill was among the first to visit the Continent after the invasion. The chaos in the chain of command, resulting from the struggle between Army and Party leaders—sharply contrasting with the "leadership principle"—hampered any attempt to give clear-cut orders and led to divided authority. It was the soldier at the front who paid the price.

Instead of confidence between officers and men, there was

compulsion, falsehood, political trials, and courts-martial. There was no more of that eagerness among junior officers to accept responsibility and take the initiative that was once the trademark of the German soldier. As things stood, and taking into consideration the comparative strength of the opponents—quite apart from political solutions—only large-scale strategy could have offered hope of salvation. Instead, fighting went on simultaneously in all theaters of war. Strategic decisions made at the proper time would have averted the most annihilating blows of the enemy: in the east, the front should have been drastically shortened and strengthened, and a strong reserve built up; in the south, there should have been withdrawal to the Pisa-Florence-Adria line and then to the line of the Alps; in the west, first of all, France south of the Seine should have been abandoned, a striking force formed on the eastern flank, and forethought given to rearward lines which could receive the retreating troops and could then be defended.

Hitler's Failures and Fantasies

But Hitler, unable to compromise politically or in his propaganda, devoid of any sober clarity of thought, ordered the troops to hold their ground at any cost and abandoned 200,000 men in his "fortresses." The fighting man was thus physically, spiritually, and morally overburdened. There began a bleeding of the German Army similar to that which took place in the Russian winter of 1942–43. The defensive war had to be fought without adequate firepower and without the support of the other two services—it was a beggars' war.

As for the technical conduct of operations, Hitler was not accustomed to giving long-range orders. He issued piecemeal tactical orders and often interfered on even the lowest levels of command. Usually his orders were not applicable to the situation by the time they were received. There could never be that degree of confidence in him that the strain of battle demanded; his methods ignored the dignity of the soldier and of the human being.

The war on the western front in the summer of 1944 must have cost Germany half a million casualties, including those trapped in the fortress areas. The losses of matériel cannot be estimated. There were only 40,000 dead in the west in the campaign of 1940.

In the western campaign Hitler was unable to perceive the moment of climax. He deceived others, but he deceived himself most terribly of all, when he tried to veil the inescapable facts and raise false hopes in his "miracle weapons," instead of recognizing Germany's actual position and drawing the necessary political consequences therefrom.

Even as late as 1944, Hitler completely underestimated his enemies in the west. . . . Hitler lived in a world of fantasy without any sense of proportion, exaggerating his own will power and possessed by delusions of grandeur. He spilled the life blood of the nation both by his authoritarian methods of defense and by such offensive operations on the Normandy front as the Avranches counterattack.

The Tragedy of the German Soldier

An army ceases to be an army when it is incapable of fighting. Whenever this occurred in past wars, responsible military and political leaders drew the appropriate conclusions. . . .

This weighty decision was again necessary in the summer of 1944. Soldiers conscious of their responsibilities . . . tried to remove Hitler and bring the war to an end. Thus the revolt of July 20 was attempted, but it failed. There were no direct effects upon the front. The facts did not become known until much later; the motives, scope, and results of the revolt remained hidden from the ordinary fighting man.

Adolf Hitler consciously gave way to illusions by refusing to recognize that the war was lost. He put his hopes in the V-I, in U-boat warfare, in the collapse of the coalition between Russia and the United States. He did not, and did not wish to, draw the right conclusions.

Fateful tragedy overtook the German army. In performance and behavior the German divisions met [former German general Hans von] Seeckt's requirement "to possess icy courage and so withstand misfortune."

It is the tragedy of every German soldier and of German history that such courage was misused and sacrificed for a phantom.

A Humiliating End to an Era

Kenneth S. Davis

During World War II acclaimed biographer and author Kenneth S. Davis was a special correspondent covering General Dwight D. Eisenhower's campaign in France. In this selection, Davis explains that by the spring of 1945 the end was very near for Italian Fascist leader Benito Mussolini, Germany, and the Nazis. Davis chronicles the successful advances of the Allies into German and Italian territory and describes the flight of Mussolini and his mistress and their subsequent bloody executions by Italian partisans. Asserting that Adolf Hitler's end was "equally sordid," "nastier," and "more obscene" than that of Mussolini, Davis describes the irrational actions and fits of rage that preceded Hitler's suicide. Given the viciousness and quantity of Nazi-perpetrated horrors during the war, contends Davis, the postwar Nuremberg trial for war crimes had to take place not just to avenge the victims but also to exorcise the demons associated with the war.

The ruin at the heart of Berlin [April 13, 1945] is compounded by another RAF [British Royal Air Force] bombing raid. At midnight, fire rages through the smashed Chancellery while the incredible monster who has loosed upon the world the greatest horrors of all history huddles in his deep bunker beneath the Wilhelmplatz, a rat in a hole. Adolf Hitler, though not yet fifty-six years old (he will be next week, on April 20), has now the appearance and many of the traits of a senile man. His face is gray and slack, his eyes dull, save when insane rage (and insane rage is frequent) distorts his features and transforms his gaze into a baleful glare. Sometimes his head wobbles uncontrollably, often his hands

Excerpted from Kenneth S. Davis, *Experience of War: The United States in World War II.* Copyright © 1965 Kenneth S. Davis. Reprinted with permission from Doubleday, a division of Random House, Inc.

tremble, and his left arm . . . hangs looses and apparently useless. He has lost all contact with reality. He continuously issues orders that cannot possibly be obeyed and raves about "treason" and "betrayal" when they are not obeyed. He turns for slender comfort to astrology, striving desperately to believe that a "miracle" is forecast by the stars to occur in the latter half of April—a supernatural intervention that will save him and his Germany. Meanwhile he does his best to make sure that all Germany will go down with him into the final darkness, for he can no longer really hope. Certainly he can see no basis for hope in the news that has come to him all day from the battlefields. . . . Both to the east and to the west the enemy stands in overwhelming strength just thirty miles or so from Berlin. Soon, inevitably, the capital will be in enemy hands.

And yet, will it?

Sometime after midnight comes a ring on Hitler's private phone and he picks up the receiver to hear [propaganda minister Joseph] Goebbels' excited, exultant voice saying: "My Fuehrer, I congratulate you! Roosevelt is dead! It is written in the stars that the second half of April will be the turning point for us. This is Friday, April the thirteenth. It is the turning point!" Goebbels toasts this death in the best champagne, and others are similarly overjoyed—the Minister of Finance in Berlin, for instance, who feels "wings flutter through the room" when he hears the news, the wings of the "Angel of History" marking the "turn of fortune" for Germany. And Hitler's own crushed spirits are briefly raised.

But only briefly . . .

The End of Mussolini and Hitler

For there now fell upon the writhing, bleeding body of Nazi Germany the final flesh-shredding lashes of the war. In the north, the British struck through Bremen and on across the Elbe to Hamburg and Lübeck. The Americans, having reached the Elbe, struck southeastward into Czechoslovakia and Austria and to the German border of Switzerland. In Italy, the Anglo-American armies and the Poles struck northward into the Po Valley. . . . Simultaneously, the Russians opened their attack across the Oder and drove again westward on a front of more than two hundred miles, scoring great successes everywhere against the hardest resistance the Germans could still make. . . .

Italian Partisans in northern Italy . . . seized control of Milan, Venice, and many other cities. Mussolini, now a haggard old man, fled northward with a German convoy, ac-

"So Long, Sir"

On April 12, 1945, with America still at war, U.S. president Franklin Delano Roosevelt died unexpectedly in Warm Springs, Georgia, of a cerebral hemorrhage. This tribute to Roosevelt appeared less than a month later in the U.S. Army's weekly magazine, Yank.

Most of us in the Army have a hard time remembering any president other than Franklin D. Roosevelt. We never saw the inside of a speakeasy, because he had prohibition repealed before we were old enough to drink. When we were kids during the Depression, and the factories and stores were not taking anybody, plenty of us joined his CCCs [Civilian Conservation Corps], and the hard work in the woods felt good after those months of sleeping late and hanging around the house and the corner drugstore, too broke to go anywhere and do anything. Or we got our first jobs in his ERA [Economic Recovery Act] or WPA [Works Progress Administration] projects. That seems like a long time ago.

And since then, under President Roosevelt's leadership, we have struggled through 12 years of troubled peace and war, 12 of the toughest and most important years in our country's history. It got so that all over the world, his name meant everything that America stood for. It meant hope in London and Moscow and in occupied Paris and Athens. It was sneered at in Berlin and Tokyo. To us, wherever we were, in the combat zones or in forgotten supply and guard posts, it meant the whole works—our kind of life and freedom and the necessity for protecting it. We made cracks about it and told Roosevelt

companied by his young mistress, Clara Petacci. Though he wore a German helmet and greatcoat he was recognized and, on April 28, while ensconced in a farmhouse on Lake Como, was seized by a Partisan band. He and his mistress were stood against a wall and shot. Their bodies were then taken to the Piazza Loretto in Milan and dumped there with the bodies of a dozen other Fascists at or near the spot where fif-

---

jokes and sometimes we bitterly criticized his way of doing things. But he was still Roosevelt, the man we had grown up under and the man whom we had entrusted with the staggering responsibility of running our war. He was the commander in chief, not only of the armed forces but of our generation.

That is why it is hard to realize he is dead, even in these days, when death is a common and expected thing. We had grown accustomed to his leadership and we leaned on it heavily, as we would lean on the leadership of a good company commander who had taken us safely through several battles, getting us where we were supposed to go without doing anything foolish or cowardly. And the loss of Roosevelt hit us the same way as the loss of a good company commander. It left us a little panic-stricken, a little afraid of the future.

But the panic and fear didn't last long. We soon found out that the safety of our democracy, like the safety of a rifle company, doesn't depend on the life of any one man. A platoon leader with the same training and the same sense of timing and responsibility takes over, and the men find themselves and the company as a whole operating with the same confidence and efficiency. That's the way it will be with our government. The new president has pledged himself to carry out its plans for the successful ending of the war and the building of the peace. The program for security and peace will continue.

Franklin D. Roosevelt's death brings grief but should not bring despair. He leaves us great hope.

"So Long, Sir," in *Yank: World War II from the Guys Who Brought You Victory*, by Steven Kluger. New York: St. Martin's, 1991.

teen Partisans had been executed by the Nazi-Fascists months before. In the last view the world was to have of him he was hanging by his heels from a meat hook, his mistress beside him, being kicked and stoned and reviled by a huge crowd of the people (very different in temperament and outlook from the Germans) whom he had tricked and cajoled into disaster. Much photographed, thoroughly described in print by eye-witnesses, the scene was gruesome and shocking . . . but perhaps beneficent in its long-term impress upon the popular mind, and upon history. For in the future, whenever power-lustful young egoists animated by childish dreams of "glory" saw pictures of the great Mussolini on his balcony—strutting, arrogant, contemptuously looking down upon a sea of upturned faces—they could not but see also in their minds eye this final picture of a gaunt old man, his jaw smashed by an angry boot, hung up like butcher's meat before a huge mob that cursed and spat upon him.

Equally sordid—indeed, nastier somehow, and more obscene—was the end of the Nazi Fuehrer.

On April 28, Adolf Hitler learned via a BBC broadcast that Heinrich Himmler, whom he had always deemed the most loyal of his subordinates, had been engaged in secret negotiations with Count Bernadotte, head of the Swedish Red Cross, aimed toward a surrender of all German forces in the West to [American general Dwight D.] Eisenhower. (Even in this final hour, Himmler hoped to arrange a peace in the West which would enable German armies to concentrate against the Russians, perhaps with active Anglo-American support.) He raved, frothed at the mouth, turned purple with congested blood, then collapsed into a stupor. After that he was drained, it seemed, of all emotion save a dull, embittered despair. He began to make preparations for suicide and the destruction of his body. Very early in the morning of April 29 he went through the formality of marriage with his mistress of many years, a vapid, bovine young woman named Eva Braun who was determined to die at his side. He then dictated his last will and "Political Testament," repeating in the latter the ugly falsehoods by which he had lived. That afternoon, as the Russians, who had broken into the city on April 23, fought only a block away from the shattered Chancellery, news came to him of Mussolini's death. Everything was finished. . . .

Next day, Monday, April 30, shortly before 3:30 in the afternoon, Adolf Hitler killed himself with a pistol shot through the roof of his mouth, his bride dying beside him of self-administered poison. Their bodies, carried up into the Chancellery garden during a brief lull in the Russian shelling, were soaked with gasoline and burned.

Nazi Germany Surrenders

His "Thousand-Year" Reich died with him. All German and Italian Fascist troops in northern Italy and western Austria were surrendered unconditionally to the Allies on May 2, the instrument of surrender being signed in the palace of the Bourbon kings at Caserta, twenty miles from Naples. Next day British forces took Hamburg and on the day after that arrangements between [British commander Sir Bernard Law] Montgomery and German Admiral [Karl] Doenitz (whom Hitler had named as his successor) were concluded for the unconditional surrender of all German forces in Holland, northwest Germany, and Denmark. The terms were signed on May 5. On the same morning, the First and Nineteenth German armies surrendered to the Allied 6th Army Group in the south. Only shattered remnants of the German Seventh Army now remained in opposition to Eisenhower's forces.

On the afternoon of the following day, a German delegation arrived at Eisenhower's headquarters to arrange the unconditional surrender of *all* German forces, those on the Eastern as well as Western Fronts insofar as the two yet remained separate. The headquarters was in a trade school building in Rheims, France—a dreary, red-brick structure. . . . Hours were required to arrange the technical details of surrender but finally, at 2:25 in the morning of May 7, the discussions were completed. Correspondents were assembled in the map-walled war room and here, without ceremony . . . the Instrument of Unconditional Surrender [was signed]. It was 2:41 when the last signature was completed.

Nearly two days later, or at half an hour before midnight

of Tuesday, May 8, 1945, this Instrument of Unconditional Surrender was ratified in Berlin in a ceremony designed to express and stress the unity of the Western Allies with the Soviet Union. . . .

After five years, eight months, and seven days of war, a ruined Europe entered upon an uneasy and dubious peace. . . .

Germany lying prostrate in the dust that summer, naked and bleeding from such a scourging of war as no other major power had received since ancient Carthage, presented a spectacle that appalled mankind. Pity was evoked by it in humane breasts. How could it fail to be by the sight of women and children and old men scrabbling for food in garbage heaps among the ruins of scores of towns, dozens of once-great cities? By the sight of child prostitutes soliciting with words obscene and gestures obscene along rubble-heaped streets of night? By the sight of people without arms, without legs, without eyes, their bodies twisted and their faces scarred by explosive fire and steel? By the evidences everywhere abundant, everywhere reflected in grief-darkened eyes and terror-frozen faces, of what had been suffered by all these people, the physically uninjured along with the wounded, during the long fury that had crushed their nation? Pity was overtly asked for. [Chief of staff of the German army, Colonel General Alfred] Jodl had asked for it at the surrender table in Rheims. Granted permission to speak, after having signed the instrument of surrender, he had stood up very stiff and straight and, staring straight ahead, had said in a voice hoarse with emotion: "With this signature the German people and the German forces are, for better or worse, delivered into the victors' hands. In this war, which has lasted more than five years, both have achieved and suffered more than perhaps any other people in the world. I can only express the hope that the victors will treat them with generosity."

The Horrors of War Are Revealed

But pity was not the only emotion evoked. There was horror and disgust also as, days passing into weeks, more and more was revealed of what these poor suffering Germans had actually "achieved" during the last five and a half years.

Many square miles of countryside had been drenched with the stink of death day after day as crematorium chimneys poured forth white acrid smoke from the burning bodies of human beings killed, not one by one (that might have given their deaths some individual dignity), but in batches of a dozen to two hundred at a time. Doctors of medicine by the score had performed horrible "medical experiments" on living men and women and children and had made reports of them to meetings of medical societies, reports of no scientific value whatever that were nevertheless seriously discussed by the most eminent of the nation's medical practitioners, and with no evidence of personal revulsion. Farmers and industrialists had worked thousands of slave laborers literally to death in mines and fields and factories; bankers had stuffed their vaults with dental gold extracted from the teeth of murdered Jews. Hundreds of bleached human skulls, and of handbags and gloves and lampshades made of the skin of concentration camp victims, were displayed as souvenirs in Nazi German homes. And all these horrors, actively perpetrated by thousands and thousands of these poor suffering Germans, had been passively permitted—without protest, often with approval—by millions upon millions of others.

Such knowledge, falling heavily down upon the Western mind, plunging deep into the individual self, was like a sharp-edged stone dropped into a still pool. Ripples spread out from it in wider and ever-wider circles. "This is what *Nazis* are capable of!" one began by saying, with loathing and with scorn. Later one said, with equal loathing but less certain scorn: "This is what *Germans* are capable of!" One said at last, with loathing still but with a drastic reduction in scorn, since there was now drastically reduced that sense of otherness on which scorn depends: "This is what *men* are capable of!" And as these ripples spread horizontally the stone itself sank down and down until it struck against the very bottom of the soul, its sharp edge cutting deep, and forced upward a cry of anguish that was also a question filled with terror: "This is what *I* am capable of?"

Thus there was an inner as well as an outer necessity, a psychological as well as an objectively historical need, to round up Nazi war criminals following the unconditional surrender of Germany and to arrange for their public trial and stern punishment.

Fat Hermann Goering, long the Number Two Nazi, originator of the concentration camp and commander of the Luftwaffe, surrendered to American troops in Austria a few hours after the Berlin ratification of the instrument of Germany's surrender. By then or shortly thereafter the Allies held captive, among others, Rudolf Hess, the Number Three Nazi, long Hitler's deputy; Alfred Rosenberg, the "philosopher" of the Nazi Party; Joachim von Ribbentrop, the ruthless, overbearing Nazi Foreign Minister; Julius Streicher, notorious sadist and pornographer, editor of *Der Stürmer*; Ernst Kaltenbrunner, one of those with the highest responsibility for the mass extermination of Jews; and Robert Ley, leader of the German Labor Front, under whose administration slave laborers had suffered and died by the thousand. Heinrich Himmler, chief of the Gestapo, the greatest (under Hitler) mass murderer of all time, was captured by British troops near Hamburg on May 20 but promptly committed suicide by biting into a vial of poison concealed in his mouth. . . .

Judgment at Nuremberg

The others would be among those who sat in the prisoners' dock at Nuremberg with the camera eyes of the world focused on while their enormous crimes were spread upon the public record in frequently nauseating detail. Sitting there day after day, week after week, month after month (the trial would run from November 20, 1945, to October 1, 1946), they would be denied the possibility of future investment with such glamor of wickedness as invests, say, the mythical Mephistopheles or the historic Borgias. They would become, after a while, boring in a peculiarly horrible way, being so monotonously vicious, so gross and repetitious and unimaginative in their murderous cruelties. They would shrink then in the eyes of the world to their true dimensions as banal, shabby, nasty, craven creatures whose proper fate was to be hustled out of life as quickly as possible and shoveled into holes, like so much stinking garbage.

Nor was all this mere vengefulness: it was also exorcism. There was in it, certainly, the spirit of the Old Testament, a sense of justice as punishment and retribution, but at the same time there was not wholly absent from it the spirit of the New. For in a deep psychological sense, and in a way that might be deemed a bridge between Old and New, the Golden Rule applied insofar as those who sat in judgment did indeed do unto others as they would have others do unto them should they ever be guilty of the least of such crimes as these. The Judgment at Nuremberg, in other words—the condemnation of these sordid creatures of hate—was in part a protection of self from self on the part of those who judged. It raised another wall against the possibility that a similar evil might break out of the inner recesses of their own beings into the light and air of the actual world. . . .

The same motive was operative at the San Francisco Conference of the United Nations between April 25 and June 25, 1945. But it operated in a different way. Here too was a clear realization of the dangers of depending too exclusively upon pure self-restraint for the prevention of evil in the world, whether that restraint be exercised by individuals or by sovereign States, but here the emphasis was not upon punitive sanctions but upon the institutionalized implementation of good will, the organized reduction of the incentives and opportunities for national aggression and war. It was an emphasis sadly flawed by continuing and even growing dissension between Russia and the West.

At Issue—America's Decision to Drop the Atomic Bomb

James E. Auer and Richard Halloran

On August 6, 1945, the Americans dropped an atomic bomb on the Japanese city of Hiroshima. Three days later, they dropped a second bomb—this time on the Japanese city of Nagasaki. The bombings ended the war with Japan but set off a heated debate that continues to this day about President Harry S. Truman's decision to use the newly developed atomic bomb on Japan. In this selection, writer and former foreign and military correspondent for the *New York Times* Richard Halloran, and James E. Auer, Director of the Center for United States–Japan Studies and Cooperation at Vanderbilt University in Nashville, Tennessee, contend that President Truman made the right decision, the only decision given the times. They go on to explain why, in their opinion, the revisionist view that Truman did not have to use the atomic bomb is in error and ignores prevailing attitudes and conditions.

The great debate over the atomic bombing of Hiroshima and Nagasaki that swept across America in 1995 was partly emotional and even trivial but mainly genuine and profound. The 50th anniversary of the bombings generated at least nine books, a packet of magazine articles, radio commentaries, television shows, reminiscences by Americans who attacked and Japanese who were victims. . . .

The deliberations have subsided, but that does not mean the issues have gone away or a consensus has been reached. The fundamental question remains: Was the United States justified in dropping two bombs that immediately killed

Excerpted from James E. Auer and Richard Halloran, "Looking Back at the Bomb," *Parameters*, Spring 1996. Reprinted with permission from Richard Halloran.

200,000 people, the vast majority of them civilians? More simply, was President Truman right or wrong?

The President's Options

After studying much of the literature, we have concluded that the United States was justified and President Truman was right. We also believe that, like most human endeavors, it could have been handled better; the atomic bombing of Nagasaki so soon after Hiroshima is rightly open to question. Lastly, we recognize that, again as with most human endeavors, reasonable men and women will differ.

Sifting through this mass of material, it seems evident that Japan had been defeated by late July 1945, and that some Japanese leaders realized this. But defeat and surrender are not the same, and the issue was how to get Japan, notably the militarists who ruled the nation, to quit. In this, President Truman appeared to have six options:

- Invade Japan in two stages, prolonging the war for a year and taking large numbers of American and Allied casualties.
- Continue the aerial bombing and naval blockade until the Japanese lost the will to resist and surrendered.
- Get the Russians into the war in the hope they would crack Japanese resolve and make them sue for peace.
- Accept Japan's proposals to negotiate by modifying the demand for an unconditional surrender to permit Japan to retain the Emperor, a vital point to the Japanese, and agreeing to a minimal occupation of Japan.
- Warn that atomic bombs would be used unless Japan surrendered, and possibly detonate one as a demonstration.
- Drop the atomic bombs to shock the Japanese into quitting before more devastation was loosed on their nation.

Each option was considered, some more thoroughly than others, between 12 April 1945, when Mr. Truman became President and 24 July 1945, when he approved an order to drop the bombs after 3 August 1945. It was not a methodical process—government then was no more neat and orderly than it is today—but the decision was taken after three and a half years of a brutal, draining, desperate war.

Why the Bomb Was the Only Choice

US forces planned to invade Kyushu, Japan's southwestern island, on 1 November 1945; a second assault was planned for 1 March 1946, against Tokyo. As for expected casualties, planners knew the ratio had risen as American forces got closer to Japan and the Japanese became ever more ferocious in defending their homeland. Estimates were all over the lot, from a minimum of 40,000 on up.

Continuing to bomb and blockade aroused fears that Japan would wait out the United States in hopes of a better deal. Americans were weary and impatient to end the war. Keeping an invasion force poised for months would be hard. Allied prisoners all over Asia might be killed.

The Russians promised to enter the war in August, but there is little evidence that Japan would have quit even if the Russians had reached the southern tip of Korea. The high command in Tokyo was not relying on forces on the Asian mainland to defend Japan proper.

Negotiating on Japanese terms was seen as breaking faith with Allies and a political land mine within the United States, where the public backed unconditional surrender. The Allies relented on retaining the Emperor; a shift in the Potsdam Declaration called for the unconditional surrender of Japan's armed forces rather than Japan as a nation, a nuance that Japanese diplomats caught but militarists ignored.

Much thought was given to warning the Japanese about the atomic bomb beyond the Potsdam Declaration's promise that Japan faced "prompt and utter destruction," but some doubted the Japanese high command would believe it. A proposed demonstration was dismissed because the Japanese might shoot down the airplane carrying the bomb, because the bomb had been tested but once and might not work again, and because the Japanese might think the United States had only one.

That left dropping the bomb. On 24 July in Potsdam, Mr. Truman approved its use. The next night, he wrote in his diary: "We have discovered the most terrible bomb in the history of the world. . . . It seems to be the most terrible thing ever discovered, but it can be made useful."

Drawing Conclusions from History

Critics of Mr. Truman contend he dropped the bomb to stave off the Russians, or to justify the $2 billion expense of developing the bomb, or because he was a racist. The overwhelming evidence in several . . . books, plus that from historian David McCullough in his superb biography, *Truman*, shows that the President was driven foremost by a determination to end the war on American terms and with the least loss of life. "We have used it in order to shorten the agony of war," Mr. Truman said just after the bomb had been dropped.

With the benefit of hindsight, some of the criticism might have been forestalled if the Potsdam Declaration had included an explicit pledge that the imperial throne would be retained plus an explicit warning about the atomic bomb. No one knows, however, whether that would have been enough to make Japan surrender. No Japanese has come forward to say: "If only . . . ."

Each student of this decision may draw his or her own insights from the history of this episode. Among them might be to reinforce the conviction that moral issues do not go away, as much as a soldier might be tempted to brush them aside to get on with the mission. Another might be an understanding that the only fair way to judge a momentous decision would be in the context of the times. . . .

Still another: Personalities count, whether they be elected or appointed political leaders or serving military officers. Secretary of War Henry L. Stimson comes off as thoughtful and perceptive, while Secretary of State James Byrnes seems to have been unable to see past the next political maneuver. Even so, in this decision, civilian supremacy over the military services served the nation well. Students of this question might find enlightening a comparison between the dominating political role of the Japanese high command and the subordinate military role of the American Joint Chiefs in World War II.

Lastly, we come away from these books again discouraged by the corrosive effect of interservice rivalry. Some was natural and even constructive: Each service thought it had the better way to force Japan to surrender—the Army Air Force by bombing, the Navy by blockade, the Army by invasion. From that came consideration of all possibilities. But sometimes a reader might wonder whether General Douglas MacArthur and Admiral Chester Nimitz were more concerned with fighting each other than the Japanese.

The Revisionist View

A leader of the so-called revisionists who condemn President Truman's decision is Gar Alperovitz, a historian and

President Truman's decision to drop the atomic bomb set off a heated debate that continues to this day.

political economist at the University of Maryland. His book, *The Decision to Use the Atomic Bomb*, is an updated version of his 1965 *Atomic Diplomacy: Hiroshima and Potsdam*. Armed with scores of declassified records, including Mr. Truman's notes on Potsdam that were discovered in 1979, Alperovitz has written a long and thoroughly documented work.

He contends that Japan knew it was defeated by May 1945. In his view, if the United States had indicated more clearly that Japan could retain Emperor Hirohito, Japan would have surrendered without an American invasion or the atomic bombings. Any hesitation by Japan would have been overcome by Russia's attack, but the United States delayed the Potsdam Conference so that the Alamogordo atomic test results would be known. Then, Secretary of State Byrnes persuaded President Truman to discourage Soviet entry into the war. Alperovitz further contends that most US officials, military and civilian, other than Byrnes, who won over a wavering President Truman, and the Manhattan Project chief, Lieutenant General Leslie Groves, wanted the Potsdam Declaration to assure the Japanese that they could retain the Emperor. Despite his almost endless documentation, Alperovitz admits that critical decisions at Potsdam were not documented, including the decision on 24 July to allow the Army Air Force to use atomic bombs on cities as soon as made ready. Alperovitz says Byrnes wanted to use the bombs not to induce Japan's surrender but to make the Soviets behave. Thus, two bombs were needlessly dropped on two cities that weren't military targets. . . .

Alperovitz is hard on Truman for not listening to his Chief of Staff, Admiral William D. Leahy, who warned that atomic bombs would be in the same category as poison gas, a violation of "all of the known acts of war." The author condemns the President for having acted illegally, self-servingly overestimating the number of American lives saved, and misrepresenting Hiroshima and Nagasaki as military targets. . . .

Robert Jay Lifton, a professor of psychology at John Jay College and the City University of New York, and Greg Mitchell, a former editor of *Nuclear Times* magazine, consider the term "revisionist" to be pejorative. Even so, they are far more vituperative than Alperovitz . . . in condemning Mr. Truman and his associates in their *Hiroshima in America: Fifty Years of Denial.* They allege not only a cover-up by Truman, but a "confabulation," which they define as "an untrue belief or reconstruction that can unconsciously alter events in favor of one's own moral claim." The authors assert: "It can change what one actually did into something one's conscience can accept—and this confabulation had the specific psychological function of placing blame for the bombings entirely on the Japanese."

In the final quarter of this volume, the authors describe the "largely unexamined dimension of Hiroshima: the lasting psychological, ethical, and political impact on those who used the first nuclear weapons." They say "the bomb's contamination not only of Japanese victims and survivors, but of the American mind as well" has produced "aberrations in American life.". . .

Lifton and Mitchell assert that America's "bomb entrapment required us to violate existing ethical practices in actions aimed at harming our people and consistently lying to them about that harm." It was a "self-betrayal" of "our own history, our national entity, and ourselves." Hiroshima is the "mother of all cover-ups. . . ."

What the Revisionists Ignore

The analyses by Alperovitz . . . and . . . Lifton and Mitchell confuse power and morality. War, as Prussian military thinker Carl von Clausewitz reminds us, is a continuation of politics by other means, and those means can get very nasty. . . . Truman had to confront the problem [of the Soviet Union] immediately and saw the potential of the bomb to end the war plus deal with Soviet aggressiveness. Alperovitz and the others blame Truman and Byrnes for causing the Cold War; Lifton and Mitchell blame them for a myriad of additional ills. But none of these authors offers convincing evidence to suggest that their alternative strategies would have produced a better world.

More important, Alperovitz . . . and Lifton and Mitchell fail to note that the atomic decision was made cleanly and properly by the civilian Commander in Chief of the armed forces in accordance with the Constitution. No Dr. Strangelove appeared. . . .

Nor do the revisionists suggest that any other country possessing the bomb would not have used it. They might expect the United States to hold itself to a higher standard, but by 1945 the rigors of war weighed heavily on all combatants. And in a democracy the highest imperative, after victory itself, was to stop the killing of American men (and foreign men, women, and children, too). Woodrow Wilson ended American neutrality and entered World War I, even though he had promised not to during his election campaign, because of his outrage at Germany's use of unrestricted submarine warfare. Following Pearl Harbor, the United States used nearly unrestricted submarine warfare as an effective means of defeating Japan. The fire-bombing of Tokyo provided further evidence of American willingness to use horrific means to force Japan to surrender. Had the atomic bomb not been used, there would have been political bloodshed when the American public found out about it, especially because it *wasn't used to save American lives.*" Minoru Genda, the Japanese naval officer who planned the attack on Pearl Harbor, was asked during a visit to Annapolis, Maryland, in the 1970s whether Japan would have used the A-bomb. Despite his position as a member of the Diet, Japan's national legislature, he answered candidly that he thought so—and set off a political uproar in Japan. Revisionists do not permit themselves to see that the American decision reflected the bomb's capability to make a difference in a long and ugly war, not America's immorality. . . .

Donald . . . Kagan, a historian at Yale, is masterful in refuting the "new revisionist consensus" that the bomb was neither necessary nor a morally acceptable means to end the war, and that Americans have refused to admit this. Kagan contends, "If a moral complaint is to be fairly lodged, it must be lodged against any and all warfare that attacked innocents." He asserts: "It is right to do all we can to reduce the horrors of war. But to prevent them entirely, it will be necessary to prevent war." He concludes that Americans need not shrink from basic questions arising from Hiroshima: "An honest examination of the evidence reveals that their leaders, in the tragic predicament common to all who have engaged in wars that reach the point where every choice is repugnant, chose the least bad course. Americans may look back on that decision with sadness, but without shame."

Chapter 5

Legacies of War

Germany at War's End

Max Hastings

World War II historian Max Hastings is a war correspondent and author who has reported from more than fifty different countries for the *London Standard* and British Broadcasting Company (BBC) Television. In the following article, Hastings focuses on the challenges facing the Allies during their occupation of a defeated and humiliated Germany. The most devastating thing the Allies had to do, Hastings relates, was provide for survivors of the Nazi concentration camps, most of whom were emotionally and physically bereft. Hastings explains that many Allied soldiers, tired of the war and everything about it, found it difficult to retain their animosity toward the Germans during the early postwar period in Germany. He relates how the Allies each withdrew behind their own boundaries and describes the rapidly widening gap between Russia and the other Allies. Hastings maintains that the one point of agreement among all of the Allies after the war was the righteousness of their cause during the war.

Almost the only public act of [Grand Admiral Karl] Dönitz's brief imposture as Germany's Führer was his radio broadcast on the night of 1 May 1945, in which he advanced the grotesque deceit that Hitler had died "a hero's death," declared his determination to save his country from Bolshevism, and concluded by assuring the German people that "God will not forsake us after so much suffering and sacrifice." It was remarkable how frequently the Nazi leadership invoked the Deity in their latter days. In reality, Dönitz's absurd rump government, which had been established at Flensburg on the Danish border, was dissolved by the Allies

Excerpted from Max Hastings, *Victory in Europe: D-Day to V-E Day*. Copyright © 1985 Romadata Ltd. (text); copyright © 1985 New Liberty Productions (photos); copyright © 1985 George Stevens Jr. (intro); copyright © 1985 Richard Natkiel (cartography). Reprinted with permission from Little, Brown and Company, Inc. and George Weidenfeld & Nicholson Ltd.

on 23 May 1945. The bleak Grand Admiral and all his colleagues were arrested, and most served terms of imprisonment after the Nüremberg war crimes trials. . . . Of the lesser Nazis a few were hanged, many more were imprisoned, and yet more escaped. Perhaps partly because many of the Western Allied leaders felt uneasy sitting in joint judgement upon Germany's great criminals alongside the Russians, with their own terrible record of bloodshed, the victors' judgements upon the vanquished remained remarkable for their forbearance.

The Plight of Prisoners and Victims

Half Europe seemed to be moving along its roads that summer of 1945: forced labourers and deportees struggling to return to their homes; soldiers of the Wehrmacht and the SS making desperate, epic attempts to escape from the Russians or war crimes investigators, fleeing to their homes or beyond the reach of Allied justice; refugees displaced by bombing or ground action searching for shelter; widows and orphans bereft of family and possessions looking for the means with which to support life. As late as 10 May, the Russians complained bitterly to [American general Dwight D.] Eisenhower that German soldiers were still fighting Russians in their efforts to break through westwards and surrender to the Anglo-Americans.

All these prisoners and victims the Allied armies were compelled to examine, to control, to feed, where necessary to imprison or care for. The history of the period was eternally sullied by the Allies' forcible return of almost two million Russians in the Anglo-American zones. Many had fought in German uniform either under compulsion, or driven by bitter resentment that their own nations had been incorporated in the Soviet Union against their wishes. Some were forced labourers, some Jews, some exiles. None wished to return east, yet all were condemned to do so. . . . Most Allied soldiers detested the part that they were compelled to play, transhipping endless truck- and trainloads of men at bayonet point, most of whom knew that they were returning to die, and some of whom preferred to do so by their own hands.

Yet the most horrendous burden facing the Allies was that of tending the surviving inmates of the concentration camps. Shocked American troops had liberated Dachau on 29 April, after a brief battle with an SS rearguard. They found "freight cars full of piled cadavers . . . bloody heaps at the rail car doors where weakened prisoners, trying to get out, were machine-gunned to death . . . rooms stacked almost to the ceiling high with tangled human bodies. . . ." The scenes were repeated at Belsen, Buchenwald, Ravensbrück and all the other Nazi industrialized mass murder plants. Most of the survivors were too shocked and broken even to comprehend their deliverance. Those who did so sought terrible and summary revenge upon their former guards, indeed any uniformed German within their reach. A British nurse caring for some of the former inmates in a military hospital

Churchill Urges the British to Finish the Task

On May 13, 1945, British prime minister Winston S. Churchill addressed the British people in a radio broadcast. He spoke of the great Allied victory in Europe and, with the following words, told the British that they had more to do before victory was complete.

I wish I could tell you tonight that all our toils and troubles were over. Then indeed I could end my five years' service happily, and if you thought that you had had enough of me and that I ought to be put out to grass I tell you I would take it with the best of grace. But, on the contrary, I must warn you, as I did when I began this five years' task—and no one knew then that it would last so long—that there is still a lot to do, and that you must be prepared for further efforts of mind and body and further sacrifices to great causes if you are not to fall back into the rut of inertia, the confusion of aim, and "the craven fear of being great." You must not weaken in any way in your alert and vigilant frame of mind. Though holiday rejoicing is necessary to the human spirit, yet it must add to the strength and resilience with which every man and woman turns again to the work they have to do, and also to the outlook and watch they wrote: "The dead eyes rarely kindled a response. . . . Although the patients had the freedom to wander at will within the compounds of the hospital, they were always back in the ward at mealtimes, no matter where they had strayed, silently converging on the food trolley with their tin plates, eyes rivetted on the containers full of meat and vegetables. The helpings had to be small at first, for their shrunken stomachs could not take normal rations. Despite the regular meals, Sister Davies and I would find, while making the beds, a slice of corned beef, a potato or a piece of bread hidden under a pillow, for they could not yet be sure that another day would bring more food. Sometimes we despaired for these men. What future was there for them? No one knew where their families were and they seemed to have forgotten that they ever had wives or children. They only cared

have to keep on public affairs.

On the continent of Europe we have yet to make sure that the simple and honourable purposes for which we entered the war are not brushed aside or overlooked in the months following our success, and that the words "freedom," "democracy," and "liberation" are not distorted from their true meaning as we have understood them. There would be little use in punishing the Hitlerites for their crimes if law and justice did not rule, and if totalitarian or police Governments were to take the place of the German invaders. We seek nothing for ourselves. But we must make sure that those causes which we fought for find recognition at the peace table in facts as well as words, and above all we must labour that the World Organisation which the United Nations are creating at San Francisco does not become an idle name, does not become a shield for the strong and a mockery for the weak. It is the victors who must search their hearts in their glowing hours, and be worthy by their nobility of the immense forces that they wield.

Winston S. Churchill, *The Second World War: Triumph and Tragedy.* Boston: Houghton Mifflin, 1953.

for the food trolley. Every other instinct or emotion had been suppressed except the will to survive."

Occupied Germany

Eisenhower set up his headquarters in the former I.G. Farben building in Frankfurt, [Germany], and set about the rigid enforcement of Allied non-fraternization orders. In the words of his biographer: "His hatred of the Germans was wide-ranging and ran very deep. He definitely wanted them punished, humiliated, made to pay. He blamed the Germans for starting the war and for prolonging it." Yet even after the terrible revelations of the concentration camps, the six million Jews killed, many Allied soldiers found it difficult to sustain their hostility to the Germans in the pitiful circumstances of their defeat. The victors were weary of killing, and tired of fear and bitterness, propaganda and national causes. . . .

From the moment of the surrender, the government of Germany posed an enormous problem for the Allies. In 1918, the entire bureaucracy, the fabric of authority in the country, had been left intact by the victors. In 1945, policy decreed that Nazis must be banished from all positions in the bureaucracy and in government. At a stroke, the controlling forces of the nation were almost eliminated. A long-prepared, yet at once overstretched, structure of Allied military government replaced it. Germany entered the sordid, gloomy postwar era of hunger and the black market; of families picking over mountains of rubble for salvage; Allied officers and men making a twilight living selling petrol, tyres, cigarettes; widespread prostitution; men and women of all nationalities urgently seeking papers, any papers or identity documents that would enable them to cross a frontier, purchase food, or lose a past. . . .

On 1 July 1945, the Allied armies began to withdraw behind the boundaries of the occupation zones. . . . For the British and Americans, this involved large-scale movements of men across great distances. The four-party occupation of Berlin was secured across the Russian zone by a 20-mile-wide air corridor, and a road and railway link. The Russians rapidly began the systematic plundering of their own zone, the removal of vast quantities of industrial plant to their homeland. While the Allied armies were under strict order to take no food from the western zones where the local inhabitants were already in desperate need of it, the Red Army in eastern Germany lived ruthlessly off the land.

On 15 July, the last great conference of the war—for the struggle continued against Japan—took place between the Allied powers in Potsdam. In its midst, on 26 July, [Prime Minister Winston] Churchill learned that his government had been defeated in Britain's first General Election in a decade. It was Clement Atlee who returned to Britain's seat at the conference table. The agreement that finally emerged from Potsdam, committing the Allies to uniform treatment of their respective zones of Germany, was the last for which they achieved joint consent for years to come. The common peace treaty with Germany which they pledged themselves to prepare was never attained. The East-West occupation boundaries of Germany became the frontier of the two post-war German nations. The ending of the war with Japan on 15 August 1945, following the dropping of the atomic bombs on Hiroshima and Nagasaki, passed almost unnoticed in the defeated land where Hitler's people prepared to face a winter of near-starvation without coal to heat their homes, without adequate shelter or clothing, amid absolute lack of employment except in vital services.

A Just, Good War: Evil Defeated

Yet if the anticlimax that followed V-E Day, the first frosts of the Cold War and the descent of the Iron Curtain, seemed a bitter ending to the great Allied "crusade for democracy," the lasting fruits of victory were much less bitter. For all the odium heaped upon the division of Germany between East and West, in their hearts most democrats in the Western World came to believe that partition had at last solved "the German problem," the century-old threat to the stability of Europe. Most of those who had fought returned home to demobilization cherishing the knowledge that the Second World War had not been "just another war," but a genuine struggle to defeat a great evil. When [Georgy] Zhukov came to Frankfurt in the late summer of 1945, Eisenhower played host at a banquet for the Russian marshal, perhaps more than any other one man the victor of the struggle against Germany. The Supreme Commander declared with justice in his speech afterwards: "This war was a holy war, more than any other in history this war has been an array of the forces of evil against those of righteousness." History has thus far endorsed his verdict, and acknowledged V-E Day as a just moment for celebration among the nations of the West.

Epilogue to War

Martin Gilbert

Since 1945 much of the world has considered May 8, 1945—VE-Day—the day World War II ended in Europe. According to noted historian, biographer, and author Martin Gilbert, the war ended on no single day; in fact, in the minds of some, it never ended. Gilbert explains that the early postwar period was a difficult time of change and adjustment, especially for Germany. He chronicles the long-term impact the postwar division of Germany had— not just on the defeated Germans but on all of Europe. Gilbert elaborates on the new world order that emerged, with the United States and the Soviet Union becoming the dominant global powers, and the militarization that evolved out of their intense rivalry. Gilbert was Winston Churchill's official biographer and has authored numerous works about World Wars I and II, including a definitive history of the Holocaust.

On VE-Day 1945 [the day World War II ended in Europe] millions of men, women and children were caught up in the celebrations: singing, dancing and carousing into the night. As on Armistice Day 1918 the immediate impact of the end to the fighting was one of relief and rejoicing. Yet many, including those who vividly recall the unbridled celebrations, also remember the doubts and problems remaining; the uncertainties which did not necessarily end with the ending of the war against Japan. I myself remember the long wait for the return of my cousin Simmy Gordon, who had been captured by the Japanese at Singapore and had been held a prisoner-of-war for more than three and a half years. On his return we glimpsed, as tens of thousands of families glimpsed, a hint of

Excerpted from Martin Gilbert, *The Day the War Ended* (London: HarperCollins, 1995). Reprinted with permission from A.P. Watt Ltd. on behalf of Sir Martin Gilbert CBE.

the ordeal through which those held captive by the Japanese had passed. In common with so many former prisoners-of-war, Simmy never fully recovered from his experiences, which were the subject of innumerable nightmares. In one sense, his war never ended: for him the day the war ended was more of a date in the history books than a part of real life. . . .

The injustices of the war bedevilled the post-war years. Many in Britain felt uneasy at the inability of their country to maintain an independent Poland. "Tomorrow we celebrate our victory," [British prime minister] Harold Macmillan wrote . . . on 7 June 1946, more than a year after VE-Day and nearly ten months after the defeat of Japan. "With my colleagues in Mr Churchill's Government, I shall be at the saluting stand to watch the parade. I tell you this frankly; with all the legitimate joy and pride in every British heart will be mingled much sorrow and even shame." The personal sorrows and sadnesses of the war could likewise not be totally dissipated even by time. . . .

It was only after the end of the war that many children saw their fathers for the first time, nor was the homecoming always a happy one. Of the Australian servicemen who returned after the war, among them her own father, [author] Germaine Greer has written: "Thousands of them came home to live out their lives as walking wounded, carrying out their masculine duties in a sort of dream, trying not to hear the children who asked, 'Mummy, why does that man have to sleep in your bed?'" . . .

War Goes On After Victory

The death toll in the Second World War was higher than in any war of recorded history. On the day the war ended, the parents, widows, children, families and friends of the dead were those for whom the ending was sad and bitter. These, Paul Fussell has written, were "the survivors, those whose lives are ruined by their sons', husbands', fathers' sacrifices for ideologies. The men don't feel anything: they're out of it. It's the living who are the casualties."

The living sought different forms of solace. Forgetfulness was one, made more difficult in our day as the passage of time brings back past memories in sharp relief. Reconciliation was another, hard for those whose lives were uprooted and crippled by suffering and loss. Retribution was a third, pursued through the courts at the Nuremberg Trials and in dozens of other trials in all the countries that were occupied, and in Germany itself. Several thousand camp commandants, guards, torturers and collaborators were executed, some after trials, some after drum-head courts, some without any trial. Many thousands more were brought to trial and imprisoned, albeit often for short terms. More than forty years after the end of the war, Britain, Canada and Australia put laws on their statute books (the British law in 1991) which give the jurisdiction to local courts to try crimes committed during the war years by individuals who emigrated after the war.

There was no single day on which the Second World War ended, not even on the battlefield. Individual stories of liberation, and areas of continued fighting, cover a wide range of moments in time. Circumstances and moods, as much as calendars and geography, also determined the day on which an individual felt his or her moment of individual relief. Roger Peacock, for whom more than four years as a prisoner-of-war had made the celebrating of VE-Day so difficult, wrote: "Governments must of necessity draw a line across the calendar and ordain a VE-Day, or two, and a VJ-Day, ditto. But for many participants such lines were of limited personal significance. It will be recalled that a quarter of a century after 1945, a solitary Japanese soldier was still hiding out in some Pacific jungle, inflexibly convinced that talk of peace was hostile propaganda. He put down his weaponry, reluctantly, only after a relative had been flown out from Japan, equipped with a few relevant newspapers, and had convinced him. We Europeans, on the other hand, needed no such convincing: all over the world Allies and Germans alike accepted gladly the cessation of hostilities."

Even the defeat of Japan did not mark the end of fighting. Despite the Japanese surrender the British decided, because of considerable uncertainty that outlying Japanese troops might disobey the surrender orders from Tokyo, to continue with the planned invasion of Malaya. On September 12 [1945] a landing was made at Port Dickson, after which the

troops began to fan out in Malaya. Hardly had this movement begun than the 23rd Indian Division, one of the two
assault divisions involved, was ordered to embark for Java.
Alfred Doulton, who had fought against the Japanese in
Burma with the 23rd Indian Division, later recalled: "Not
even VJ-Day was the end of WW II for us, as the Division
was sent to Java where it fell to our lot to try and keep apart
the Dutch, who thought they were returning to reclaim their
Empire, and the Indonesians, who had, through the machi-
nations of the Japanese, recently declared their independence. In the process we suffered quite heavy casualties.". . .

Germany: Forever Changed

Echoes of [the] war persist after half a century. On 23 September 1994 *The Times* reported that the bodies of more
than two hundred Italian prisoners-of-war who had died in
Magdeburg, in eastern Germany, after Italy had left the Axis,
"are being repatriated after lying buried under army training
grounds for fifty years."

For the Allies, the day the war ended in Europe was the
day on which good triumphed over evil. This exhilaration
inevitably found an immediate echo in the art, literature,
films and the history books of their respective nations. As
the decades advanced, cynicism, disillusion and doubt were
to tarnish the image of the "good" war. For those who had
been defeated, it was harder than for the victorious powers
to confront the reality of so much destruction and so much
loss, which could not easily be presented in a heroic fight.

Ten years after the German surrender, the first Chancellor of the Federal Republic of Germany, Konrad Adenauer,
reflected on the meaning of May 8. It had, he said, represented the defeat of the evil forces of Nazism. When Mayor
of Cologne, he had been an opponent of Nazism, was dismissed from office in 1933, and twice imprisoned. "But," he
added, "May 8, 1945, will also be recorded by history as the
day when the division of Germany began. This division has
created a source of disquietude in the heart of Europe. The
obliteration of the unnatural boundary between West and
Central Germany will be the primary concern of every Ger-

man Government. Reunification can only be achieved by peaceful means. Until it is accomplished the German people will have no domestic peace and no means of livelihood, nor will the population of the Soviet occupation zone attain freedom from want and liberty of thought."

The Central Germany to which Adenauer referred was what had become in 1945 East Germany, and the reunification to which he looked forward did eventually take place. But the "East Germany" of his characterisation had come under Polish and Russian rule in 1945. He made no claim to those lands, which had been a part of the nineteenth- and early twentieth-century German patrimony. The completeness of the Russian victory over Germany in 1945, the expulsion of millions of Germans from those eastern lands, and their re-population by Poles and Russians, created demographic facts that are unlikely to be reversed. For a decade after the Allied victory they were often challenged. . . . But, however much the Russian and Polish ideologies move towards the western European pattern, the lands they took in 1945 are no longer a part of the negotiable frontier changes envisaged by rulers and politicians. Breslau, the city that held out under siege almost to the last day, one of the great German cities, is unlikely to become German again. As Wroclaw, it has become as Polish a city as Warsaw or Cracow, its guide books reflecting recent Polish history, its German days of glory erased. . . .

In *The Times* on VE-Day there had been three attempts, given prominence in readers' letters, to look forward to a renewal of German life on a basis of hope. One letter was from Robert Birley, a distinguished headmaster, who wrote of the "unavoidable duty" of re-educating the German people. Re-education for responsibility could lead to a Germany that was "capable of producing a stable democratic government.". . .

The Western Allies were determined to restore German democracy. Germans imprisoned by the Nazis or fleeing from the Third Reich were to emerge as leaders. De-nazification and re-education were instituted as crucial elements in the creation of a new German ethic. Far from becoming a pariah nation, West Germany was to take a lead in the creation of a

European community and, after reunification, in the political deliberations, economic prosperity and peace-pursuing ideology of the European Union. Of all the transformations that fifty years . . . wrought in Europe, the transformation of Germany from the terror of the continent to an integral, democratic and peace-loving partner was probably the greatest, and certainly the most welcome to those who had suffered most, whether as nations or individuals.

A Lifetime of Nightmares

German totalitarianism had been destroyed, but national aspirations and global ideologies made the period after the war a time of continuing violence and loss of life, starting when the war ended and continuing in some lands for many years. For many individuals, the post-war period was one in which recovery from their experiences was extremely difficult. . . .

There were many in all armies for whom the pain of combat or captivity was to result in a lifetime of nightmares. With the wide newspaper coverage in June 1994 of the fiftieth anniversary of D-Day, this mental anguish was intensified. Major Colin Crawford, the director of a British charity which cares for mental health of veterans said, as both VE-Day and VJ-Day celebrations loomed on the horizon, "many patients suffer from nightmares every night. They are reminded all their waking lives about events they can never forget. The more they recall the events that caused them stress, the more they are distressed. . . . Many old soldiers—about four per cent are women—suffer from post-traumatic stress syndrome. Newsreel film of fifty-year-old battles can trigger feelings of guilt: they ask why they survived when comrades died."

Major Crawford reflected that as the veteran soldiers get older, "they find it less easy to cope with their memories. Many have now retired and have no more help from their colleagues at work. They have more time to brood. Some are now widowed, and have no one to care for them.". . .

A New World Order

All those who remembered VE-Day, or whose letters and diaries survive, looked to the future with mixed feelings of hope and foreboding, and with aspiration they were determined to see fulfilled, whether of housing and jobs, education, or an end to wars. This latter hope had been strong in 1918. Those who held it in 1945 held it no less strongly. The "war to end war" of 1914–18 had failed utterly to live up to that particular designation. Those born nine months after the exuberances of Armistice Day 1918 were just twenty years old when war broke out again in 1939. . . .

The new war, which many saw as a continuation of the quarrels and unfinished business of the old one, was limited at first to fighting between Germany, Poland, Britain and France. There were many who thought, or hoped, that it need not spread to them. . . . But within two years Germany had attacked Belgium, Holland, Denmark, Norway, Greece and the Soviet Union. Within days of the Japanese attack on Pearl Harbour, Germany had declared war on the United States.

The European war that ended on 8 May 1945 had been total war on land, in the air and at sea, fought by the armies, navies and air forces of more than twenty States, and waged mercilessly on civilians. Unlike the ending of war in 1918, the Germany of 1945 had been occupied by its enemies, and its eastern territories stripped away, including two whole provinces, East Prussia and Silesia. Unlike 1918, the victorious powers had no intention of allowing a revived Germany to threaten them militarily. The Soviet Union sought to attain this by strict political control over what was now East Germany, the Western Allies by encouraging a democratic and demilitarized regime in West Germany, later the Federal Republic. Another safeguard was the division of Germany into two halves: a division that came, ironically, to symbolize not the end of Nazi Germany but the deep gulf of belief and practice between the former Allies.

German reunification came forty-five years after VE-Day. Throughout that period it had been unthinkable: the Soviet Union had represented it as the ultimate danger to the stability of the continent. Suddenly, as the Soviet Union itself began to lose the iron bonds of communist discipline and belief, the two Germanies came together, in a spontaneous outpouring of national unity totally lacking the nationalist extremism that characterized the Third Reich. Although economically as strong as at any time in her history, the new Germany no longer represented a force to be feared on the battlefield.

Within fifty years of VE-Day, the United States and the Soviet Union, the two Great Powers which had built up their rival strengths in Europe and had filled Europe with their arsenals from the day the war ended, came to an agreement that they would no longer confront each other in Europe's territory. The whole apparatus of confrontation established and maintained at such high material and psychological cost, was dismantled. At the beginning of 1994, just over two years after the collapse of the Soviet Union, NATO [the North Atlantic Treaty Organization], the main instrument of Western defence, established Partnership for Peace: this envisaged an individual partnership agreement between NATO and any country on the Eurasian land mass that wished to join. Each agreement offered the newly participating country a wide range of joint military activities. Among the objectives which each country agreed to pursue was the democratic control of defence forces.

More than twenty former communist countries, including Poland, Hungary and . . . the former Soviet republic of Armenia, had signed partnership agreements by the end of 1994. . . .

From Militarization to Economic Cooperation

The East-West divisions of the Cold War, and the confrontation that was so intense as the Second World War ended, dissolved almost overnight. Fifty years after the end of the war in Europe, the militarization of the continent was being replaced by economic cooperation. The political debates of the European Union . . . is a far cry from the military confrontations that twice plunged the whole continent into war in the twentieth century.

On 1 September 1994 the last Russian troops (they were no longer Soviet troops, for the Soviet Union was no more) left Berlin, the city they had reached as conquerors nearly half a century earlier, and in which they had since 1945 been the dominant military presence. They left the city by train from the suburb of Karlshorst, the very place in which the final act of unconditional surrender had been signed on 8 May 1945.

On 25 January 1995 President [Boris] Yeltsin of Russia issued a decree formally rehabilitating all Russian civilians and former prisoners-of-war, several million people in all, who . . . had been imprisoned in the gulag immediately on their return to the Soviet Union. "The Government has been instructed to make compensation payments to the former Soviet prisoners-of-war on a par with the citizens who were victims of Nazi reprisals," the official announcement stated. Former soldiers would receive some monetary compensation and special cards reinstating them as war veterans. The unfinished business of The Day the War Ended never ends.

World War II: A Retrospective

Mark Arnold-Forster

Significant outcomes of World War II are the primary focus of this selection from journalist and author Mark Arnold-Forster's *The World at War.* Arnold-Forster views the invention of nuclear weapons as a major outcome of the war. He writes that the bomb, together with the partition of Germany and the establishment of Russian satellite states in Eastern Europe, were instrumental in preventing a third world war. He explains how Yugoslavia and Berlin differed from the other countries and cities caught up in the Allied postwar "carve-up" of Europe. Another major outcome of the war, contends Arnold-Forster, was the ending of colonialism, which seriously diminished British influence and economic power. Arnold-Forster also asserts that the war strengthened the United States and made it wealthy enough to offer aid through the Marshall Plan to countries in need.

World War One was supposed to be the war to end all wars, but it wasn't. The resentments and injustices that it generated were one cause of World War Two, which followed it twenty-one years later. For all their imperfections and fresh injustices, the peace settlements that followed World War Two were more effective in preventing another worldwide conflict. Another outcome of World War Two, perhaps more important than the peace settlements themselves, was the invention of nuclear weapons. The partition of Germany, the establishment of Russian satellite States in Eastern Europe, and the bomb, combined to prevent the outbreak of a third world conflict. This is not to say that the World War Two settlements were morally defensible. The bomb was a weapon of terror. The absorption into an extended Soviet empire of the East European States violated the principle of self-determination (by which peoples are supposed to be allowed to choose their own form of government) and contravened directly, specifically, and unashamedly the provisions of the Atlantic Charter which all the major Allies had signed. Nevertheless the bomb and the Yalta and Teheran agreements about Eastern Europe did help to keep the peace.

The bomb helped to keep the peace because it multiplied hideously and enormously man's power to destroy his own kind. It made the likely consequences of another world conflict so horrifying that even the most ruthless statesmen were afraid to risk one. It was only necessary for one bomber to get through if it was carrying a nuclear weapon. For the first years after World War Two ended only the United States possessed this new power of destruction. Later, when the Russians acquired it too, these two super powers came to realize in mutual fear that the risks involved in armed conflict were now so much greater than they had ever been before that no cause could be imagined that might justify full-scale war. . . .

Dealing with Yugoslavia and Berlin

The Yalta and Teheran agreements—which gave Russia a free hand in Eastern Europe and which partitioned Germany— were like the nineteenth-century agreements between the European colonial powers, Britain, France, Germany and Belgium, to respect each other's "spheres of influence" in Africa. The proposition that the great powers had any right to claim dominion over smaller ones, let alone to make a bargain among themselves about which smaller power should be dominated by which larger one, ran counter to the spirit of the Atlantic Charter. Nevertheless the deals were made. Perhaps the clearest and most candid was [Winston] Churchill's deal with [Joseph] Stalin under which the Soviet Union undertook not to interfere in Greece in return for a British pledge not to interfere in Rumania. The bargain was kept. So was the much larger bargain between the Western Allies and

Russia about the future of Eastern Europe as a whole. The "iron curtain," as Churchill called it, divided a Russian sphere of influence in Eastern Europe from an Anglo-American one in the West. Bulgaria, Rumania, Czechoslovakia, Poland and Eastern Germany were to be Russian satellite States whose governments, however chosen, were to be subservient in all things to the Soviet Union. Western Germany and the western part of Berlin were Allied spheres of influence. Turkey, which had been neutral in the war, was left to itself. So, in effect, was Austria.

There were two exceptions to this European carve-up—Berlin and Yugoslavia. Yugoslavia's position was different from that of the other East European States in four ways. It was the furthest Communist State from Russia; Yugoslav territory was not occupied by the Red Army and the leading Yugoslav Communists had not been trained in Moscow. Above all, however, the Yugoslavs did not owe their liberation to the Red Army or to any other ally. They owed it to their own efforts. The Yugoslavs were the only people whose country had been totally occupied by the Germans and the Italians and who had, by themselves, chased their enemies out. It is true that they had received aid from Britain, principally, and from the other Allies, but they had done their own planning, their own fighting, and their own suffering. It is also true that Yugoslavia was governed by the Communist parties of the various States of the Yugoslav Federation, united behind Tito. But, Communists or not, the post-war rulers of Yugoslavia supported by the people saw no reason why they should exchange German domination for Russian. In 1948 the non-conformist Yugoslavian Communists were expelled from the Cominform, the international organization of Communist parties through which at that time the Soviet Union sought to impose its will on other European countries. The Russians denounced the Yugoslavs bitterly and continuously, and cut off all commercial ties with their country. The tame Communist governments of Eastern Europe followed suit. Yugoslavia was isolated but undaunted. The Russians could do nothing to bring it to heel.

Berlin produced a tenser situation. It lay well within the

agreed Soviet zone of occupation in Germany, therefore well within the Soviet sphere of influence. The westward displacement of both Polish frontiers had put Berlin within forty minutes' drive of Poland. Nevertheless it had been the capital of Prussia and of Hitler's Reich. So on paper, at any rate, the Allies agreed at their Potsdam Conference to establish a four-power council—representing the Soviet Union, the United States, Britain, and France . . . —which would rule Germany from Berlin. This meant that each of the four powers must have a '"presence" there. The city was divided into four sectors each of which, initially, was under the direct control of an Allied military government. The British, French and American sectors constituted a Western island in the middle of the Soviet sphere of influence. But the Russians on the one hand and the three Western Allies on the other had different ideas about how to govern Germany in the immediate post-war period. The Russians demanded and got reparations. They did not encourage or allow the East Germans to raise their standard of living which, at this time, was miserable. The Western Allies, while demanding reparations initially, were genuinely concerned that the West Germans and the West Berliners should be able to recover economically and to raise their standard of living. There was thus a direct conflict between Russian policy towards Germany and the policies of the Western Allies. Berlin, deep in the heart of the Soviet zone of Germany, became an embarrassment to the Russians. West Berlin began to prosper more than East Berlin, and West Berliners enjoyed greater liberty. The attempt to govern Germany jointly broke down. The Russians decided to try to get the Western Allies out of their sphere of influence.

The Russian Blockade of Berlin

In the early summer of 1948 the Western Allies put into operation a British plan for the reform of the West German currency. The Germans were still using Hitler's money which had lost virtually all its value. The West German "currency reform" was to lay the foundations for West Germany's post-war recovery and for its subsequent prosperity.

The introduction of the new money—the Deutschmark—cured inflation at a stroke and began almost immediately to widen the gap in prosperity between West and East Germany and between West and East Berlin. Without waiting for this to happen the Russians made the introduction of the new currency an excuse for blockading Berlin.

Under the agreements which had established four-power rule the Western Allies had rights of access from West Germany to Berlin through air corridors, along specified super highways, by rail, and along specified canals. The Russians cut all these surface links. . . . Short of declaring war on Russia and fighting their way through, there was nothing the Western Allies could do to restore land communications. The Russians did not, however, interfere with the air corridors to Berlin. These were West Berlin's only link with Western Europe, and, to most people, they appeared inadequate. In 1948 no one supposed that it would be possible to supply two and a quarter million city-dwellers with food, fuel, and raw materials for their industries by air. But two Western statesmen in particular thought it could be done—President [Harry] Truman and the British Foreign Secretary, Ernest Bevin. Truman and Bevin were right. American, British, Australian, French, and Canadian pilots succeeded in supplying a city by air for nearly one year—a year which included an inclement winter.

The blockade of Berlin lasted until the spring of 1949 and it failed. The Russians could not drive the Western Allies out. They reopened the surface communication routes. West Berlin could breathe again. But it remained for the Russians a dangerous gap in the Iron Curtain. Through it the people of East Germany and of East Berlin could observe another, more prosperous, freer society. . . .

The blockade of Berlin marked the active beginning of what became known as the "Cold War" between the Soviet Union and her satellites in East Europe, and the Western Allies and their friends in the West. It was a period of suspicion and of hostility short of war during which the Soviet leaders strengthened their hold over their satellite States. . . . Eastern Europe was Russia's vassal.

The End of Colonialism

On the other hand the Russians made no serious attempt to interfere in Western Europe. They may have intended to interfere, but in the event they did not act They did not encourage the strong French and Italian Communist parties to foment revolution. They maintained diplomatic relations which were formally cordial with the French and Italian Governments. To the extent that the Teheran and Yalta Agreements constituted a bargain sealed by the Iron Curtain, the Russians kept their side of it.

Eastern Europe had been one potentially dangerous source of renewed conflict. The colonial empires of the European powers were another. World War Two was followed by many small colonial wars and by a few larger ones. By the 1940's the colonial empires won by the European powers in the nineteenth century were no longer tenable. World War Two had been about liberty. The Indian Army, for example, had fought valiantly with the British to liberate Italy, France, and the other enslaved European countries. British and French African colonial troops had fought for the same cause. Why, when the war was over, should India, Burma, and the African colonial empires remain subject to European masters?

World War Two did not of itself bring about the end of colonialism but it was the catalyst which started the process and which hastened it. The man who probably first saw most clearly what the war had done to the colonial concept was Lord [Louis] Mountbatten. As Supreme Allied Commander in South-East Asia it fell to him to accept the surrender of the Japanese forces in what had been French Indo-China. In a despatch to the British Foreign Office . . . Mountbatten warned that the French could not simply return to Saigon and resume colonial government as if nothing had happened. He found the country being governed not by the Japanese but by the Vietnamese themselves, led by the North Vietnamese Communist, Ho Chih Minh. Mountbatten found a similar situation in Indonesia. Again he warned the Dutch that they could not expect to resume business as if the war had never happened. The French and the Dutch paid no heed, though the Dutch were quicker to learn from experience and soon gave up trying to restore colonial rule in Indonesia. The French, more stubbornly, continued the struggle until their defeat at the hands of the Vietnamese at Dien Bien Phu in 1954.

The British, meanwhile, had resolved to grant self-government to India and Burma. The decision to do this was taken by the new, post-war Labour Government led by Clement Attlee and executed with despatch by Mountbatten himself in 1947. The outcome was the birth of three new Asian States—India, Burma, and Pakistan, which last comprised the Muslim areas of what had formerly been British India.

Colonialism died more slowly in Africa and more slowly still in the Middle East. . . . But the process that began with the granting of independence to India, Burma, and Pakistan was unstoppable. . . . Colonialism ended in a welter of small, bitter wars which the colonial powers lost, not necessarily for lack of military might but because they did not have the will to sustain an untenable situation for ever. . . .

NATO and the United Nations

In Europe World War Two left behind the nucleus of two organizations—the North Atlantic Treaty Organization [NATO] and the Warsaw Pact—which sustained a balance of power of a sort on either side of the Iron Curtain but which also, and much more importantly, involved non-European powers in the defence of Western Europe. When the war ended Britain, the United States, Canada, and France all were providing sizeable contingents of troops in Western Germany. As time wore on and Western Germany became self-governing, the "occupying powers" and their forces were transformed into Allied powers and Allied forces. The North Atlantic Treaty was a mutual defence pact between the United States with its nuclear arsenal and America's World War Two Allies and some other countries. NATO's stated purpose was to defend democracy. Its main and guiding principle was that an attack on one member of NATO would be deemed to be an attack on all and that the "all" included the United States with its power of nuclear retaliation. . . .

The United Nations Organization, a direct descendant of the Atlantic Charter Agreement, did not of itself play a peace-keeping role in Europe but it was occasionally effective elsewhere. The United Nations was more efficient than its predecessor, the League of Nations, for two main reasons. The United Nations' constitution does not assume, as the League's had assumed, that a majority of small, peace-loving nations can coerce a minority of larger, more bellicose countries to abandon their war-like plans. The second main difference is that the United States was a founder member of the United Nations and did not abdicate its place in the nations' councils as President [Woodrow] Wilson's America had done in the 1920's. . . .

America Becomes an Economic Power

The [1956] Suez war demonstrated for the first time clearly and publicly the extent to which Britain's economic power and therefore her influence had diminished. There were many reasons for this decline but one of them—a main one—had been the effect of World War Two on the British economy. The British were at war for longer than any other nation. They also organized themselves better and more completely for war than any other nation. The British devoted everything they had to the fight. But they themselves did not realize the cost until later.

Towards the end of 1943 the British Government was dismayed to learn from a private report by its chief economic adviser, John Maynard Keynes, that Britain was running out of money. Victory—or something like it—would have to come in 1944 or the war effort would have to be curtailed. British resources, human and other, were fully stretched. In spite of lend-lease and the sale of her foreign assets, Britain was virtually a pauper whereas the United States had become an economic giant.

The United States was large enough and rich enough to take World War Two in its economic stride. America, for the first time, had measured its own economic and industrial strength and had found it to be vast. The American standard of living actually rose during World War Two, partly because more people were employed, partly because under the stress of war the Americans had discovered new resources to exploit. In 1945 Keynes compared the losses suffered by the two nations. British casualties were two and three quarter times as great as those of the United States, with losses in killed and missing three and a half times as great. 55% of Britain's total labour force was engaged in war production by June 1944, compared with 40% in America. Britain had lost 35 times as much capital invested overseas as had the United States. The consumption of goods and services by civilians decreased by 16% in Britain whereas it had increased by 16% in the United States. British and British Commonwealth merchant shipping losses had reduced the total size of the fleet from 40 million tons to 19 million 500 thousand tons, whereas American merchant shipping had increased fourfold to 50 million tons.

The United States emerged from the war stronger than she had gone into it. In 1945, rather to their own surprise, the Americans discovered that they were richer than any other nation had ever been before. The Americans' reaction to this discovery was imaginative and generous. General [George C.] Marshall, by now Secretary of State, secured Congressional approval for the plan which bears his name. The United States offered aid to those countries which needed it, Germany included, because of losses suffered during the war. [President Theodore] Roosevelt's lend-lease principle was extended for peaceful purposes in peacetime. The offer was open to all. Only the Soviet Union and the East European Russian satellites refused it.

Marshall Aid was a great act of national generosity but it was also sensible. By giving away her wealth, the United States was able to avoid the slump which would have followed an abrupt cessation of her vast war production. In the event, American wealth was re-distributed widely and generously while, at the same time, the United States continued to prosper. Inevitably, too, the United States became the dominant economic power in the post-war years. Americans became involved commercially as well as diplomatically with the rest of the world to an extent that had no precedent in

American history. The new circumstances in which the United States found itself, including its new wealth, had made isolationism impractical as well as out of date. One of the things that World War Two did to America was to introduce that rich and resourceful country into a new role as the generally benevolent regulator of the economies of the Western world.

Nuremberg

Michael R. Marrus

> On November 20, 1945, a court set up by the Allies in
> Nuremberg, Germany, tried twenty-two former Nazi of-
> ficials for war crimes. Historian and author Michael R.
> Marrus contends that Nuremberg was a product of its
> time and place and should not be viewed as a policy to
> praise or condemn. According to Marrus, the only other
> alternative Allied decision makers seriously considered to
> determine guilt and punishment was a quick trial and im-
> mediate punishment, which is what the majority of people
> from Allied countries wanted. Marrus acknowledges that
> the charges brought against the Nazis on trial were com-
> plicated and flawed but contends that they were just.

"The greatest trial in history," as Sir Norman Birkett, the as-
sociate British judge on the International Military Tribunal
referred to the trial of the major German war criminals at
Nuremberg, has inevitably been exposed to a wave of historical scrutiny flying under the flag of "revisionism"—a de-
mythologizing of important episodes of the Second World
War. . . . While applauding in principle a re-examination of
old myths, I, as a professional historian, want to report my
unease with some of the furor that has attended upon some
so-called revisionist controversies in popular forums. More
often than not, purported exposes . . . have breathlessly announced findings long known to researchers in the field; and
have also prompted unwarranted moral judgments that apply
our standards, our appreciations, our sensibilities, our knowledge, and our hindsight to the events of half a century ago.

Nuremberg is a case in point. Ultimately, it seems to me,

Excerpted from Michael R. Marrus, "The Nuremberg Trial: Fifty Years After,"
American Scholar, vol. 66, no. 4, Autumn 1997. Copyright © 1997 Michael R. Marrus. Reprinted with permission from the author.

there comes a time when we have to distance ourselves from the events of the past in an effort to understand. . . .

How the Nuremberg Trial Came to Be

How did the Nuremberg Trial come about? From the Anglo-American standpoint, Nuremberg arose from a circumstance that revisionist historians have actively addressed over the past twenty years or more—the failure of Western governments to respond in any significant way to the insistent pleas of the victims of Nazi atrocities in occupied Europe. Since the beginning of the war, and particularly from mid-1942, appeals rained down on Western capitals from governments in exile, Jewish representatives, and humanitarian organizations to do something about Nazi atrocities—to retaliate, mount rescue operations, welcome refugees, or whatever else was possible. Little or nothing was done. Reluctant to disturb warmaking priorities, London and Washington contented themselves with issuing statements. These statements, however, pointed unambiguously to post-war retribution. "The American people not only sympathize with all victims of Nazi crimes," President Franklin Roosevelt wrote to Rabbi Stephen Wise, president of the American Jewish Congress in July 1942, "but will hold the perpetrators of these crimes to strict accountability in a day of reckoning which will surely come." Individuals would be held responsible, FDR and Winston Churchill repeatedly assured all who would listen. "None who participate in these acts of savagery shall go unpunished," Roosevelt insisted two years later. "The United Nations have made it clear that they will pursue the guilty and deliver them up in order that justice be done."

Fearing that they would trigger German retaliation by punishing war criminals before hostilities ended, the Western Allies refused to define their intentions more precisely. The Soviets, already bearing the most ferocious Nazi atrocities, were less reluctant, and indeed moved on their own to try some German criminals in the latter part of the war. In the autumn of 1943, however, all three Allied leaders were ready to take another step on war crimes. In November the Big Three declared that those responsible for Nazi atrocities "will be sent back to the countries in which their abominable deeds were done, in order that they may be judged and punished according to the laws of these liberated countries and of the free Governments which will be created therein." Further: "Major criminals whose offenses have no particular geographic localization" were to be "punished by the joint declaration of the Governments of the Allies."

As the war drew to a close, the British and the Americans debated how to achieve these ends. London seemed reluctant to punish major Nazi war criminals through judicial proceedings. Uneasy about how a trial of the highest ranking Nazis would unfold . . . and uncertain about legal questions, the British favored "executive action"—proceeding summarily to identify high-ranking Nazi criminals, after which they would be shot. On the American side, the question of what to do with the Nazi leaders was caught up in the wider dispute over how to deal with the defeated Axis countries. . . .

Harry Truman promptly accepted the wisdom of a trial, based on a model proposed by the War Department, and he convinced the British, the Russians, and the French, who were brought into the discussions. . . . On August 8, 1945, the representatives reached agreement on a charter establishing an International Military Tribunal (IMT) "for the just and prompt trial and punishment of the major war criminals of the European Axis." Article 6 of the charter declared that the following were "crimes coming within the jurisdiction of the Tribunal": "Crimes against Peace," "War Crimes," and "Crimes against Humanity." The course was set for the Nuremberg Trial.

Alternatives to the Trial

Note an important point from this very hurried sketch of the origins of the Nuremberg Trial: the contemporary alternative to a judicial proceeding, the alternative presented at the time, that is, was not a differently balanced judicial solution. . . . The most energetically pursued alternative to the IMT was, quite simply, swift execution.

A word, for a moment, about some other alternatives that critics have proposed over the years. Some have suggested that the trial should have been turned over to neutral countries and that it would have been fairer to have had judges from such countries on the bench. Never, so far as I can tell, was such a proposal advanced in the discussions leading to the IMT, and it is impossible to imagine any of the Allies agreeing to such an idea. . . .

Should German judges have participated, or should the entire business have been turned over to them? Once again, there is no indication that this notion was ever countenanced at the time. Feeling in every Allied country ran strongly against the defeated Germans, and public opinion would have likely revolted against the idea of German participation—even that of anti-Nazi judges, assuming that these could have been found. Very much on the minds of Western representatives was their experience following the First World War when . . . the adjudication of war criminals was assigned to the German supreme court, sitting in Leipzig. The Leipzig trials produced the most meager results imaginable: of nine hundred suspected criminals on the original Allied list, only twelve were eventually tried; of that number six were convicted and sentenced to terms of imprisonment ranging from four years to a mere two months. As a result, this model was repeatedly scorned as one that should be rejected—a "farce," it was frequently called. . . .

None of these alternatives, one must repeat, even occurred to Allied decision makers at the time. In Washington, London, Paris, and Moscow, the trial of German war criminals was understood as part of the wider and more difficult problem of how to deal with the defeated Nazi state. Germany's unconditional surrender, it was understood, entitled the four victorious Allies to act as "supreme authority with respect to Germany"—with rights to legislate, adjudicate, and administer. The responsibility was theirs, and having been persuaded, with some difficulty, that summary execution was not a desirable solution, the way was cleared for the Nuremberg Trial.

The Validity of the Charges

Were there fundamental flaws in the charges against the twenty-two German leaders put on trial? More specifically, were the accused obliged to answer for actions rendered illegal afterwards . . . violating . . . a fundamental principle of justice? Without going deeply into the legal side of this accusation, which was vigorously contested by the prosecution and which was discussed in the judgment, a few points may put it into historical perspective. As we shall see, the prosecuting lawyers never conceded that the acts for which the accused were indicted were not illegal at the time that they were committed. Indeed, they took great pains to establish that the charges in the Nuremberg Indictment were grounded in international law . . . not the acts of an international legislature, which did not exist, but rather a body of law that had evolved over the course of time, particularly during the interwar period, through treaties and other international agreements. Learned opinion divided on this question, but in the United States at least, where this question was extensively debated in scholarly periodicals as well as more popular journals, the prosecutors could point to a very solid body of opinion that told in their favor.

Perhaps more important, few contemporary observers considered that . . . the Nuremberg Trials had been rendered unfair. This charge, after all, rested on the idea that the accused, when they committed what were later called crimes, had no idea that they were acting illegally. So heinous were the deeds that they were alleged to have done, and so solemn were the warnings issued during the war against those who committed these acts, that, in general terms at least, this criticism seemed widely to have been without merit. One American expert, Sheldon Glueck of Harvard, made the point in the *Harvard Law Review*:

> Surely . . . Hitler . . . and the rest of the unholy alliance in supreme authority in Nazi Germany knew full well that murder is murder, whether wholesale or retail, whether committed in pursuance of a gigantic conspiracy to disregard all treaties and wage lawless wars or of a smaller conspiracy evolved by a group of domestic murderers. Surely, also, the accused knew that they could be executed for their deeds without being granted the privilege of any trial at all. Can

they now be heard to complain that they had no notice that they would have to stand trial under an interpretation of international law which they do not like because they deem it to involve retroactivity?

This is not to say that the charges against the accused were equally grounded in custom, precedent, and legal enactment. Nor is it the case that the accused were equally guilty, as charged. After a year of courtroom sessions the judgment of the IMT made important distinctions, failed to accept some of the prosecutors' contentions while accepting others and passed judgment variously on the accused. While twelve of those indicted were sentenced to death, three were acquitted. Some sense of the complications and shortcomings of the charges may be seen by looking at each of the counts with which defendants were charged.

The most conventional of these, Count Three, was War Crimes. . . . About the legality of these charges, which applied to atrocities committed against both military personnel and civilians, there was little dispute. And there has been little challenge since, save, as we shall see, over the question of tu quoque ("you did it too").

Weaker Counts—Crimes Against Humanity and Peace

Count Four, Crimes against Humanity, was a novel charge, later seen by some to be the major innovation of Nuremberg and a significant advance in the codification of international law. For reasons having largely to do with terminology, I think, Crimes against Humanity was wrongly seen to designate crimes of unprecedented magnitude, such as the murder of European Jews, deeds that in their singular inhumanity represented what the French prosecutor, Francois de Menthon, called "crimes against the human status." In fact, Crimes against Humanity were conceived of for largely technical reasons: they were an effort to include among the indictable offenses the persecution of various groups (such as German Jews, for example)—acts that might otherwise, because of the victims' nationality, escape prosecution. . . .

Coming in practice to stand largely for the crimes against the Jews, the effect of the evidence of this slaughter on the court was so devastating that the legality of the charge itself went largely unchallenged. Instead, some defendants indicted on this count contended that they had not done what they were accused of doing. Sixteen defendants were found guilty of this charge, and two who were indicted . . . were acquitted.

The charges brought against the Nazis, though complicated and flawed, were just.

Much weaker, from a legal point of view, was Count Two of the indictment, Crimes against Peace, in which defendants were charged with participation in the planning, preparation, initiation, and waging of specific wars in violations of international treaties. Open to tu quoque arguments as well as to accusations that these charges were based on an ex post facto definition of criminality, this count was never understood or accepted by the French, and carried with it the obvious potential of embarrassing the Russians. It was the United States that had insisted upon this charge. During the negotiations in preparation for the trial, the American chief prosecutor and Supreme Court Justice Robert H. Jackson insisted that the trial vindicate Washington's decision to pursue the war against Nazi Germany. The United States had fought, he told his listeners, to stop aggression. Aggression was the criminal core of Nazism, from which everything else flowed. "Our view," he told his British, French, and Soviet counterparts, "is that this isn't merely a case of showing that these Nazi Hitlerite people failed to be gentlemen in war; it is a matter of their having designed an illegal attack on the international peace . . . and the other atrocities were all preparatory to it or done in execution of it."

In both law and evidence, the weakest count against the accused was the first, that which charged defendants with conspiring to commit the other crimes. Even more than Crimes against the Peace, this charge was an American product from first to last, having emerged from planners in the United States War Department with a view to addressing some of the problems facing the Americans with subsequent trials of Nazi criminals. The idea was that the accused Nazi leaders would stand in the dock in their own right but also in some sense as "representatives" of the major Reich organizations from which they came. Evidence used against those indicted would establish that these were criminal organizations, agents of a criminal conspiracy. And once this had been established, so the plan went, it would be easy, in subsequent trials, to declare others who had been part of those organizations similarly guilty. . . .

In practice, Count One unnecessarily complicated the trial and failed to serve the purpose for which it was intended. While familiar to American and British lawyers, the concept of conspiracy was not understood in Continental legal practice. Not only did the German defense lawyers protest against the whole idea, the French and Russians also seemed to have trouble with the concept. Inevitably, evidence presented on Count One spilled across the rest of the prosecution's case—particularly Count Two, Crimes against Peace. The emphasis on conspiracy badly distorted the historical interpretation of Nazism presented to the IMT, putting undue emphasis on the coherence and foresight associated with Nazi criminality. The conspiracy charge, by general consensus, did not serve the cause of history well. On the other hand, Count One does not seem to have told heavily against the defense. The indictment charged all the defendants with this offense; in the end the Tribunal convicted only eight and acquitted twelve.

Finally, the indictment referred to six major organs of the Third Reich: the Reich Cabinet, Party leadership, the SS, the Gestapo, the General Staff, and the SA. Each was represented by counsel, and tens of thousands of Germans who had been members made submissions to the court. In retrospect, the identification of some of these groups seems to have been the result of overly hasty or careless research on the part of the prosecutors and reflected some misunderstanding of how the Reich worked. In the end, the judges found that three of the six were criminal within the meaning of the charter. The judgment distinguished among classes of members and nature of membership for future determination of individual guilt.

Tu Quoque as a Defense

While bound by the terms of the charter and the indictment of the accused, defense lawyers repeatedly claimed that leaders of the countries that had organized the trial and were represented on the IMT were themselves guilty of crimes with which the Nazi leaders were charged. "Tu quoque," or "You did it too!" they said in effect. "If we are pronounced guilty, then you should be as well." Since the Nuremberg Trial, commentators have returned often to this claim and have benefited from evidence on the Allied prosecution of the war that has since come to light. . . .

Then, as now, there were two implied alternatives: either the Germans ought not to have been indicted for these crimes, or Allied leaders ought also to have been brought to justice. Viewed historically, however, these criticisms seem utterly unreal. The Allied course was set in the direction of a trial at the end of the war. Given the depth of feeling on the subject of Axis war crimes in the broadest sense, there was simply no prospect, in 1945, that the authorities concerned would have accepted these alternatives. No responsible authority proposed that Nuremberg be constituted as a general inquiry into the conduct of the Second World War. Any such suggestion would have been considered outlandish at the time, and would not have secured the participation of any of the four victorious powers. That is why the IMT was established, in the words of the Nuremberg Charter, "for the just and prompt trial and punishment of the major war criminals of the European Axis."

"Do two wrongs make a right?" British Chief Prosecutor Sir Hartley Shawcross asked rhetorically in his summation. "Not in that international law which this Tribunal will administer," was his reply. This was the prosecution's chief response—along with angry denials of illegality by the Russians or embarrassed silence by the Westerners on the particularly obvious cases of Soviet wrongdoing. For historians, some of the most interesting parts of the Nuremberg proceedings are those in which the defense attorneys battled against all odds to have tu quoque arguments accepted. But from a legal standpoint, . . . this insistence on "clean hands" has little legal standing—and thus was given little heed at the time. Such arguments . . . can be leveled against any type of terrestrial justice. A potent historical point, and perhaps a case for diminishing the historic standing of the IMT, it carried no weight at all as an argument on behalf of the twenty-two accused. The claim that "you did it too," that is to say, seems convincing only as a pointer to what Nuremberg might have been if the world had been an utterly different place than it was.

A Need for Perspective

After half a century, I think we can consider Nuremberg as the product of its own time and place, rather than as a policy to be praised or condemned. Politically, the Nuremberg Trial occurred in a post-war climate in which Allied opinion ran powerfully against Germans and the German state. Everywhere in the Allied world the question of what to do with the Nazi leadership posed itself insistently in the last months of the war. And everywhere responses to the question of what to do were extremely harsh. . . . Opinion everywhere, particularly in the occupied countries, favored a very harsh treatment of Germany. Judicial proceedings were always the view of a minority, and sometimes a tiny minority.

So in practical terms, the real alternative to Nuremberg was not a wider inquiry into war crimes committed by victors as well as vanquished, or a new venture into international adjudication by incorporating judges from countries that had not participated in the struggle—let alone judges from the defeated Axis powers. The real alternative, and what most people from Allied countries probably preferred, was a summary proceeding followed by speedy punishment—in all likelihood, death. Without American pressure against it, this would probably have taken place.

Critics of Nuremberg have made much of the presence of the Russians on the bench and the Tribunal's silence on the wartime atrocities of Stalin and his henchmen. Western participants were not unaware of these crimes. But Nuremberg, they felt, was not the place to deal with them. Mostly, they saw the trial as a last act of the Allied coalition against Nazi Germany. In retrospect, we should understand Nuremberg as occurring just as the Cold War storm was gathering—as tensions were rising and disputes were evident, but when the Allies, certainly many Americans among them, were eagerly hoping that these difficulties would be resolved. That is the most important reason why Westerners responsible for the trial were prepared to look the other way when it came to the Russians. They were not blind, but they preferred not to scrutinize their Soviet interlocutors too closely.

In this sense, there was a measure of idealism at Nuremberg that extended into other areas as well—the hope to lay the foundation for a new world order in which aggressive war would be universally condemned, in which the major powers, including the Russians, would work together in the interests of world peace, and in which the unity achieved in a common purpose could be extended to other areas of human affairs. Each of the great powers saw this new order somewhat differently. But each hoped to maintain some measure of collective action. A trial of the major German war criminals seemed like a reasonable project with which to begin.

In legal terms, there were undoubted flaws—pointed out

at the time and subsequently. German critics of Nuremberg complained of the severe imbalance between the prosecution and the defense and challenged court procedures as well as the wider conception of the trial. At Nuremberg, they claimed, probably with some justice, the defense was at a significant disadvantage. More generally, Nuremberg was not everyone's sense of justice well administered. . . .

Nuremberg Is a Landmark

A more serious question is what effect these and other flaws had upon the outcome of the trial. So far as the law is concerned, learned disputation was part of the trial itself, flourished in its wake, and is likely to continue indefinitely on the most fundamental questions. Examined historically, however, much of this debate may seem beside the point. For example, given the circumstances of 1945–46, it is highly implausible that any court judging high-ranking Nazis would have allowed a searching exploration of the injustices of the Treaty of Versailles in 1919—to take what was the demand most insistently pressed upon the IMT by defense lawyers. Defense attorneys repeatedly asked to present evidence on this great evil that they contended was at the root of Nazism; they should not have been surprised that they were forbidden to make this case. . . .

Nuremberg should be understood within the framework of Allied worries about the continuing threat of Nazism to Germany and to Europe—a threat embodied in the courtroom by the swaggering, sometimes brilliant presence of the former Reichsmarschall Hermann Goering, for many the leading personality of the Nuremberg Trial. Hundreds of thousands of Nazi-sympathizing officers, judges, police, bureaucrats, and industrialists remained part of the German scene in 1945, and in the West, at least, it was assumed that they were an inescapable part of the future Germany. Nuremberg prosecutors and judges were highly conscious of their responsibilities for the future of Germany and Europe to pronounce a stern verdict against Nazism.

Finally, Nuremberg may be seen in what I would call a cultural context—a landmark. . . . No doubt, the trial of the major war criminals has entered into our culture, and this too prompts some historical reflection. Inevitably, with the passage of time, our views of Nazism, the Holocaust, and the Second World War are becoming more historical—freed progressively from the grip of partisanship, from a perspective overwhelmed by grief or anger. Not only inevitable, I believe, this process is worth supporting in itself. Coming to terms with these great scars in our century is one of the significant challenges of our time, and if we really believe we are capable of preventing such catastrophes in the future, we had better ensure that we have as objective an evaluation as possible of what went so wrong in the past.

In this, Nuremberg has had an important place, first, by having brought forward an extraordinarily vast body of documentation. . . . More than many of the organizers even hoped, Nuremberg was a voice for history—in the form of thousands of documents on the Third Reich assembled by the court and released for the scrutiny of historians and writers with every possible viewpoint. The prosecution, but also the defense (though to a lesser degree) used the trial to introduce evidence that has been pondered by a whole generation. . . . "There is no parallel in history," wrote one participant, "to this baring of contemporary official papers to the public eye and to expert scrutiny."

In considering the most highly charged of historical events, Nuremberg at its best moments set an example for a kind of international judgment—impartial, but not necessarily dispassionate; fair-minded, but not without moral compass; searching in its quest for truth, while recognizing the formal limitations that attend to the endeavor in an adversary proceeding. Nuremberg was not perfect, by any means, and it is possible to believe that its warts and blemishes—or even its structural faults—may be the most important aspects of it worthy of discussion today. But most would agree that there are other dimensions, too, and that some of these speak to timeless concerns that justice and fairness prevail.

Image of a New Nation

Mark Jonathan Harris, Franklin D. Mitchell, and Steven J. Schechter

According to authors Mark Jonathan Harris, Franklin D. Mitchell, and Steven J. Schechter, World War II altered the character of life in America and brought the nation into a new age. In their collaborative work *The Homefront: America During World War II*, award-winning documentary filmmaker Harris, director/producer Schechter, and historian and retired professor of history Mitchell explain that America, unlike the other major powers involved in World War II, emerged from the war a much stronger nation. The wartime economy, the authors write, brought prosperity to many Americans and made social and economic change the hallmark of postwar America. Equally important, according to Harris, Mitchell, and Schechter, the war had a major effect on the expectations and status of women, African Americans, and other minorities that greatly impacted their roles and their rights from that point forward.

Although the United States was spared the massive destruction of lives and property that occurred in the homelands of other countries, the nation and the American people were still profoundly changed by World War II. Most nations emerged from the war poorer and weaker than when they entered it—their economies shattered, their industrial plants destroyed. Among the major powers only the United States—never bombed, never invaded—emerged from the war stronger than before.

A modern Rip Van Winkle who dozed off to sleep in 1939 and awoke in 1945 would hardly have believed that the six years of America's mobilization for war could have so altered the character of life in this country. In both foreign and domestic affairs, the nation witnessed the end of an old order and the beginning of a new age.

The Wartime Economy

The economic and social forces generated by the nation's response to war brought the Great Depression to a resounding end, completing the recovery that the New Deal of the thirties had begun. The tremendous production achieved by industry, labor and agriculture reaffirmed people's faith in capitalism and American political and social institutions. At the same time, however, a vast array of developments in demography, social mobility, race relations, large-scale organization, the status of women, family structure, science and technology either transformed aspects of society or carried the promise of transforming change. The war years in America uprooted millions of Americans and transported them to a new age.

Wartime spending—$186 billion in federal expenditures for war production alone—brought full employment and booming prosperity to the nation. The widespread prosperity refurbished the middle class and added millions of people to its ranks. A postwar depression would have reversed these developments, but the pent-up demand of returning veterans and civilian workers, along with astute reconversion policies of the federal government, fueled a strong postwar boom. Millions eager to purchase a new home, a new car, modern appliances and other goods of the mass-production/mass-consumption society now had the means to do so. Affluence was so pervasive that most people did not see that minorities and working women had a limited share of the postwar prosperity. No one could have envisioned that the economic recovery of World War II would carry forward with only minor setbacks for forty years until the great recession of the early 1980s.

The wartime economy accelerated the prewar trend of bigness in business, labor, agriculture and government. Large corporations, awarded about eighty percent of the federal-government defense contracts, entered the postwar era with the capital, technology, production capacity and organizational skills to dominate the market at home and abroad. Labor, particularly the Congress of Industrial Organizations (CIO) that had organized unskilled workers in the nation's major industries, benefited from the labor shortages and expansion of the work force during the war. After the war, fifteen million union members effectively pursued their interests in both the economic and political arenas. The family farm remained the most common economic unit in agriculture after the war, but the high cost of land, livestock and machinery assured the continuing development of large-scale corporate farming. Finally, the federal government continued to exert a major influence over the economy despite the rapid dismantling of the mammoth wartime agencies. Big government and huge federal budgets were here to stay. The postwar economy, highly complex and interrelated with world resources and markets, was the strongest in the world.

Altered Self-Images and Expectations

The mobilization of people for the military and the home-front war-production effort had uprooted millions of Americans. In 1945, fifteen million Americans were living somewhere other than where they had been on December 7, 1941. People migrated from country to city, from South to North, above all from East to West. The result was an extraordinary redistribution of the population. When the war was over, many were eager to return to the familiar surroundings of their home communities; but others, attracted to the opportunities and lifestyles of a new locality, never went back to their former homes. Both groups found that something was lost and something gained in the postwar society, and disillusionment was the partner of great expectations.

The war had also altered the status of blacks and other minorities by lowering social and economic barriers to their advancement. The notable exception to this development, of course, were the Japanese Americans who were subjected to relocation and internment. Minority and civil-rights groups were proud of their wartime accomplishments and were determined to keep and expand these gains after the war. Many whites were equally determined to maintain segregation and discrimination. The most notable victories for minorities came not at the grass-roots level, but from the federal government. President Harry S. Truman led the way in 1948 by ordering the desegregation of the armed forces and a ban on discrimination in federal employment. The Supreme Court broadened the assault on second-class citizenship in 1954 by striking down the "separate but equal" doctrine, thus inaugurating the slow but measured desegregation of public schools. The civil-rights movement that emerged in the sixties was impelled in part by the frustration among blacks that the expectations raised by the war remained unfulfilled.

Women who had worked in defense industries or who had lived alone while their servicemen husbands were away were another group whose expectations and self-image were altered by their wartime experiences. Many were unprepared for the abrupt change in their lives that occurred with the coming of peace. The swift closing of many war industries literally left millions of women unemployed overnight. Their efforts to continue their employment in nontraditional jobs were largely unsuccessful, although some returned to work in defense industries during the Korean War of the 1950s. Women employed outside the home after the war usually had to settle for low wages for working on the assembly line or as cook, dishwasher, waitress or secretary. Many became full-time homemakers, with the intent of being happy wives and mothers, only later to have their marriages end in divorce, often on their initiative. No one knows how many marriages were terminated because the wife's expectation of life had been altered by her experiences of wartime, but the divorce rate skyrocketed to a historic high in 1946, setting a record that stood until the 1970s. The women who seemed to have profited most from their wartime economic independence may also have been the most determined to retain their independence after the war. Indeed, some may have passed on their liberation from an unequal union and from traditional pursuits to their daughters and granddaughters.

Finally, America's mobilization and involvement in World War II transformed the nation's foreign and defense policies. In foreign affairs, the United States embarked upon an international course of unparalleled dimension and scope. Isolationism was firmly relegated to the past. The country joined the United Nations and provided that international organization a permanent home as well. American soldiers joined in the Allied occupation of Germany and presided alone over the reconstruction of defeated Japan. Economic and military aid flowed to both Europe and Asia shortly after the war, followed by formal alliances. The breakdown of wartime cooperation with the Soviet Union gave an anti-Communist character to U.S. foreign policy, spawning the Cold War between the two countries. The Cold War in turn necessitated the buildup of the nation's armed forces, including the development of nuclear weapons and the planes and missiles to deliver them. Paradoxically, as America's military might increased, the nation's security decreased in the face of new technology and weaponry.

The many complexities and paradoxes of postwar life have encouraged Americans to look back wistfully upon the World War II years. Life seemed much simpler then, and it was. The war itself presented a contrast between good and evil that left few doubts about the righteousness of America's cause. Many of the wartime generation miss the love of country and the national unity that flourished during World War II. They remember when America's triumph over its enemies was unconditional and conclusive. They still consider those years our country's finest hour. This nostalgic view of the past, mixing reality with illusion, influences both national life and the life of individuals and becomes, in its own way, a legacy of World War II.

Appendix of Documents

Document 1: Neville Chamberlain and the British Reaction to the Nazi Invasion of Poland

In September 1938, Britain, France, and Germany signed the Munich Pact, in which German leader Adolf Hitler promised to respect Czechoslovakia's sovereignty and not seize any more European territory. British prime minister Neville Chamberlain, who had represented his country at the Munich conference, told the British people that they could trust Hitler and proclaimed "peace in our time." Less than six months later, Hitler's armies invaded western Czechoslovakia. On September 1, 1939, Hitler invaded Poland. A few hours after the invasion, Chamberlain gave this speech to the British House of Commons.

I do not propose to say many words tonight. The time has come when action rather than speech is required. Eighteen months ago in this House I prayed that the responsibility might not fall upon me to ask this country to accept the awful arbitrament of war. I fear that I may not be able to avoid that responsibility.

But, at any rate, I cannot wish for conditions in which such a burden should fall upon me in which I should feel clearer than I do today as to where my duty lies.

No man can say that the Government could have done more to try to keep open the way for an honorable and equitable settlement of the dispute between Germany and Poland. Nor have we neglected any means of making it crystal clear to the German Government that if they insisted on using force again in the manner in which they had used it in the past we were resolved to oppose them by force.

Now that all the relevant documents are being made public we shall stand at the bar of history knowing that the responsibility for this terrible catastrophe lies on the shoulders of one man, the German Chancellor, who has not hesitated to plunge the world into misery in order to serve his own senseless ambitions. . . .

Only last night the Polish Ambassador did see the German Foreign Secretary, Herr von Ribbentrop. Once again he expressed to him what, indeed, the Polish Government had already said publicly, that they were willing to negotiate with Germany about their disputes on an equal basis.

What was the reply of the German Government? The reply was

that without another word the German troops crossed the Polish frontier this morning at dawn and are since reported to be bombing open towns. In these circumstances there is only one course open to us.

His Majesty's Ambassador in Berlin and the French Ambassador have been instructed to hand to the German Government the following document:

"Early this morning the German Chancellor issued a proclamation to the German Army which indicated that he was about to attack Poland. Information which has reached His Majesty's Government in the United Kingdom and the French Government indicates that attacks upon Polish towns are proceeding. In these circumstances it appears to the Governments of the United Kingdom and France that by their action the German Government have created conditions, namely, an aggressive act of force against Poland threatening the independence of Poland, which call for the implementation by the Government of the United Kingdom and France of the undertaking to Poland to come to her assistance. I am accordingly to inform your Excellency that unless the German Government are prepared to give His Majesty's Government satisfactory assurances that the German Government have suspended all aggressive action against Poland and are prepared promptly to withdraw their forces from Polish territory, His Majesty's Government in the United Kingdom will without hesitation fulfill their obligations to Poland."

If a reply to this last warning is unfavorable, and I do not suggest that it is likely to be otherwise, His Majesty's Ambassador is instructed to ask for his passports. In that case we are ready.

Yesterday, we took further steps towards the completion of our defensive preparation. This morning we ordered complete mobilization of the whole of the Royal Navy, Army and Royal Air Force. We have also taken a number of other measures, both at home and abroad, which the House will not perhaps expect me to specify in detail. Briefly, they represent the final steps in accordance with pre-arranged plans. These last can be put into force rapidly, and are of such a nature that they can be deferred until war seems inevitable. Steps have also been taken under the powers conferred by the House last week to safeguard the position in regard to stocks of commodities of various kinds. . . .

There is one other allusion which I should like to make before I end my speech, and that is to record my satisfaction of His Majesty's Government, that throughout these last days of crisis Signor [Benito] Mussolini also has been doing his best to reach a solution. It now only remains for us to set our teeth and to enter upon this struggle, which we ourselves earnestly endeavored to avoid, with determination to see it through to the end.

We shall enter it with a clear conscience, with the support of the Dominions and the British Empire, and the moral approval of the greater part of the world.

We have no quarrel with the German people, except that they allow themselves to be governed by a Nazi Government. As long as that Government exists and pursues the methods it has so persistently followed during the last two years, there will be no peace in Europe. We shall merely pass from one crisis to another, and see one country after another attacked by methods which have now become familiar to us in their sickening technique.

We are resolved that these methods must come to an end. If out of the struggle we again re-establish in the world the rules of good faith and the renunciation of force, why, then even the sacrifices that will be entailed upon us will find their fullest justification.

Neville Chamberlain, speech to British House of Commons, September 1, 1939.

Document 2: "Blood, Toil, Tears, and Sweat"

On May 13, 1940, recently appointed British prime minister Winston Churchill addressed his nation's House of Commons. With these words, Churchill warns the members of the House—and the British Empire as a whole—that they had a major ordeal ahead of them and makes clear that the only acceptable conclusion is total victory.

On Friday evening last I received His Majesty's Commission to form a new Administration. It was the evident wish and will of Parliament and the nation that this should be conceived on the broadest possible basis and that it should include all parties, both those who supported the late Government and also the parties of the Opposition. I have completed the most important part of this task. A War Cabinet has been formed of five Members, representing, with the Opposition Liberals, the unity of the nation. The three party Leaders have agreed to serve, either in the War Cabinet or in high executive office. The three Fighting Services have been filled. It was necessary that this should be done in one single day, on account of the extreme urgency and rigor of events. A number of other positions, key positions, were filled yesterday, and I am submitting a further list to His Majesty tonight. I hope to complete the appointment of the principal Ministers during tomorrow. The appointment of the other Ministers usually takes a little longer, but I trust that, when Parliament meets again, this part of my task will be complete and that the Administration will be complete in all respects.

I considered it in the public interest to suggest that the House should be summoned to meet today. Mr. Speaker agreed, and took the necessary steps, in accordance with the powers conferred upon him by the Resolution of the House. At the end of the proceedings today, the Adjournment of the House will be proposed until Tuesday, 21st May, with, of course, provision for earlier meeting if need be. The business to be considered during that week will be notified to Members at the earliest opportunity. I now invite the House, by the Motion which stands in my name, to record its approval of the steps taken and to declare its confidence in the new Government.

To form an Administration of this scale and complexity is a serious undertaking in itself, but it must be remembered that we are in the preliminary stage of one of the greatest battles in history, that we are in action at many points in Norway and in Holland, that we have to be prepared in the Mediterranean, that the air battle is continuous and that many preparations, . . . have to be made here at home. In this crisis I hope I may be pardoned if I do not address the House at any length today. I hope that any of my friends and colleagues, or former colleagues, who are affected by the political reconstruction, all make allowance, all allowance, for any lack of ceremony with which it has been necessary to act. I would say the House, as I said to those who have joined this Government: "I have nothing to offer but blood, toil, tears and sweat."

We have before us an ordeal of the most grievous kind. We have before us many, many long months of struggle and of suffering. You ask, what is our policy? I will say: it is to wage war, by sea, land, and air, with all our might and with all the strength that God can give us: to wage war against a monstrous tyranny, never surpassed in the dark, lamentable catalogue of human crime. That is our policy. You ask, what is our aim? I can answer in one word: It is victory, victory at all costs, victory in spite of all terror, victory, however long and hard the road may be; for without victory, there is no survival. Let that be realized; no survival for the British Empire; no survival for all that the British Empire has stood for, no survival for the urge and impulse of the ages, that mankind will move forward towards its goal. But I take up my task with buoyancy and hope. I feel sure that our cause will not be suffered to fail among men. At this time I feel entitled to claim the aid of all, and I say, "Come then, let us go forward together with our united strength."

Winston Churchill, "Blood, Toil, Tears and Sweat" Speech to British House of Commons, May 13, 1940.

Document 3: Hitler's Rationale for Invading the Soviet Union

On June 22, 1941, Germany, Italy, and Rumania declared war on the Soviet Union. That same day, German troops invaded Soviet territory. The day before, Adolf Hitler wrote this letter to Italian leader Benito Mussolini—Il Duce—explaining why it was in their best interests to invade their former ally.

I am writing this letter to you at a moment when months of anxious deliberation and continuous nerve-racking waiting are ending in the hardest decision of my life. I believe—after seeing the latest Russian situation map and after appraisal of numerous other reports—that I cannot take the responsibility for waiting longer, and above all, I believe that there is no other way of obviating this danger—unless it be further waiting, which, however, would necessarily lead to disaster in this or the next year at the latest.

The situation: England has lost this war. With the right of the drowning person, she grasps at every straw which, in her imagination, might serve as a sheet anchor. Nevertheless, some of her hopes are naturally not without a certain logic. England has thus far always conducted her wars with help from the Continent. The destruction of France—fact, the elimination of all west-European positions—directing the glances of the British warmongers continually to the place from which they tried to start the war: to Soviet Russia.

Both countries, Soviet Russia and England, are equally interested in a Europe fallen into ruin, rendered prostrate by a long war. Behind these two countries stands the North American Union goading them on and watchfully waiting. Since the liquidation of Poland, there is evident in Soviet Russia a consistent trend, which, even if cleverly and cautiously, is nevertheless reverting firmly to the old Bolshevist tendency to expansion of the Soviet State. The prolongation of the war necessary for this purpose is to be achieved by tying up German forces in the East, so that—particularly in the air—the German Command can no longer vouch for a large-scale attack in the West. I declared to you only recently, Duce, that it was precisely the success of the experiment in Crete that demonstrated how necessary it is to make use of every single airplane in the much greater project against England. It may well happen that in this decisive battle we would win with a superiority of only a few squadrons. I shall not hesitate a moment to undertake such a responsibility if, aside from all other conditions, I at least possess the one certainty that I will not then suddenly be attacked or even threatened from the East. The concentration of Russian forces . . . is tremendous. Really, all available Russian forces are at our border. Moreover, since the approach of warm weather, work has been proceeding on numerous defenses. If circumstances should give me cause to employ the German air force against England, there is danger that Russia will then begin its strategy of extortion in the South and North, to which I would have to yield in silence, simply from a feeling of air inferiority. It would, above all, not then be possible for me without adequate support from an air force, to attack the Russian fortifications with the divisions stationed in the East. If I do not wish to expose myself to this danger, then perhaps the whole year of 1941 will go by without any change in the general situation. On the contrary. England will be all the less ready for peace, for it will be able to pin its hopes on the Russian partner. Indeed, this hope must naturally even grow with the progress in preparedness of the Russian armed forces. And behind this is the mass delivery of war material from America which they hope to get in 1942.

Aside from this, Duce, it is not even certain whether I shall have this time, for with so gigantic a concentration of forces on both sides . . . there is the possibility that the shooting will start spontaneously at any moment. A withdrawal on my part would, however, entail a serious loss of prestige for us. This would be particularly unpleasant in its possible effect on Japan. I have, therefore, after constantly racking my brains, finally reached the decision to cut the noose before it can be drawn tight. I believe, Duce, that I am hereby rendering probably the best possible service to our joint conduct of the war this year. . . .

I waited until this moment, Duce, to send you this information, it is because the final decision itself will not be made until 7 o'clock tonight. I earnestly beg you, therefore, to refrain, above all, from making any explanation to your Ambassador at Moscow, for there is no absolute guarantee that our coded reports cannot be decoded. I, too, shall wait until the last moment to have my own Ambassador informed of the decisions reached.

The material that I now contemplate publishing gradually, is so exhaustive that the world will have more occasion to wonder at our forbearance than at our decision, except for that part of the world which opposes us on principle and for which, therefore, arguments are of no use.

Whatever may now come, Duce, our situation cannot become worse as a result of this step; it can only improve. Even if I should be obliged at the end of this year to leave 60 or 70 divisions in Russia, that is only a fraction of the forces that I am now continually using on the eastern front. Should England nevertheless not draw any conclusions from the hard facts that present themselves, then we can, with our rear secured, apply ourselves with increased strength to the dispatching of our opponent. I can promise you, Duce, that what lies in our German power, will be done. . . .

In conclusion, let me say one more thing, Duce. Since I struggled through to this decision, I again feel spiritually free. The partnership with the Soviet Union, in spite of the complete sincerity of the efforts to bring about a final conciliation, was nevertheless often very irksome to me, for in some way or other it seemed to me to be a break with my whole origin, my concepts, and my former obligations. I am happy now to be relieved of these mental agonies.

Adolf Hitler, letter to Benito Mussolini, June 21, 1941, in United States, Department of State, Publication No. 3023, *Nazi-Soviet Relations 1939–1941. Documents from the Archives of the German Foreign Office.* Washington, DC: Government Printing Office, 1948.

Document 4: A Call for an End to Nazi Tyranny

In August 1941 British prime minister Winston Churchill and U.S. president Franklin Delano Roosevelt met face-to-face for the first time off the coast of Newfoundland in the North Atlantic. On August 14 they issued the Atlantic Charter, an eight-point program calling for "the final destruction of Nazi tyranny" and emphasizing freedom of trade and the right of a people to choose their own government.

The President of the United States of America and the Prime Minister, Mr. Churchill, representing His Majesty's Government in the United Kingdom, being met together, deem it right to make known certain common principles in the national policies of their respective countries on which they base their hopes for a better future for the world.

First, their countries seek no aggrandizement, territorial or other;

Second, they desire to see no territorial changes that do not accord with the freely expressed wishes of the peoples concerned;

Third, they respect the right of all peoples to choose the form of government under which they will live; and they wish to see sovereign rights and self government restored to those who have been forcibly deprived of them;

Fourth, they will endeavor, with due respect for their existing obligations, to further the enjoyment by all States, great or small, victor or vanquished, of access, on equal terms, to the trade and to the raw materials of the world which are needed for their economic prosperity;

Fifth, they desire to bring about the fullest collaboration between all nations in the economic field with the object of securing, for all, improved labor standards, economic advancement and social security;

Sixth, after the final destruction of the Nazi tyranny, they hope to see established a peace which will afford to all nations the means of dwelling in safety within their own boundaries, and which will afford assurance that all the men in all lands may live out their lives in freedom from fear and want;

Seventh, such a peace should enable all men to traverse the high seas and oceans without hindrance;

Eighth, they believe that all of the nations of the world, for realistic as well as spiritual reasons must come to the abandonment of the use of force. Since no future peace can be maintained if land, sea or air armaments continue to be employed by nations which threaten, or may threaten, aggression outside of their frontiers, they believe, pending the establishment of a wider and permanent system of general security, that the disarmament of such nations is essential. They will likewise aid and encourage all other practicable measures which will lighten for peace-loving peoples the crushing burden of armaments.

Winston Churchill and Franklin Delano Roosevelt, "Atlantic Charter," August 14, 1941.

Document 5: Stalin Calls the Soviet People to Arms Against Germany

In June 1941 Hitler turned against his Soviet allies and invaded Russia. Soviet premier Joseph Stalin was determined that Nazi leader Adolf Hitler's troops would not conquer his people, no matter what sacrifices they had to make to ensure victory. In this July 1941 radio broadcast, he tells the Soviet people what has to be done to "put an end to the danger hovering over our country" and precisely what measures must be taken to defeat the Germans.

Above all, it is essential that our people, the Soviet people, should understand the full immensity of the danger that threatens our country and should abandon all complacency, all heedlessness, all those moods of peaceful constructive work which were so natural before the war, but which are fatal today when war has fundamentally changed everything.

The enemy is cruel and implacable. He is out to seize our lands, watered with our sweat, to seize our grain and oil secured by our labor. He is out to restore the rule of landlords, to restore Tsarism, to destroy national culture and the national state existence of the Russians . . . and the other free people of the Soviet Union, to Germanize them, to convert them into the slaves of German princes and barons.

Thus the issue is one of life or death for the Soviet State, for the peoples of the USSR; the issue is whether the peoples of the Soviet Union shall remain free or fall into slavery.

The Soviet people must realize this and abandon all heedlessness, they must mobilize themselves and reorganize all their work on new, wartime bases, when there can be no mercy to the enemy.

Further, there must be no room in our ranks for whimperers and cowards, for panic-mongers and deserters. . . .

All our work must be immediately reconstructed on a war footing, everything must be subordinated to the interests of the front and the task of organizing the demolition of the enemy. . . .

The peoples of the Soviet Union must rise against the enemy and defend their rights and their land. The Red Army, Red Navy and all citizens of the Soviet Union must defend every inch of Soviet soil, must fight to the last drop of blood for our towns and villages, must display the daring initiative and intelligence that are inherent in our people.

We must organize all-round assistance for the Red Army, ensure powerful reinforcements for its ranks and the supply of everything it requires, we must organize the rapid transport of troops and military freight and extensive aid to the wounded.

We must strengthen the Red Army's rear, subordinating all our work to this cause. All our industries must be got to work with greater intensity to produce more rifles, machine-guns, artillery, bullets, shells, airplanes; we must organize the guarding of factories, power-stations, telephonic and telegraphic communications and arrange effective air raid precautions in all localities. . . .

All who by their panic-mongering and cowardice hinder the work of defence, no matter who they are, must be immediately hauled before the military tribunal. In case of forced retreat of Red

Army units, all rolling stock must be evacuated, the enemy must not be left a single engine, a single railway car, not a single pound of grain or a gallon of fuel.

The collective farmers must drive off all their cattle, and turn over their grain to the safe-keeping of State authorities for transportation to the rear. All valuable property, including non-ferrous metals, grain and fuel which cannot be withdrawn, must without fail be destroyed.

In areas occupied by the enemy, guerrilla units, mounted and on foot, must be formed, diversionist groups must be organized to combat the enemy troops, to foment guerrilla warfare everywhere, to blow up bridges and roads, damage telephone and telegraph lines, set fire to forests, stores, transports.

In the occupied regions conditions must be made unbearable for the enemy and all his accomplices. They must be hounded and annihilated at every step, and all their measures frustrated.

This war with fascist Germany cannot be considered an ordinary war. It is not only a war between two armies, it is also a great war of the entire Soviet people against the German fascist forces.

The aim of this national war in defense of our country against the fascist oppressors is not only elimination of the danger hanging over our country, but also aid to all European peoples groaning under the yoke of German fascism.

In this war of liberation we shall not be alone. In this great war we shall have loyal allies in the peoples of Europe and America, including the German people who are enslaved by the Hitlerite despots.

Our war for the freedom of our country will merge with the struggle of the peoples of Europe and America for their independence, for democratic liberties.

It will be a united front of peoples standing for freedom and against enslavement and threats of enslavement by Hitler's fascist armies.

Joseph Stalin, broadcast to the Soviet people, July 3, 1941, from *Soviet Russia Today*, August 1941.

Document 6: The Role of the German Soldier in the Soviet Union

German military leaders, concerned that their troops in the Soviet Union were not being tough enough on the Soviets, made sure the soldiers of the Wehrmacht knew what was expected of them. According to this document that Field Marshal Walter von Reichenau issued to his troops in 1941, soldiers were to cease any kindnesses to natives and prisoners of war and do everything in their power to suppress Communism and Soviet Jewry.

Regarding the conduct of troops towards the bolshevistic system, vague ideas are still prevalent in many cases. The most essential aim of war against the Jewish-bolshevistic system is a complete destruction of their means of power and the elimination of Asiatic influence from the European culture. In this connection the troops are facing tasks which exceed the one-sided routine of soldiering. The soldier in the Eastern territories is not merely a fighter according to the rules of the art of war but also a bearer of ruthless national ideology and the avenger of bestialities which have been inflicted upon German and racially related nations.

Therefore the soldier must have full understanding for the necessity of a severe but just revenge on subhuman Jewry. The Army has to aim at another purpose, i.e. the annihilation of revolts in the hinterland, which, as experience proves, have always been caused by Jews.

The combating of the enemy behind the front line is still not being taken seriously enough. Treacherous, cruel partisans and degenerate women are still being made prisoners-of-war and guerilla fighters dressed partly in uniform or plain clothes and vagabonds are still being treated as proper soldiers, and sent to prisoner-of-war camps. In fact, captured Russian officers talk even mockingly about Soviet agents moving openly about the roads and very often eating at German field kitchens. Such an attitude of the troops can only be explained by complete thoughtlessness, so it is now high time for the commanders to clarify the meaning of the pressing struggle.

The feeding of the natives and of prisoners-of-war who are not working for the Armed forces from Army kitchens is an equally misunderstood humanitarian act as is the giving of cigarettes and bread. Things which the people at home can spare under great sacrifices and things which are being brought by the command to the front under great difficulties, should not be given to the enemy by the soldier even if they originate from booty. It is an important part of our supply.

When retreating the Soviets have often set buildings on fire. The troops should be interested in extinguishing of fires only as far as it is necessary to secure sufficient numbers of billets. Otherwise the disappearance of symbols of the former bolshevistic rule even in the form of buildings is part of the struggle of destruction. Neither historic nor artistic considerations are of any importance in the Eastern territories. The command issues the necessary directives for the securing of raw material and plants, essential for war economy. The complete disarming of the civilian population in the rear of the fighting troops is imperative considering the long vulnerable lines of communications. Where possible, captured weapons and ammunition should be stored and guarded. Should this be impossible because of the situation of the battle, the weapons and ammunition will be rendered useless. If isolated partisans are found using firearms in the rear of the army drastic measures are to be taken. These measures will be extended to that part of the male population who were in a position to hinder or report the attacks. The indifference of numerous apparently anti-Soviet elements which originates from a "wait and see" attitude, must give way to a clear decision for active collaboration. If not, no one can complain about being judged and treated a member of the Soviet system.

The fear of German counter-measures must be stronger than threats of the wandering bolshevistic remnants. Regardless of all future political considerations the soldier has to fulfill two tasks:

1. Complete annihilation of the false Bolshevist doctrine of the Soviet State and its armed forces.
2. The pitiless extermination of foreign treachery and cruelty and thus the protection of the lives of military personnel in Russia.

This is the only way to fulfill our historic task to liberate the German people once and for all from the Asiatic-Jewish danger.

Field Marshal Walter von Reichenau, "Conduct of Troops in Eastern Territories," October 10, 1941.

Document 7: President Roosevelt Appeals to the Japanese Emperor

Grave concern about the increase in the number of Japanese troops and military bases in southern Indochina led American president Franklin Roosevelt to send this message to the Emperor of Japan. In the message, Roosevelt explains why recent developments in the Pacific might well lead to the end of peace between the United States and Japan and appeals to the emperor to avoid conflict by withdrawing Japanese forces from the South Pacific.

Almost a century ago the President of the United States addressed to the Emperor of Japan a message extending an offer of friendship of the people of the United States to the people of Japan.

That offer was accepted, and in the long period of unbroken peace and friendship which has followed, our respective nations, through the virtues of their peoples and the wisdom of their rulers have prospered and have substantially helped humanity.

Only in situations of extraordinary importance to our two countries need I address to Your Majesty messages on matters of state. I feel I should now so address you because of the deep and far-reaching emergency which appears to be in formation.

Developments are occurring in the Pacific area which threaten to deprive each of our nations and all humanity of the beneficial influence of the long peace between our two countries. Those developments contain tragic possibilities.

The people of the United States, believing in peace and in the right of nations to live and let live, have eagerly watched the conversations between our two Governments during these past months. We have hoped for a termination of the present conflict between Japan and China. We have hoped that a peace of the Pacific could be consummated in such a way that nationalities of many diverse peoples could exist side by side without fear of invasion; that unbearable burdens of armaments could be lifted for them all; and that all peoples would resume commerce without discrimination against or in favor of any nation.

I am certain that it will be clear to Your Majesty, as it is to me, that in seeking these great objectives both Japan and the United States should agree to eliminate any form of military threat. This seemed essential to the attainment of the high objectives.

More than a year ago Your Majesty's Government concluded an agreement with the Vichy Government by which five or six thousand Japanese troops were permitted to enter into Northern French Indo-China for the protection of Japanese troops which were operating against China further north. And this Spring and Summer the Vichy Government permitted further Japanese military forces to enter into Southern French Indo-China for the common defense of French Indo-China. I think I am correct in saying that no attack has been made upon Indo-China, nor that any has been contemplated.

During the past few weeks it has become clear to the world that Japanese military, naval and air forces have been sent to Southern Indo-China in such large numbers as to create a reasonable doubt on the part of other nations that this continuing concentration in Indo-China is not defensive in its character.

Because these continuing concentrations in Indo-China have

reached such large proportions and because they extend now to the southeast and the southwest corners of that Peninsula, it is only reasonable that the people of the Philippines, of the hundreds of Islands of the East Indies, of Malaya and of Thailand itself are asking themselves whether these forces of Japan are preparing or intending to make attack in one or more of these many directions.

I am sure that Your Majesty will understand that the fear of all these peoples is a legitimate fear inasmuch as it involves their peace and their national existence. I am sure that Your Majesty will understand why the people of the United States in such large numbers look askance at the establishment of military, naval and air bases manned and equipped so greatly as to constitute armed forces capable of measures of offense.

It is clear that a continuance of such a situation is unthinkable.

None of the peoples whom I have spoken of above can sit either indefinitely or permanently on a keg of dynamite.

There is absolutely no thought on the part of the United States of invading Indo-China if every Japanese soldier or sailor were to be withdrawn therefrom.

I think that we can obtain the same assurance from the Governments of the East Indies, the Governments of Malaya and the Government of Thailand. I would even undertake to ask for the same assurance on the part of the Government of China. Thus a withdrawal of the Japanese forces from Indo-China would result in the assurance of peace throughout the whole of the South Pacific area.

I address myself to Your Majesty at this moment in the fervent hope that Your Majesty may, as I am doing, give thought in this definite emergency a way of dispelling the dark clouds. I am confident that both of us, for the sake of the peoples not only of our own great countries but for the sake of humanity in neighboring territories, have a sacred duty to restore traditional amity and prevent further death and destruction in the world.

Franklin D. Roosevelt, Message to the Emperor of Japan, *Department of State Bulletin*, Vol. V, No. 129, December 13, 1941.

Document 8: Adolf Hitler Tells the French Germany Is Not Their Enemy

On November 11, 1942, German troops occupied Vichy France. The day before, in this address to the French people, German chancellor Adolf Hitler explained that Germany bore no animosity toward the French. He advised the French that only by cutting across unoccupied France could German troops stop any British and American landing attempts.

Frenchmen, officers and men of the French Army:

On Sept. 3, 1939, the British government without cause or reason declared war upon Germany. Those responsible for this war unfortunately succeeded at that time in instigating the French government to join the declaration of war.

For Germany this constituted an unbearable provocation. The German government had never made any claims on her which might have caused her offense. The German people, who then had to face this aggression while sacrificing the blood of its sons, never felt any hatred for France.

Nevertheless, this war started in this fashion and involved a great many families of the two countries in grief and sorrow.

After the crumbling of the Anglo-French front which, after the flight of the British to Dunkerque, developed into a catastrophe, France asked Germany for an armistice. Under the armistice Germany asked nothing which might be incompatible with the honor of the French Army. Precautions, however, had to be taken in order to prevent the fight from being started again in the interests of the British war-mongers by means of paid agents.

Germany had no intention whatsoever of humiliating France or of infringing on the integrity of the French Empire. She hoped by a subsequent reasonable peace to achieve an atmosphere of mutual understanding in Europe.

Since that time, Great Britain and now also the United States have sought to set foot again on French soil in order to continue the war, as suits their interests, on French territory.

After several attempts had come to a lamentable end, the Anglo-American attack was launched against the colonists of North and West Africa.

Having regard to the weakness of the French forces in those parts the enemy would find it an easier ground for operations than in the west, where the country is protected by Germany.

The German government has known for twenty-four hours that plans of these operations provide that the next attack will be made against Corsica, in order to occupy that island, and against the south coast of France.

In these circumstances I felt compelled to order the German Army immediately to march through the unoccupied zone—and this is now being done—and to march to the point aimed at by the Anglo-American landing troops.

The German Army does not come as an enemy of the French people nor of its soldiers, nor does it intend to govern these territories. It has a single aim—to repel together with its allies any landing attempt by the Anglo-American forces.

Marshal Petain and his government are entirely free and are in the position to fulfill their duty as in the past. From now on nothing stands in the way of realization of their requests, made earlier, to come to Versailles to govern France from there.

The German forces have been ordered to see to it that the French people are inconvenienced as little as possible.

The French people must, however, bear in mind that by the attitude of their government in 1939 the German people were thrown into a grievous war which threw hundreds of thousands of families into peril and grief.

The German government no less than its soldiers has every wish within bounds of what is possible not only to protect the frontiers of France jointly with the French Army but also before all to assist in preserving in the future the African possessions of European nations against acts of brigandage.

Only where blind fanaticism or agents in the pay of Britain oppose the advance of our troops will the decision be left to the force of arms.

Numerous Frenchmen will, on the other hand, show an understandable desire to be delivered from occupation, but they should all know that the German soldier, too, would prefer to live and work peacefully in his own country by the side of his wife and his children in his paternal home.

The sooner this power, which in the past so often has plundered France and which in this moment is again trying to rob her, will be annihilated, the sooner the wishes of Frenchmen of the occupied zone and of the German soldiers will find together their realization.

All particular questions are regulated and will find their solution in agreement with French authorities.

Adolf Hitler, *Inter-Allied Review*, November 10, 1942.

Document 9: A Plane Comes Home

Anyone stationed at an airfield during World War II knew that not all the planes and crews that went out would come back. But knowing did not make their responses any less emotional. Reporter Ernie Pyle describes the mood swing from desolation to elation at an airdrome in North Africa when a Flying Fortress reported missing returned hours after all the other planes—with all the crew aboard and alive.

It was late afternoon at our desert airdrome. The sun was lazy, the air was warm, and a faint haze of propeller dust hung over the field, giving it softness. It was time for the planes to start coming back from their mission, and one by one they did come—big Flying Fortresses and fiery little Lightnings. Nobody paid a great deal of attention, for this returning was a daily routine thing.

Finally they were all in—all that is, except one. Operations reported a Fortress missing. Returning pilots said it had lagged behind and lost altitude just after leaving the target. The last report said the Fortress couldn't stay in the air more than five minutes. Hours had passed since then. So it was gone.

Ten men were in that plane. The day's accomplishments had been great, but the thought of ten lost friends cast a pall over us. . . .

After the last report, half a dozen of us went to the high control tower. We went there every evening, for two things—to watch the sunset, and to get word on the progress of the German bombers that frequently came just after dusk to blast our airdrome. . . .

As we stood on the tower looking down over this scene, the day began folding itself up. Fighter planes, which had patrolled the field all day, were coming in. All the soldiers in the tent camps had finished supper. That noiseless peace that sometimes comes just before dusk hung over the airdrome. Men talked in low tones. . . .

And then an electric thing happened. Far off in the dusk a red flare shot into the sky. It made an arc against the dark background of the mountains and fell to the earth. It couldn't be anything else. It had to be. The ten dead men were coming home!

"Where's the flare gun? Gimme a green flare!" yelled an officer.

He ran to the edge of the tower, shouted, "Look out below!" and fired a green rocket into the air. Then we saw the plane—just a tiny black speck. It seemed almost on the ground, it was so low, and in the first glance we could sense that it was barely moving, barely staying in the air. Crippled and alone, two hours behind all the rest, it was dragging itself home.

I was a layman, and no longer of the fraternity that flies, but I could feel. And at that moment I felt something close to human love for that faithful, battered machine, that far dark speck struggling toward us with such pathetic slowness.

All of us stood tense, hardly remembering anyone else was there. With all our nerves we seemed to pull the plane toward us. I suspect a photograph would have shown us all leaning slightly to the left. Not one of us thought the plane would ever make the field, but on it came—so slowly that it was cruel to watch.

It reached the far end of the airdrome, still holding its pathetic little altitude. It skimmed over the tops of parked planes, and kept on, actually reaching out—it seemed to us—for the runway.

A few hundred yards more now. Could it? Would it? Was it truly possible?

They cleared the last plane, they were over the runway. They settled slowly. The wheels touched softly. And as the plane rolled on down the runway the thousands of men around that vast field suddenly realized that they were weak and that they could hear their hearts pounding.

The last of the sunset died, and the sky turned into blackness, which would help the Germans if they came on schedule with their bombs. But nobody cared. Our ten dead men were miraculously back from the grave.

Ernie Pyle, *Here Is Your War.* New York: Henry Holt and Company, 1943.

Document 10: Himmler Admonishes the SS to Be Loyal Only to Their Own

From the beginning, Nazi leaders and their followers considered them-selves superior to everyone else in general and to Jews in particular. Aryan Germans were told that they need not be loyal to or care about anyone not of "your own blood." Heinrich Himmler, head of the Schutzstaffeln, *the Nazi Party's own armed forces known as the SS, re-inforces that attitude in this speech he made to SS group leaders early in October 1943.*

It is absolutely wrong to project our own harmless soul with its deep feelings, our kindheartedness, our idealism, upon alien peo-ples. . . . This is true, beginning with the Czechs and the Slovenes, to whom we brought their sense of nationhood. They themselves were incapable of it, but we invented it for them.

One principle must be absolute for the SS man: we must be honest, decent, loyal and comradely to members of our own blood and to no one else. What happens to the Russians, what happens to the Czechs, is a matter of utter indifference to me. Such good blood of our own kind as there may be among the nations we shall acquire for ourselves, if necessary by taking away the children and bringing them up among us. Whether the other peoples live in comfort or perish of hunger interests me only in so far as we need them as slaves for our own culture; apart from that it does not in-terest me. Whether or not 10,000 Russian women collapse from exhaustion while digging a tank ditch interests me only in so far as the tank ditch is completed for Germany. We shall never be rough or heartless where it is not necessary; that is clear. We Germans, who are the only people in the world who have a decent attitude toward animals, will also adopt a decent attitude to these human animals, but it is a crime against our own blood to worry about them and to bring them ideals.

I shall speak to you here with all frankness of a very serious subject. We shall now discuss it absolutely openly among ourselves, nevertheless we shall never speak of it in public. I mean the evacuation of the Jews, the extermination of the Jewish people. It is one of those things which is easy to say. "The Jewish people is to be exterminated," says every party member. "That's clear, it's part of our program, elimination of the Jews, extermination, right, we'll do it." And then they all come along, the eighty million good Germans, and each one has his decent Jew. Of course the others are swine, but this one is a first-class Jew. Of all those who talk like this, not one has watched, not one has stood up to it. Most of you know what it means to see a hundred corpses lying together, five hundred, or a thousand. To have gone through this and yet—apart from a few exceptions, examples of human weakness—to have remained decent, this has made us hard. This is a glorious page in our history that has never been written and shall never be written.

Heinrich Himmler, speech to SS group leaders, October 4, 1943.

Document 11: The Bataan Death March

On April 9, 1942, the Japanese overran Bataan, the northernmost island in the Philippines. The Japanese marched 76,000 prisoners they took on Bataan sixty-five miles to the north to a prisoner-of-war camp. All along the way, they brutalized their captives. At least 5,000 Filipinos and more than 600 Americans did not survive the trek, which came to be known as the Bataan Death March. Soldier-poet Jesse Knowles, who survived the march but not the captivity that followed, bared his emotions in this poem, which he wrote in 1943.

Strange things were done under the tropic sun
By the men in Khaki twill
Those tropic nights have seen some sights
That would make your heart stand still
Those mountain trails could spin some tales
That no man would ever like
But the worst of all was after the fall
When we started on that hike

T'was the 7th of December in '41

When they hit Hawaii as the day begun
T'was a Sunday morning and all was calm
When out of nowhere there came the bombs
It didn't last long but the damage was done
America was at war with the rising sun

Now over in the Philippines we heard the news
And it shook every man clean down to his shoes
It seemed like a dream to begin
But soon every soldier was a fighting man
Each branch was ready to do its part
Artillery, infantry, Nichols and Clark

And then they came on that Monday noon
They hit Clark field like a typhoon
That Monday night the moon was clear
They razed Nichols from front to rear
As the days went by more bombers came
And soon only a few P-40's remained

Then the orders came and said retreat
That no man would be seen on the city streets
So across the bay we moved at night
Away from Manila and out of sight
Deep into the jungles of Bataan
Where 15,000 were to make a stand

Here we fought as a soldier should
As the days went by we spilled our blood
Tho' the rumors came and went by night
That convoy never came in sight

April 7th was a fatal day
When the word went around that we couldn't stay
That the front line was due to fall
So the troops moved back one and all

The very next day the surrender came
Then we were men without a name
You may think here's Where the story ends
But actually here's where it begins
Tho' we fought and didn't see victory
The story of that march will go down in history

We marched along in columns of four

Living and seeing the horrors of war
And when a man fell along the way
A cold bayonet would make him pay
For those four months he fought on Bataan
Then they'd kill him 'cause he couldn't stand

The tropic sun would sweat us dry
For the pumps were few that we passed by
But on we marched to a place unknown
A place to rest and a place to call home
Home not that you might know
But home to man that suffered a blow

Then to O'Donnell Camp en masse
Some never back thru' those gates to pass
In Nipa huts we lived like beast
Bad rice and camotes were called a feast

Our minds went back to days gone by
When our throats were never dry
Of our wives, our mothers, and friends
Of our by-gone days and our many sins
And about four thousand passed away
And how many more no man can say
For no tomb stone marks the spot
Where thirty to fifty were buried in lot
Piled together as a rubbish heap
The remains of men
Who were forced to retreat

Jesse Knowles, "They," April 1943.

Document 12: Operation Overlord: Eisenhower's Great Crusade

Operation Overlord, the Allied invasion of France, began June 6, 1944, when Allied Expeditionary Forces commanded by American general Dwight D. Eisenhower landed on the beaches of Normandy. Eisenhower believed without a doubt that the invasion would bring a quick end to the war. In this message to the troops the morning of the invasion, he tells the soldiers, sailors, and airmen of the Expeditionary Forces that they are about to mount a Great Crusade, which they can win in spite of the odds and which will result in an end to the war and to Nazi power.

Soldiers, Sailors and Airmen of the Allied Expeditionary Forces:
You are about to embark upon the Great Crusade, toward which

we have striven these many months. The eyes of the world are upon you. The hopes and prayers of liberty-loving people everywhere march with you. In company with our brave Allies and brothers-in-arms on other Fronts you will bring about the destruction of the German war machine, the elimination of Nazi tyranny over oppressed peoples of Europe, and security for ourselves in a free world.

Your task will not be an easy one. Your enemy is well trained, well equipped and battle-hardened. He will fight savagely.

But this is the year 1944! Much has happened since the Nazi triumphs of 1940–41. The United Nations have inflicted upon the Germans great defeats, in open battle, man-to-man. Our air offensive has seriously reduced their strength in the air and their capacity to wage war on the ground. Our Home Fronts have given us an overwhelming superiority in weapons and munitions of war, and placed at our disposal great reserves of trained fighting men. The tide has turned! The free men of the world are marching together to Victory!

I have full confidence in your courage, devotion to duty and skill in battle. We will accept nothing less than full victory!

Good Luck! And let us all beseech the blessing of Almighty God upon this great and noble undertaking.

Dwight David Eisenhower, "The Great Crusade," June 6, 1944.

Document 13: The Interests of France First and Above All in War and Peace

French general Charles de Gaulle gained the trust of the French people and recognition as leader of the Free French forces during the war. In his mind, France had been and still was, the temporary setback resulting from the war notwithstanding, the foremost country of Europe. In this 1945 broadcast to the French people, de Gaulle reminds them of the glory of France and makes clear his intention not to allow France to be bound by any postwar decisions made without French participation and agreement.

On the Oder and Rhine Rivers the Allies are now in contact with the German body proper. In spite of the telling reverses sustained by the enemy, we must, nevertheless, expect him to resist desperately. Germany's present leaders cannot doubt that they have lost the war. But they persist in hoping that they can make the struggle last until some event will cause either division or weariness among her adversaries—in which case Germany would find a favorable solution. In case they should not have this chance of salvation, they are preparing a policy of total defeat, hoping that chaos in Germany—coming in a world that is exhausted and divided—could lead to upheaval and antagonism in other countries, thereby placing them on the same level as Germany. Hitler and his entourage, who can judge the extent of their country's misfortune, intend to retain until the very end the appearance of unconquerable leaders, whose nostalgic memory may some day haunt the dreams of a great and desperate people.

In this supreme phase of the struggle as in the peace which will follow, the rights and duties of France are in the front rank of all rights and duties. In spite of all that France has suffered by a temporary setback, her power is obviously necessary on the Western front to crush enemy resistance deep within Germany. . . .

Tomorrow, France's effort will be relatively greater, since in three months' time we shall have doubled the number of units we had in line last December. We must also add that our seaports, railways and our air fields are the backbone of the common battle.

Concerning the total occupation of German territory, which will necessarily follow the hostilities, it is obvious that the French army will gradually become the dominant element in the West.

Whatever may be the duration and vicissitudes of this war, it is needless to add that the settlements which emerge from it will be of vital importance to France. For more than one and a half centuries our country has never ceased to grow weaker in comparison to other countries, inasmuch as she has had to withstand gigantic wars which have cost her much more than any nation in the world.

Naturally, her political balance, her economic and demographic development, her vital progress, and above all the unity of her citizens, which is the condition for balance, development, and progress, were seriously compromised by these wars. In short, our national life, within France and abroad, has gone from upheaval to upheaval for generations and each of these upheavals has been more ruinous than the preceding one. This time France nearly perished as a free nation and the sources of her activity have been cruelly affected. The rest of the world, and above all, the nations of Europe, have greatly suffered because of her weakness, since it is a kind of law that no one is safe when France is in trouble. . . .

As for the future peace settlement or any other arrangement that would concern it, we have informed our Allies and we have said publicly that France would, of course, be bound by nothing that she had not had the opportunity to discuss and approve on the same grounds as the other nations. . . .

When the vise-like grip of the battles of Europe and Asia has been relaxed, when we shall have regained our freedom of action and all our territories, we shall be ready to participate spiritedly in the vast programs and negotiations from which a world peace organization will emerge. . . .

This is France's immediate plan for war and peace. Circumstances are such that, if we are determined and act accordingly, we shall carry out this plan.

By achieving our aim we will create general conditions of dignity, power and security for our country. These conditions have been lacking for so long, since the misunderstanding of realities, deprived us of them after the exhausting victory of 1918, and consequently we have been living in an atmosphere of discontent, uncertainty and threats, all of which are contrary to a nation's rebirth. However, even if on this supreme occasion we succeeded in creating ideal conditions for our country among other nations, even if we help build the finest possible construction for world co-operation, all this would be in vain if we did not achieve an internal rebirth which is essential for our return to the front rank of the great nations.

We must make a great effort to raise ourselves to the rank where we wish to be. For the time being, it is quite true that the necessities, trials and ruins of war are limiting us in this field and forcing us to cope with the most urgent problems; in other words, we must fight to live. But as the sun of victory is gradually rising on the horizon, the nation is discovering the future, and is wondering about the road that she must follow to rebuild and develop herself politically, economically, socially, demographically, and morally.

Charles de Gaulle, Broadcast on French Policy in War and Peace, French Press and Information Service, February 2, 1945.

Document 14: Big Three Agreement at Yalta

In February 1945, with victory in sight, Allied leaders Joseph Stalin, Winston Churchill, and Franklin Roosevelt met at Yalta in the Crimea from February 4–11 to plan the postwar reorganization of Europe. They set a date and ground rules for a United Nations conference for a new world organization and agreed that France would join the United States, Britain, and the Soviet Union in the occupation of postwar Germany, that the Soviet Union would fight Japan if they would receive occupation areas in the East, and that the Allies would install a representative government in Poland. These and other decisions were spelled out in this Protocol of Proceedings of Crimea Conference.

II. DECLARATION OF LIBERATED EUROPE

The following declaration has been approved:

The Premier of the Union of Soviet Socialist Republics, the Prime Minister of the United Kingdom and the President of the United States of America have consulted with each other in the common interests of the people of their countries and those of liberated Europe. They jointly declare their mutual agreement to concert during the temporary period of instability in liberated Europe the policies of their three Governments in assisting the peoples liberated from the domination of Nazi Germany and the peoples of the former Axis satellite states of Europe to solve by democratic means their pressing political and economic problems.

The establishment of order in Europe and the rebuilding of national economic life must be achieved by processes which will enable the liberated peoples to destroy the last vestiges of nazism and fascism and to create democratic institutions of their own choice. This is a principle of the Atlantic Charter—the right of all people to choose the form of government under which they will live—the restoration of sovereign rights and self-government to those peoples who have been forcibly deprived to them by the aggressor nations.

To foster the conditions in which the liberated people may exercise these rights, the three governments will jointly assist the people in any European liberated state or former Axis state in Europe where, in their judgment conditions require,

(a) to establish conditions of internal peace; (b) to carry out emergency relief measures for the relief of distressed peoples; (c) to form interim governmental authorities broadly representative of all democratic elements in the population and pledged to the earliest possible establishment through free elections of Governments responsive to the will of the people; and (d) to facilitate where necessary the holding of such elections.

The three Governments will consult the other United Nations and provisional authorities or other Governments in Europe when matters of direct interest to them are under consideration.

When, in the opinion of the three Governments, conditions in any European liberated state or former Axis satellite in Europe make such action necessary, they will immediately consult together on the measure necessary to discharge the joint responsibilities set forth in this declaration.

By this declaration we reaffirm our faith in the principles of the Atlantic Charter, our pledge in the Declaration by the United Nations and our determination to build in cooperation with other peace-loving nations world order, under law, dedicated to peace, security, freedom and general well-being of all mankind.

In issuing this declaration, the three powers express the hope that the Provisional Government of the French Republic may be associated with them in the procedure suggested.

[End first section published February 13, 1945.]

III. DISMEMBERMENT OF GERMANY

It was agreed that Article 12 (a) of the Surrender terms for Germany should be amended to read as follows:

"The United Kingdom, the United States of America and the Union of Soviet Socialist Republics shall possess supreme authority with respect to Germany. In the exercise of such authority they will take such steps, including the complete dismemberment of Germany as they deem requisite for future peace and security.". . .

V. REPARATION

1. Germany must pay in kind for the losses caused by her to the Allied nations in the course of the war. Reparations are to be received in the first instance by those countries which have borne the main burden of the war, have suffered the heaviest losses and have organized victory over the enemy.

2. Reparation in kind is to be exacted from Germany in three following forms:

(a) Removals within two years from the surrender of Germany or the cessation of organized resistance from the national wealth of Germany located on the territory of Germany herself as well as outside her territory (equipment, machine tools, ships, rolling stock, German investments abroad, shares of industrial, transport and other enterprises in Germany, etc.), these removals to be carried out chiefly for the purpose of destroying the war potential of Germany. (b) Annual deliveries of goods from current production for a period to be fixed. (c) Use of German labor.

3. For the working out on the above principles of a detailed plan for exaction of reparation from Germany an Allied reparation commission will be set up in Moscow. It will consist of three representatives—one from the Union of Soviet Socialist Republics, one from the United Kingdom and one from the United States of America.

4. With regard to the fixing of the total sum of the reparation as well as the distribution of it among the countries which suffered from the German aggression, the Soviet and American delegations agreed as follows:

"The Moscow reparation commission should take in its initial studies as a basis for discussion the suggestion of the Soviet Government that the total sum of the reparation in accordance with the points (a) and (b) of the Paragraph 2 should be 22 billion dollars and that 50 per cent should go to the Union of Soviet Socialist Republics."

"Protocol of Proceedings of Crimea Conference," February 11, 1945, *A Decade of American Foreign Policy: Basic Documents, 1941–49*, Prepared at the request of the Senate Committee on Foreign Relations by the Staff of the Committee and the Department of State. Washington, DC: Government Printing Office, 1950.

Document 15: Memories of the Liberation of Buchenwald

Adolf Hitler sought to create a Master Aryan Race that would rule the world for 1,000 years as the Third Reich, or third German Empire. His belief that all non-Aryans and other "undesirables" had to be purged resulted in the establishment of concentration camps in which millions of Jews, communists, gypsies, homosexuals, political enemies, and other "undesirables" were imprisoned, brutalized, and put to death. On April 11, 1945, nineteen-year-old Army private Harry Herder was among the American soldiers sent to "liberate" the Buchenwald camp in Germany. What the liberators discovered there stunned them profoundly.

When we started there was no way for those of us at the bottom of the ladder to have any idea at all where we were going or what we were up to. What I do remember is that we eventually drove up some gentle valley where there were trees on either side of us, when we made a sharp left turn. . . . There it was: a great high barbed wire fence at least ten feet high. Between us and the fence and running parallel to the fence was a dirt road, with high guard towers every fifty yards or so. Beyond the fence were two more layers of barbed wire fence not quite as tall. There seemed to be about five yards between those fences. The barbed wire in those fences was laced in a fine mesh, so finely meshed no one was going to get through it. Our tanks slowed down, but they did not stop; they blew straight at and through the barbed wire. . . . When we broke through the first of those fences we got a clue, the first clue as to what we had come upon, but we had no real comprehension at all of what was to assault our senses for the next hours, the next days.

We hit those fences with enough speed so that it was unclear to me whether it was the first level, or the second, or the third, but at least one of those levels was hot with electricity. We hit the fences, blew through them, and shorted out whichever it was on the damp ground. Once we were through the fences we turned left a bit and took off up a gentle cleared hill toward a concentration of buildings. . . .

I remember scouting out the area in front of us quickly with my eyes. There were no great details, but I saw that over to the left, next to, and just inside of the fence, and to our front, were some major buildings, and next to one of those buildings was a monster of a chimney, a monster both in diameter and in height. Black smoke was pouring out of it, and blowing away from us, but we could still smell it. An ugly horrible smell. A vicious smell.

The tank which we were riding, along with two other tanks in our column, wheeled to the left so that the three of them made a front. Two more columns containing the rest of our company, off to our right, made the same maneuver so that all of us presented one front. Our Company Commander and the commander of the tank destroyer outfit were riding in a jeep somewhere near the middle of all of that mess. . . .

Slowly, as we formed up, a ragged group of human beings started to creep out of and from between the buildings in front of us. As we watched these men, the number and the different types of buildings came to my attention. From them came these human beings, timidly, slowly, deliberately showing their hands, all in a sort of uniform, or bits and pieces of a uniform, made from horribly coarse cloth with stripes running vertically. The stripes alternating a dull gray with a dark blue. Some of those human beings wore pants made of the material, some had shirt/jackets, and some had hats. Some only had one piece of the uniform, others had two, many had all three parts. They came out of the buildings and just stood there. . . .

The jeeps, our company commander's and a few others, rolled forward very slowly toward these people, and, as they parted, drove slowly through them, to the brick building next to that tall chimney, and our officers disappeared inside. Our platoon sergeant had us form up some and relax, then signaled that horde of human beings to stand fast; he just held both hands up, palms out, and motioned them backwards slowly. Everything was very quiet. The tanks were all in slow idle.

Hesitatingly we inched closer to that strange group as they also started inching closer to us. Some of them spoke English, and asked, "Are you American?" We said we were, and the reaction of the whole mass was immediate: simultaneously on their faces were relaxation, ease, joy, and they all began chattering to us in a babble of tongues that we couldn't answer. . . .

It was then that the smell of the place started to get to me. Our noses, rebelling against the surroundings they were constantly subjected to were not functioning anywhere near normally. But now there was a new odor, thick and hanging, and it assaulted the senses.

There was still space between us and the group in front of us, the people on both sides now relaxed, one side considerably more jubilant than the other, but all of the tensions were gone. We were inching closer together when our platoon sergeant was called back to one of the tanks and got on the radio. He wasn't there but a few minutes, came back, formed up our platoon, and took us back away, toward the place where we had entered the camp, back toward the fences through which we had ripped holes. At each hole in the fence he left two of us. . . . We hadn't the vaguest idea what we had run into. Not yet. . . .

Containing the prisoners was not expected to be any trouble because they understood the need, and they were being provided for in every way that we could think of: the field hospital had just arrived, a big mess unit was on the way, loads of PX rations were coming. Sergeant Blowers told us that some of the prisoners spoke English. Then he got even quieter, looked at the ground for a moment, raised his eyes, and looking over our heads, began very softly, so softly we could barely hear him. He told us that this is what was called a "concentration camp", that we were about to see things we were in no way prepared for. He told us to look, to look as long as our stomachs lasted, and then to get out of there for a walk in the woods. . . .

Bill, Tim, and I started off through the trees, down the hill to the front gate which was only a couple of hundred yards away. The gate was a rectangular hole through the solid face of the building over which was office space and a hallway. High up above the opening for the gate was a heavy wooden beam with words carved into it in German script, Arbeit Macht Frei. In a clumsy way I attempted to translate the inscription to Bill and Tim as, "Work will make you free". The three of us headed through the gate, through the twenty or thirty feet to the other side of the building. We were slightly apprehensive of what we might see. . . . The lane we were walking on bent to the right as we cleared the building. We had barely made the turn, and there it was. In front of us a good bit, but plainly visible.

The bodies of human beings were stacked like cord wood. All of them dead. All of them stripped. The inspection I made of the pile was not very close, but the corpses seemed to be all male. The bottom layer of the bodies had a north/south orientation, the next layer went east/west, and they continued alternating. The stack was about five feet high, maybe a little more; I could see over the top. They extended down the hill, only a slight hill, for fifty to seventy-five feet. Human bodies neatly stacked, naked, ready for disposal. The arms and legs were neatly arranged, but an occasional limb dangled oddly. The bodies we could see were all face up. There was an aisle, then another stack, and another aisle, and more stacks. The Lord only knows how many there were.

Just looking at these bodies made one believe they had been starved to death. They appeared to be skin covering bones and nothing more. The eyes on some were closed, on others open. Bill, Tim, and I grew very quiet. I think my only comment was, "Jesus Christ.". . .

The three of us looked, and we walked down the edge of those stacks. I know I didn't count them—it wouldn't have mattered. We looked and said not a word. A group of guys from the company noticed us and said, "Wait till you see in there."

They pointed to a long building which was about two stories high, and butted up tightly to the chimney. It had two barn-like doors on either end of the building we were looking at, and the doors were standing open. . . . We moved . . . through the doors and felt the warmth immediately. Not far from the doors, and parallel to the front of the building, there was a brick wall, solid to the top of the building. In the wall were small openings fitted with iron doors. Those doors were a little more than two feet wide and about two and a half feet high; the tops of the doors had curved shapes much like the entrances to churches. Those iron doors were in sets, three high. There must have been more than ten of those sets, extending down that brick wall. Most of the doors were closed, but down near the middle a few stood open. Heavy metal trays had been pulled out of those openings, and on those trays were partially burned bodies. On one tray was a skull partially burned through, with a hole in the top; other trays held partially disintegrated arms and legs. It appeared that those trays could hold three bodies at a time. And the odor, my God, the odor.

I had enough. I couldn't take it any more. I left the building with Bill and Tim close behind me. As we passed through the door someone from the company said, "the crematorium." Until then I had no idea what a crematorium was.

It dawned on me much later—the number of bodies which could be burned at one time, three bodies to a tray, at least thirty trays—

and the Germans still couldn't keep up. The bodies on the stacks outside were growing at a faster rate than they could be burned. . . .

All of the German guards had packed up and moved out about three hours before our arrival. . . . When the Germans left, the crematorium was still going full blast, burning up a storm, the chimney belching out that black smoke. Our First Sergeant, Sergeant Blowers, our Company Commander, and the Leader of the TD group found the source of the fuel, and played around with one thing and another until they figured out how to turn the damned thing off.

That was the start. That was just the "openers". There was more, but it was impossible to assimilate it all at once.

Harry Herder Jr., "Liberation of Buchenwald," *Liberators*, http://remember.org/witness/herder.html.

Document 16: An Unlikely Hero

Not everyone of military age was willing to physically join the fight against the Axis. Although many of these people were patriots that sincerely believed that the Nazis and the Japanese must be stopped, some declined to render military service on the grounds of moral principle or religious belief. American Congressional Medal of Honor winner Desmond T. Doss, who served as a medical corpsman in several battles in the Pacific, was one of these conscientious objectors.

When World War II finally came along and presented his country's claim for services to a certain young Richmond, Va. citizen, by name Desmond T. Doss, that individual in turn presented some definite personal resistance to the whole idea. He was doing very nicely as a builder of ship's doors, stairways, and other woodwork—in short, as a "ship joiner"—and furthermore he belonged to a religious cult whose tenets forbade all carrying of arms, warfare, and killing.

In other words, Desmond T. Doss was . . . a conscientious objector. Though he refused to touch a weapon, however, he did not refuse his country's call altogether. Instead of a fighter, he became a medical corpsman, and in 1945 found himself in the thick of combat with the 77th Division, first at Guam, and later at Leyte and Okinawa. Wherever casualties were thickest, the figure of Pfc. Doss, in his white-circled helmet with its red crosses, was always in evidence; and for his devotion to duty under fire in the Leyte campaign he received the Bronze Star.

It was on Okinawa, bloodiest of Pacific battlegrounds, that this quiet, bespectacled pacifist in uniform rose to the top heights of personal heroism. There, on April 29, 1945, he was with the medical detachment when the 307th infantry desperately assaulted the Japs entrenched behind precipitous cliffs. Swept by heavy artillery, mortar, and machine-gun fire, the Americans were forced back, leaving 75 casualties behind them. But not Pfc. Desmond Doss. One by one, he managed to remove his wounded comrades from the inferno around them, and by means of a rope-supported litter lowered them over the cliff edge.

Three days later, he again distinguished himself by rescuing a wounded American 200 yards beyond the lines, in spite of constant enemy gunfire; and three days later still, assisted an artillery officer to the accompaniment of an enemy barrage from shells and small arms. Not content with that, discovering a badly hurt American lying within 25 feet of a cave-concealed Jap position, he crawled to the spot, bound up his wounds, and carried him a hundred yards back to safety.

That was on May 5th. Came the night of May 21st, and Doss found himself in a furious night attack near Shuri. Intrepid as always, he remained in the open, giving first aid to his injured fellow-soldiers—only to be himself dangerously wounded by a grenade. As the litter-bearers were carrying him away, came a sudden tank attack by the Japanese. Spying a more critically wounded man than himself nearby, Doss crawled off his litter and insisted that the bearers give priority attention to his comrade. While waiting for the litter men to return, he was hit a second time, but fortunately later recovered from both wounds.

This splendid record of a Pfc. who never bore arms for his country, yet heroically eased the pain and saved the lives of those who did, was made public property in a formal War Department citation; and on October 12, 1945, 26-year-old Desmond T. Doss, of Richmond, Va., had the honor of being awarded by President Truman the first Congressional Medal of Honor ever bestowed on a conscientious objector.

Lister R. Alwood, *Pick-Ups.* Chicago: Pick Hotels Corporation, 1947.

Document 17: 1945: A General's Victory Order

On June 6, 1944, the Allies invaded Europe. With the Russians advancing in the east and other Allied forces advancing from the south, they defeated the Germans and brought the war in Europe to an end. On May 8, 1945, the New York Times *published Supreme Allied Commander in Europe Dwight D. Eisenhower's Victory Order of the Day, which cel-*

ebrates the victory in Europe, applauds the participants' efforts and sacrifices, and advises everyone to remember that the war was won by a cooperative effort.

The crusade on which we embarked in the early summer of 1944 has reached its glorious conclusion. It is my especial privilege, in the name of all nations represented in this theatre of war, to commend each of you for the valiant performance of duty.

Though these words are feeble, they come from the bottom of a heart overflowing with pride in your loyal service and admiration for you as warriors. Your accomplishments at sea, in the air, on the ground and in the field of supply have astonished the world.

Even before the final week of the conflict you had put 5,000,000 of the enemy permanently out of the war. You have taken in stride military tasks so difficult as to be classed by many doubters as impossible. You have confused, defeated and destroyed your savagely fighting foe. On the road to victory you have endured every discomfort and privation and have surmounted every obstacle that ingenuity and desperation could throw in your path. You did not pause until our front was firmly joined up with the great Red Army coming from the east and other Allied forces coming from the south.

Full victory in Europe has been attained. Working and fighting together in single and indestructible partnership you have achieved a perfection in the unification of air, ground and naval power that will stand as a model in our time.

The route you have traveled through hundreds of miles is marked by the graves of former comrades. From them have been exacted the ultimate sacrifice. The blood of many nations—American, British, Canadian, French, Polish and others—has helped to gain the victory. Each of the fallen died as a member of a team to which you belong, bound together by a common love of liberty and a refusal to submit to enslavement. No monument of stone, no memorial of whatever magnitude could so well express our respect and veneration for their sacrifice as would the perpetuation of the spirit of comradeship in which they died.

As we celebrate victory in Europe let us remind ourselves that our common problems of the immediate and distant future can be best solved in the same conceptions of cooperation and devotion to the cause of human freedom as have made this Expeditionary Force such a mighty engine of righteous destruction. Let us have no part in the profitless quarrels in which other men will inevitably engage as to what country and what service won the European war.

Every man and every woman of every nation here represented has served according to his or her ability and efforts and each has contributed to the outcome. This we shall remember and in doing so we shall be revering each honored grave and be sending comfort to the loved ones of comrades who could not live to see this day.

Dwight D. Eisenhower, "Victory Order of the Day." *New York Times*, May 8, 1945.

Document 18: The Allied Powers Assume Supreme Authority over Germany

On June 5, 1945, following unconditional surrender by the Germans, the Allies released a fifteen-article Declaration that clearly delineated Allied expectations and requirements for Germany. The introductory portion of the Declaration, combined with Articles 1, 2, 12, and 13, sum up the nonmonetary costs to Germany.

The German armed forces on land, at sea and in the air have been completely defeated and have surrendered unconditionally and Germany, which bears responsibility for the war, is no longer capable of resisting the will of the victorious Powers. The unconditional surrender of Germany has thereby been effected, and Germany has become subject to such requirements as may now or hereafter be imposed upon her.

There is no central Government or authority in Germany capable of accepting responsibility for the maintenance of order, the administration of the country and compliance with the requirements of the victorious Powers.

It is in these circumstances necessary, without prejudice to any subsequent decisions that may be taken respecting Germany, to make provision for the cessation of any further hostilities on the part of the German armed forces, for the maintenance of order in Germany and for the administration of the country, and to announce the immediate requirements with which Germany must comply.

The Representatives of the Supreme Commands of the United States of America, the Union of Soviet Socialist Republics, the United Kingdom and the French Republic, hereinafter called the "Allied Representatives," acting by authority of their respective Governments and in the interests of the United Nations, accordingly make the following Declaration:

The Governments of the United States of America, the Union of Soviet Socialist Republics and the United Kingdom, and the Provisional Government of the French Republic, hereby assume supreme authority with respect to Germany, including all the powers possessed by the German Government, the High Command and any state, municipal, or local government or authority. The assumption, for the purposes stated above, of the said authority and powers does not affect the annexation of Germany.

The Governments of the United States of America, the Union of Soviet Socialist Republics and the United Kingdom, and the Provisional Government of the French Republic, will hereafter determine the boundaries of Germany or any part thereof and the status of Germany or of any area at present being part of German territory.

In virtue of the supreme authority and powers thus assumed by the four Governments, the Allied Representatives announce the following requirements arising from the complete defeat and unconditional surrender of Germany with which Germany must comply:

ARTICLE 1

Germany, and all German military, naval and air authorities and all forces under German control shall immediately cease hostilities in all theatres of war against the forces of the United Nations on land, at sea and in the air.

ARTICLE 2

(a) All armed forces of Germany or under German control, wherever they may be situated . . . shall be completely disarmed. . . .

(b) The personnel of the formations and units of all the forces referred to in paragraph (a) above shall, at the discretion of the Commander-in-Chief of the Armed Forces of the Allied State concerned, be declared to be prisoners of war. . . .

ARTICLE 12

The Allied Representatives will station forces and civil agencies in any or all parts of Germany as they may determine.

ARTICLE 13

(a) In the exercise of the supreme authority with respect to Germany assumed by the Governments of the United States of America, the Union of Soviet Socialist Republics and the United Kingdom, and the Provisional Government of the French Republic, the four Allied Governments will take such steps, including the complete disarmament and demilitarization of Germany, as they deem requisite for future peace and security.

(b) The Allied Representatives will impose on Germany additional political, administrative, economic, financial, military and other requirements arising from the complete defeat of Germany. The Allied Representatives, or persons or agencies duly designated to act on their authority, will issue proclamations, orders, ordinances and instructions for the purpose of laying down such additional requirements, and of giving effect to the other provisions of this Declaration. All German authorities and the German people shall carry out unconditionally the requirements of the Allied Representatives, and shall fully comply with all such proclamations, orders, ordinances and instructions.

"Declaration Regarding the Defeat of Germany and the Assumption of Supreme Authority by Allied Powers," June 5, 1945, in *Treaties and Other International Agreements of the United States of America 1776–1949*, compiled under the direction of Charles I. Bevans. Washington, DC: Government Printing Office, 1969.

Document 19: Japanese Emperor Hirohito Acknowledges Surrender by Japan

At midnight of August 14, 1945, after four years of fighting, the Japanese people stood in front of their radios to hear a message of surrender recorded earlier that day by their emperor. For the first time ever, they heard the voice of their emperor over the air. In this transcript of the broadcast, Emperor Hirohito apologizes to his people and their allies and explains why he agreed to the surrender.

To our good and loyal subjects: After pondering deeply the general trends of the world and the actual conditions obtaining in our empire today, we have decided to effect a settlement of the present situation by resorting to an extraordinary measure.

We have ordered our Government to communicate to the Governments of the United States, Great Britain, China and the Soviet Union that our empire accepts the provisions of their joint declaration.

To strive for the common prosperity and happiness of all nations as well as the security and well-being of our subjects is the solemn obligation which has been handed down by our imperial ancestors and which we lay close to the heart.

Indeed, we declared war on America and Britain out of our sincere desire to insure Japan's self-preservation and the stabilization of East Asia, it being far from our thought either to infringe upon the sovereignty of other nations or to embark upon territorial aggrandizement.

But now the war has lasted for nearly four years. Despite the best that has been done by everyone—the gallant fighting of our military and naval forces, the diligence and assiduity of our servants of the State and the devoted service of our 100,000,000 people—the war situation has developed not necessarily to Japan's advantage, while the general trends of the world have all turned against her interest.

Moreover, the enemy has begun to employ a new and most cruel bomb, the power of which to do damage is, indeed, incalculable, taking the toll of many innocent lives. Should we continue to fight, it would not only result in an ultimate collapse and obliteration of the Japanese nation, but also it would lead to the total extinction of human civilization.

Such being the case, how are we to save the millions of our subjects, nor to atone ourselves before the hallowed spirits of our imperial ancestors? This is the reason why we have ordered the acceptance of the provisions of the joint declaration of the powers.

We cannot but express the deepest sense of regret to our allied nations of East Asia, who have consistently cooperated with the Empire toward the emancipation of East Asia.

The thought of those officers and men as well as others who have fallen in the fields of battle, those who died at their posts of duty, or those who met death [otherwise] and all their bereaved families, pains our heart night and day.

The welfare of the wounded and the war sufferers and of those who lost their homes and livelihood is the object of our profound solicitude. The hardships and sufferings to which our nation is to be subjected hereafter will be certainly great.

We are keenly aware of the inmost feelings of all of you, our subjects. However, it is according to the dictates of time and fate that we have resolved to pave the way for a grand peace for all the generations to come by enduring the [unavoidable] and suffering what is unsufferable. Having been able to save and maintain the structure of the Imperial State, we are always with you, our good and loyal subjects, relying upon your sincerity and integrity.

Beware most strictly of any outbursts of emotion that may engender needless complications, of any fraternal contention and strife that may create confusion, lead you astray and cause you to lose the confidence of the world.

Let the entire nation continue as one family from generation to generation, ever firm in its faith of the imperishableness of its divine land, and mindful of its heavy burden of responsibilities, and the long road before it. Unite your total strength to be devoted to the construction for the future. Cultivate the ways of rectitude, nobility of spirit, and work with resolution so that you may enhance the innate glory of the Imperial State and keep pace with the progress of the world.

Hirohito, Emperor of Japan, radio broadcast speech transmitted by Domei and recorded by the Federal Communications Commission, August 14, 1945.

Document 20: An "Iron Curtain" Has Descended

On March 5, 1946, British prime minister Winston Churchill was awarded an honorary degree by Westminster College in Fulton, Missouri. In this excerpt from what is now considered one of the most important speeches in history, he speaks of the necessity for world unity and warns of the "iron curtain" that has fallen between the Communist nations of Eastern and central Europe and the non-Communist ones of Western Europe because of the Soviet push for dominance.

A shadow has fallen upon the scenes so lately lighted by the Allied victory. Nobody knows what Soviet Russia and its Communist international organisation intends to do in the immediate future, or what are the limits, if any, to their expansive and proselytising tendencies. I have a strong admiration and regard for the valiant Russian people and for my wartime comrade, Marshal Stalin. There is deep sympathy and goodwill in Britain—and I doubt not here also—towards the peoples of all the Russias and a resolve to persevere through many differences and rebuffs in establishing lasting friendships. We understand the Russian need to be secure on her western frontiers by the removal of all possibility of German aggression. We welcome Russia to her rightful place among the leading nations of the world. We welcome her flag upon the seas. Above all, we welcome constant, frequent and growing contacts between the Russian people and our own people on both sides of the Atlantic. It is my duty however, for I am sure you would wish me to state the facts as I see them to you, to place before you certain facts about the present position in Europe.

From Stettin in the Baltic to Trieste in the Adriatic, an iron curtain has descended across the Continent. Behind that line lie all the capitals of the ancient states of Central and Eastern Europe. Warsaw, Berlin, Prague, Vienna, Budapest, Belgrade, Bucharest and Sofia, all these famous cities and the populations around them lie in what I must call the Soviet sphere, and all are subject in one form or another, not only to Soviet influence but to a very high and, in many cases, increasing measure of control from Moscow. Athens alone—Greece with its immortal glories—is free to decide its future at an election under British, American and French observation. The Russian-dominated Polish Government has been encouraged to make enormous and wrongful inroads upon Germany, and mass expulsions of millions of Germans on a scale grievous and undreamed-of are now taking place. The Communist parties, which were very small in all these Eastern States of Europe, have been raised to pre-eminence and power far beyond their numbers and are seeking everywhere to obtain totalitarian control. Police governments are prevailing in nearly every case, and so far, except in Czechoslovakia, there is no true democracy.

Turkey and Persia are both profoundly alarmed and disturbed at the claims which are being made upon them and at the pressure being exerted by the Moscow Government. An attempt is being made by the Russians in Berlin to build up a quasi-Communist party in their zone of Occupied Germany by showing special favours to groups of left-wing German leaders. At the end of the fighting last June, the American and British Armies withdrew westwards, in accordance with an earlier agreement, to a depth at some points of 150 miles upon a front of nearly four hundred miles, in order to allow our Russian allies to occupy this vast expanse of territory which the Western Democracies had conquered.

If now the Soviet Government tries, by separate action, to build up a pro-Communist Germany in their areas, this will cause new serious difficulties in the British and American zones, and will give the defeated Germans the power of putting themselves up to auction between the Soviets and the Western Democracies. Whatever conclusions may be drawn from these facts—and facts they are—this is certainly not the Liberated Europe we fought to build up. Nor is it one which contains the essentials of permanent peace.

Winston Churchill, "Sinews of Peace" Speech, Westminster College, Fulton, Missouri, March 5, 1946.

Chronology

1932

November 8—Franklin Delano Roosevelt is elected president of the United States.

1933

January 30—Adolf Hitler becomes chancellor of Germany.

July 14—The Nazi Party is declared the only political party in Germany.

1934

August 19—Adolf Hitler becomes Führer of Germany.

1935

October 3—Italy invades Ethiopia.

1936

March 7—German troops occupy the Rhineland.

July 17—Civil war breaks out in Spain.

October 25—Rome-Berlin Axis is signed.

November 25—Japan signs Anti-Comitern Pact with Germany.

1938

March 12–13—Germany invades and announces *Anschluss*, union, with Austria.

September 30—England, France, Italy, and Germany sign the Munich Pact, which gives Hitler the Sudetenland, the western third of Czechoslovakia, in return for a promise not to take any more land.

October 15—German troops occupy the Sudetenland and the Czech government resigns.

1939

March 15–16—Germany takes control of Czechoslovakia.

May 22—Germany and Italy sign the "Pact of Steel."

August 23—Soviet Union signs non-aggression pact with Germany.

September 1—Germany invades Poland.

September 3—Britain, France, Australia, and New Zealand declare war against Germany.

September 10—Canada declares war on Germany. Battle of the Atlantic begins.

September 17—Soviet Union invades Poland.

September 27—Warsaw, Poland, surrenders to Germany.

November 30—Soviet Union invades Finland.

1940

April 9—Germany invades Denmark and Norway.

May 10—Germany invades France, Belgium, Luxembourg, and the Netherlands. Winston Churchill becomes Prime Minister of Great Britain.

May 20—German troops reach the English Channel.

May 26–June 4—British Expeditionary Force is evacuated from Dunkirk. Belgium surrenders to Germany.

June 10–11—Norway surrenders to Germany. Italy declares war on Britain and France.

June 14—Paris falls.

June 15—Soviet Union begins occupation of Lithuania, Latvia, and Estonia.

June 16—Marshal Pétain becomes French Prime Minister.

June 22—France signs an armistice with Germany.

July 10–September 15—Battle of Britain begins over English Channel and ends with heavy blitzing of London that goes on until May 1941.

August 5—Italy invades British Somaliland.

September 3—Adolf Hitler plans the invasion of Britain.

September 13—Italy invades Egypt.

September 27—Japan joins the Axis.

October 7—German troops enter Rumania.

October 28—Italy invades Greece.

November 5—Franklin D. Roosevelt is reelected President of the United States.

November 20–22—Hungary and Rumania join the Axis.

December 9–10—British begin western desert offensive in North Africa against the Italians.

1941

January 22—Tobruk in North Africa falls to the British and the Australians.

February 6—German General Erwin Rommel crosses from Italy to Africa to take command of German troops.

February 7—The Allies defeat the Italians in Libya.

February 14—Germany's Afrika Korps arrives in North Africa.

March 11—The Lend-Lease Act becomes law in the United States, which starts supplying war materials to the Allies.

March 25—Yugoslavia joins the Axis.

April 6—Germany invades Yugoslavia and Greece. The British occupy Addis Ababa, the Ethiopian capital.

April 13—Soviet Union and Japan sign a five-year nonaggression pact.

April 17—Yugoslavia surrenders to Germany.

April 27—Greece surrenders to Germany.

May 10–11—Nazi bombers damage the House of Commons, Westminster Abbey, and Big Ben in London.

May 27—The British Navy sinks the German *Bismarck* off the French coast.

June 22—Germany, Italy, and Rumania declare war on the Soviet Union. Germany invades the Soviet Union.

July 3—Stalin calls for a "scorched earth defense" policy.

July 24–26—Japan occupies French Indochina. The United States stops trade with Japan.

July 27—President Roosevelt proclaims a national emergency in the United States because of what is happening in Europe and Africa.

August 12—U.S. President Roosevelt and British Prime Minister Winston Churchill meet off Newfoundland and draw up the Atlantic Charter.

September 1—The Nazis order all Jews to wear yellow stars.

September 8–19—Germans lay siege to Leningrad and capture Kiev.

October 17—Hideki Tojo becomes Prime Minister of Japan.

December 5—Germany stops its attack on Moscow.

December 7–9—Japan bombs Pearl Harbor and declares war on the United States and Britain; bombs Philippines, Wake Islands, and Guam and invades Thailand, Malaya, Hong Kong, and the Gilbert Islands. United States and Britain declare war on Japan.

December 11—Germany and Italy declare war on the United States.

December 22—Japan launches a major offensive in the Philippines.

December 31—The Japanese occupy Manila, the capital of the Philippines.

1942

January 1—Twenty-six nations sign the Declaration of the United Nations in Washington, DC. The Allied nations agree not to make separate peace with Germany.

January 20—Nazi officials meet to plan the "Final Solution" to the "problem" of European Jews.

January 26—The first American troops arrive in Great Britain.

February 1—American planes bomb Japanese bases in the Marshall Islands and the Gilbert Islands.

April—Japanese-Americans living in the United States are sent to relocation centers.

April 9—American troops surrender to the Japanese on the Bataan Peninsula, Philippines.

May 7–8—The Japanese fleet suffers its first setback in the Battle of the Coral Sea.

May 16—Corregidor falls to the Japanese. All American forces in the Philippines surrender.

June 4–6—The Japanese fleet is crippled by the United States during the Battle of Midway.

June 24—American General Dwight D. Eisenhower assumes command of all American troops in Europe.

July 1–30—The first battle of El Alamein takes place.

August 7—American Marines land at Guadalcanal in the Solomon Islands.

August 12—Churchill, Stalin, U.S. representatives, and Free French representatives meet in Moscow to discuss a second front.

September 14—German troops lay siege to the Soviet city of Stalingrad.

September 22—German troops that reach the center of Stalingrad meet stiff Soviet resistance.

November 8—The United States invades North Africa.

November 11—Axis forces occupy Vichy France.

1943

January 2–3—Germany starts to withdraw from the Caucasus.

January 24—Roosevelt and Churchill meet in Casablanca to plan the Allied war strategy and call for unconditional German surrender.

January 27—The United States launches its first bombing attack on Germany.

February 2—The Germans suffer their first big defeat of the war at Stalingrad.

February 9—American troops secure Guadalcanal in the Pacific.

May 13—German and Italian troops surrender in North Africa.

June 22—The Allies win the Battle of the Atlantic.

July 9–10—The Allies land in Sicily.

July 25–26—Mussolini is arrested and Italy's Fascist government falls.

September 8—The Italian surrender is announced.

September 10—German forces occupy Rome.

September 12—The Germans rescue Mussolini.

October 13—Italy declares war on Germany.

November 6—The Soviets take back Kiev in the Ukraine.

November 28–December 1—Roosevelt, Churchill, and Stalin meet in Teheran to plan the invasion of France and formulate the postwar world structure.

December 24—American general Dwight D. Eisenhower is named to direct the invasion of Europe.

1944

January 6—Soviet troops enter Poland.

January 16—American general Dwight D. Eisenhower is appointed supreme commander of Allied forces in Europe.

January 22—The Allies land at Anzio, Italy.

January 27—The Soviets defeat the Germans at Leningrad, ending a 900-day siege.

May 12—The Germans surrender in the Crimea.

June 4—The Allies enter Rome.

June 6—D-Day: The Allies land on the beaches of Normandy, France, launching the formal liberation of Western Europe.

June 13—The Germans launch their first V–1 attack on Britain.

June 15—The United States bombs Tokyo.

June 19–20—The Japanese fleet is defeated in the Battle of the Philippine Sea.

July 20—A German attempt to assassinate Hitler fails.

August 1—Polish patriots revolt in Warsaw as Soviet troops near the city.

August 15—The Allies invade Southern France.

August 21–29—Allied representatives meet at Dumbarton Oaks in Washington, DC, to discuss forming the United Nations.

August 25—The Allies liberate Paris.

September 23—The Allies recognize Charles de Gaulle as the temporary head of the French government.

October 2—The Warsaw Uprising ends in surrender to the Germans.

October 20—American general Douglas MacArthur lands in the Philippines with American forces.

October 23–26—The American fleet totally destroys the Japanese naval fleet in the Battle of Leyte Gulf, the largest naval battle of the war.

December 16–27—The Battle of the Bulge, the last major German offensive of the war, is fought in the Ardennes.

1945

January 9—American troops invade Luzon, Philippines.

January 17—Soviet troops capture Warsaw.

January 26—Soviet troops liberate the Auschwitz concentration camp.

February 4–11—Roosevelt, Churchill, and Stalin meet at Yalta in the Crimea and agree to divide Germany into separate zones occupied by Allied forces.

February 13–14—Allied firebombs destroy the German city of Dresden.

March 3—American forces liberate Manila, Philippines.

March 7—The Allies take Cologne and the first U.S. troops cross the Rhine River at Remagen.

March 16—American forces take the island of Iwo Jima at the cost of 4,000 American lives.

April 1—American forces land on Okinawa in the Pacific.

April 12—The Allies liberate the Buchenwald and Bergen-Belsen concentration camps. President Roosevelt dies in Warm Springs, Georgia, and Vice President Harry S. Truman becomes President.

April 23—The Soviets enter Berlin.

April 28—Italian partisans capture and hang Mussolini in Como, Italy.

April 29—American troops liberate more than 32,000 prisoners in the Dachau concentration camp.

April 30—The Soviets reach the Reichstag in Berlin. Adolf Hitler commits suicide in his bunker in Berlin.

May 2—German troops in Italy surrender.

May 7—Germany formally surrenders to the Allies.

May 8—V-E (Victory in Europe) Day celebrates the end of the European war.

June 5—The Allies divide Germany into four zones of occupation.

June 26—The United Nations World Charter of Security is signed in San Francisco.

June 30—American troops liberate Luzon, Philippines.

July 1—American, British, and French troops occupy Berlin.

July 16—The first atomic bomb test is conducted at Alamogordo Air Force Base in New Mexico.

July 17–August 2—Truman, Churchill, and Stalin meet at Potsdam to plan for peace in Europe and to demand unconditional surrender from Japan.

August 6—The Americans drop an atomic bomb on Hiroshima, Japan, killing more than 50,000 people.

August 8—The Soviet Union declares war on Japan.

August 9—The Soviets invade Manchuria. The Americans drop an atomic bomb on Nagasaki, Japan, killing 40,000 people.

August 14—The Japanese surrender unconditionally.

August 15—V-J (Victory over Japan) Day celebrates Allied acceptance of Japan's unconditional surrender.

September 2—The Japanese formally sign a surrender agreement aboard the USS *Missouri* in Tokyo Bay.

October 24—The United Nations is born officially.

November 13—Charles de Gaulle is elected head of the French government.

November 20—The Nuremberg war crimes trials begin.

For Further Research

General Histories of World War II

Stephen E. Ambrose and C.I. Zulzberger, *The American Heritage New History of World War II*. New York: Penguin Putnam, Inc., 1997.

Winston S. Churchill, *The Second World War*. New York: Houghton Mifflin, 1986.

Kathlyn Gay and Martin Gay, *World War II*. New York: Twenty-First Century Books, 1995.

John Keegan, *The Second World War*. New York: Viking, 1989.

J. Lee Ready, *World War Two: Nation by Nation*. London: Arms and Armour Press, 1995.

WWII: Time-Life History of the Second World War. Barnes & Noble Books, 1995.

Perspectives and Personal Narratives

Tom Brokaw, *The Greatest Generation*. New York: Random House, 1998.

G. Jan Colijn and Marcia Sachs Little, eds., *Confronting the Holocaust: A Mandate for the 21st Century*. Lanham, MD: University Press of America, Inc., 1997.

Gottlob Herbert, Herbert Bidermann, Derek S. Zumbro, eds., *In Deadly Combat: A German Soldier's Memoir of the Eastern Front*. Lawrence: University Press of Kansas, 2000.

Erica Johnson, *Nazi Terror: The Gestapo, Jews, and Ordinary Germans*. New York: Basic Books, 1999.

John C. McManus, *The Deadly Brotherhood: The American Combat Soldier in World War II*. Novato, CA: Presidio, 1998.

Malcolm Mujir Jr., ed., *The Human Tradition in the World War II Era*. Scholarly Resources, Inc., 2000.

William L. Shirer, *Berlin Diary: The Journal of a Foreign Correspondent*. New York: Knopf, 1941.

Studs Terkel, *"The Good War": An Oral History of World War Two*. New York: Pantheon Books, 1984.

Herbert A. Werner, *Iron Coffins: A Personal Account of the German U-Boat Battles of World War II*. New York: DaCapo, 1998.

Katherine Whittemore, ed., *The World War Two Era: Perspectives on All Fronts from Harper's Magazine*. New York: Franklin Square Press, 1995.

Elie Wiesel, *Night*. Translated by Stella Rodway. New York: Bantam Books, 1982.

World War II in Europe

Stephen E. Ambrose, *Citizen Soldiers: The U.S. Army from the Normandy Beaches to the Bulge to the Surrender of Germany, June 7, 1944 to May 7, 1945*. New York: Simon & Schuster, 1998.

Stephen E. Ambrose, *From the Normandy Beaches to the Bulge to the Surrender of Germany, June 7, 1944–May 7, 1945*. New York: Simon & Schuster, 1997.

Antony Beevor, *Stalingrad*. New York: Viking, 1998.

Angus Calder, *The People's War: Britain 1939–1945*. New York: Pantheon Books, 1969.

Thomas Childers, *The Air War in Europe*. New York: Henry Holt, 2000.

Len Deighton, *Blitzkrieg: From the Rise of Hitler to the Fall of Dunkirk*. New York: Knopf, 1980.

Theodore S. Hamerow, *On the Road to the Wolf's Lair: German Resistance to Hitler*. Cambridge, MA: Belknap Press of Harvard University Press, 1997.

Edwin Palmer Hoyt, *199 Days: The Battle for Stalingrad*. New York: Forge, 1999.

Anthony Kemp, *D-Day and the Invasion of Normandy*. New York: Harry N. Abrams, Inc., 1994.

James Sidney Lucas, *War on the Eastern Front: The German Soldier in Russia 1941–45*. London: Greenhill Books, 1998.

Ernest R. May, *Strange Victory: Hitler's Conquest of France*. New York: Hill & Wang, 2000.

G.E. Patrick Murray, *Victory in Western Europe: From D-Day to the Nazi Surrender*. New York: Metro Books, 1999.

Joseph E. Perisco, *Nuremberg: Infamy on Trial*, New York: Viking Penguin, 1995.

Laurence Rees, *The Nazis: A Warning from History*. New York: New Press, 1997.

Harrison Evans Salisbury, *The 900 Days: The Siege of Leningrad*. New York: Da Capo, 1985.

William L. Shirer, *The Rise and Fall of the Third Reich: A History Of Nazi Germany*. New York: Simon & Schuster, 1960.

Gordon Williamson, *Afrikakorps 1941–1943*. London: Osprey, 1991.

World War II in the Pacific

James Bradley with Ron Powers. *Flags of Our Fathers*. New York: Bantam Books, 2000.

Iris Chang, *The Rape of Nanking: The Forgotten Holocaust of World War II*. New York: Viking Penguin, 1998.

John W. Dower, *Embracing Defeat: Japan in the Wake of World War II*. New York: Norton, 2000.

Michael Green, *MacArthur in the Pacific: From the Philippines to the Fall of Japan*. Osceola, WI: Motorbooks International Publishers and Wholesalers, 1996.

Edwin P. Hoyt, *Blue Skies and Blood: The Battle of the Coral Sea*. New York: Paul S. Erikson, Inc., 1975.

Masatake Okumiya and Jiro Horikoshi with Martin Caidin, *Zero!* New York, Ballantine Books, 1956.

Christopher Shores and Brian Cull, B*loody Shambles: The Drift to War to the Fall of Singapore*. London: Grub St., 1992.

Charles W. Sweeney with James A. Antonucci and Marion K. Antonucci, *War's End: An Eyewitness Account of America's Last Atomic Mission*. New York: Avon Books, 1997.

John Toland, *The Rising Sun: The Rise and Fall of the Japanese Empire*. New York: Random House, 1970.

The Home Front

Doris Kearns Goodwin, *No Ordinary Time: Franklin and Eleanor Roosevelt: The Home Front in World War II*. Simon & Schuster Trade, 1995.

Jeanne W. Houston and James D. Houston, *Farewell to Manzanar: A True Story of Japanese American Experience During and After the World War II Internment*. New York: Bantam Books, 1981.

Geoffrey Perrett, *Days of Sadness, Years of Triumph: The American*

People 1939–1945. New York: Coward, McCann & Geoghegan, Inc., 1973.

Philip Ziegler, *London at War, 1939–1945*. New York: Knopf, 1995.

Individuals Who Shaped World War II

Mark Mayo Boatner, *Biographical Dictionary of World War II*. Novato, CA: Presidio, 1999.

Frank Freidel, *Franklin D. Roosevelt: A Rendezvous with Destiny*. New York: Little, Brown, 1991.

Martin Gilbert, *Churchill: A Life*. New York: Henry Holt, 1992.

Konrad Heiden et al, *The Fuhrer: Hitler's Rise to Power*. New York: Carroll & Graf Publishers, Inc., 1999.

Robert Edwin Herzstein, *Roosevelt and Hitler: Prelude to War*. New York: John Wiley and Sons, 1994.

David McCullough, *Truman*. New York: Simon & Schuster, 1992.

John Toland, *Adolf Hitler*. Garden City, NY: Doubleday, 1976.

Desmond Young, *Rommel, The Desert Fox*. New York: Quill, 1978.

Index